T0301402

Leadership as Stewardship

NEW HORIZONS IN LEADERSHIP STUDIES

Series Editor: Joanne B. Ciulla, *Director, Institute for Ethical Leadership and Professor of Leadership Ethics, Department of Management and Global Business, Rutgers Business School, USA*

This important series is designed to make a significant contribution to the development of leadership studies. This field has expanded dramatically in recent years and the series provides an invaluable forum for the publication of high-quality works of scholarship and shows the diversity of leadership issues and practices around the world.

The main emphasis of the series is on the development and application of new and original ideas in leadership studies. It pays particular attention to leadership in business, economics and public policy and incorporates the wide range of disciplines which are now part of the field. Global in its approach, it includes some of the best theoretical and empirical work with contributions to fundamental principles, rigorous evaluations of existing concepts and competing theories, historical surveys and future visions.

For a full list of Edward Elgar published titles, including the titles in this series, visit our website at www.e-elgar.com.

Leadership as Stewardship

Honouring Our Past While Ensuring Our Future

Marian Iszatt-White

Department of Entrepreneurship and Strategy, Lancaster University Management School, UK

NEW HORIZONS IN LEADERSHIP STUDIES

 Edward Elgar
PUBLISHING

Cheltenham, UK • Northampton, MA, USA

Published by
Edward Elgar Publishing Limited
The Lypiatts
15 Lansdown Road
Cheltenham
Glos GL50 2JA
UK

Edward Elgar Publishing, Inc.
William Pratt House
9 Dewey Court
Northampton
Massachusetts 01060
USA

A catalogue record for this book
is available from the British Library

Library of Congress Control Number: 2024939190

This book is available electronically in the **Elgar**online
Business subject collection
http://dx.doi.org/10.4337/9781035319428

ISBN 978 1 0353 1941 1 (cased)
ISBN 978 1 0353 1942 8 (eBook)

Printed and bound by CPI G roup (UK) Ltd, Croydon, CR0 4YY

Contents

Tables

1. Introduction: why stewardship?

INTRODUCTION

In the context of responsible leadership, Maak and Pless (2006: 108) define a steward as someone who understands themselves 'as a custodian of social, moral and environmental values and resources', trusted with their protection and enrichment, and guided by the question 'What am I passing on to [] future generation[s]?' In introducing what follows, this chapter sets out the case for the salience of stewardship as a concept with the ability to combat perceived failings in leadership as both a construct and a practice. Specifically, these failings are seen as relating to (a) the need to counteract the shift in recent leadership scholarship from inquiry to advocacy, (b) the consequent promulgation of a range of aspirational forms of leadership (including responsible) that cumulatively add to the perceived burden on practicing leaders, and (c) the problematic role of leadership as a handmaiden of ideas and values deriving from both Enlightenment and capitalist thinking.

Taking the last of these first, it is increasingly being recognized that leadership as a construct is inextricably bound up with capitalist hegemonies – such as 'growth' and 'progress' (Banerjee and Arjaliès, 2021) – that have been forced upon it by academics and practitioners alike. The work of Kempster et al. (2011) in relation to 'leadership as purpose' highlights the increasing recognition of the capitalist drivers of modern organizational leadership and the imbalance between capitalist goals and the emerging sustainability agenda. The result, I will argue, is that the term 'leadership' – described by Kelly (2014) as an 'empty signifier' to which we can ascribe whatever meanings we find useful – has become too full of accreted 'baggage' to offer meaningful guidance to individuals, organizations and even societies. To use Alvesson and Sandberg's terminology (2020), leadership has become a 'hegemonic ambiguous big concept' or 'hembig'; that is:

> a scientific concept characterized by its broad scope and ambiguous meanings, which at the same time, and somewhat paradoxically, through its dominance crowds out other less fashionable concepts or prevents the development of a more precise terminology' (2020: 1292).

The choice of stewardship as a 'decluttered' alternative signifier for our leadership aspirations – and hence as a concept that is ripe for extensive academic and practitioner consideration – is suggested by its status as a construct that is already full of rich, empirical meanings across a range of research domains.

A key underpinning of the arguments presented in this chapter is the premise that there has been a shift in recent leadership scholarship, away from inquiry into how to do leadership better and towards advocacy of a range of 'aspirational' forms of leadership or purposes that leadership 'should' serve. Whilst it is clearly important to consider the purposes to which leadership is put – and there is a growing and thought-provoking body of literature on 'leadership as purpose' (Kempster et al., 2011) – this is arguably the domain of philosophers rather than leadership scholars. The danger arising from this growth in advocacy – often insufficiently underpinned by either empirical evidence or theoretical determinateness – is that it provides neither a solid foundation for future scholarship nor workable 'scaffolding' for the enactment of practical leadership. As noted above, the rich empirical groundings of stewardship thus have the potential to anchor leadership theory and practice back to a more inquiry-led foundation.

As a result of this shift from inquiry to advocacy a constant stream of 'adjective' leadership approaches – ethical (Ciulla, 2004), authentic (Walumbwa et al., 2008), responsible (Pless and Maak, 2011) and sustainable (Avery and Bergsteiner, 2010) leadership – have arisen which, arguably, have been ineffectual in their attempts to bolster the leadership construct's flagging status. Collectively, these aspirational forms of leadership thus tend to be long on aspiration and short on practical detail. For practitioners, they pile ever-increasing burdens on those attempting to enact it, without necessarily offering supportive 'scaffolding' for its successful accomplishment or restoring confidence in its value and relevance. For academics, these aspirational theories highlight leadership's struggle for relevance in the broader management research pantheon, rather than providing genuine credibility for the field. As a result, faith in the efficacy of leadership – particularly political leadership – seems to be at an all-time low, and the discipline is struggling to command a 'seat at the table' in large-scale, interdisciplinary research projects aimed at addressing global challenges. As such, aspirational forms of leadership – along with the accompanying shift towards advocacy rather than inquiry in leadership scholarship – suggest a loss of direction in the field of leadership research rather than a purposeful advance.

This chapter sets the scene for those which follow by proposing the emergence of stewardship as a promising and timely alternative to aspirational forms of leadership. In recent years the management literature relating to stewardship has expanded to embrace the troubled trajectory of corporate social responsibility (CSR) (Klettner, 2021; Kuttner et al., 2021) and the broader commitment to the United Nations' (UN's) Sustainable Development Goals (Williams and Whiteman, 2021). This growing trend represents a shift away from the historical focus on growth fuelled by consumerism, and – in its most hard-line form – challenges the ability of Western, Enlightenment-based thinking to solve global issues created by that same Western, Enlightenment thinking (Banerjee and Arjaliès, 2021). Riding this wave of expansion, this book explores the notion of 'stewardship' (Davis et al., 1997) across a broad range of academic literature, contexts and worldviews with the aim of understanding the different meanings which stewardship has across these different research domains and for different stakeholders to the concept. Drawing on the relational ontologies of both Western and Indigenous worldviews (Walsh et al., 2021; Banerjee and Arjaliès, 2021; Spiller, 2021) as a sense-making lens, it then explores stewardship's connections with leadership and its potential for revitalizing this tired construct. As evidence that this revitalization process is not without hope, it also draws on exciting research currently being undertaken relating to leadership in the context of corporate biosphere stewardship, to develop arguments and propositions about how corporate leaders can become biosphere stewards and where this sits in relation to existing capitalist, market-economy, hegemonies.

LEADERSHIP NOW: THE RISE OF 'ASPIRATIONAL' LEADERSHIP

The trajectory of leadership scholarship has come a long way from its early attempts to identify the traits belonging to 'great men' (Carlyle, 1846) and other essentialist approaches, but – as is so often the case – not all change is progress. Whilst progress has been made over the years in recognizing the motivational (Bass and Avolio, 1990) and relational (Uhl-Bien, 2006) foundations of leadership, recent trends have seen a shift in emphasis in leadership scholarship that is less clearly helpful. Specifically, we have seen the rise of 'aspirational' forms of leadership that often have more to do with what leadership is *for* than with how to enact or accomplish it. As a point of departure for establishing why an alternative approach is needed, this section considers some of the most prevalent aspirational forays by leadership scholars, through an overview of ethical (Ciulla, 2004), authentic (Walumbwa et al., 2008), responsible (Pless and Maak, 2011) and sustainable (Avery and Bergsteiner, 2010) leadership and their interconnections.

Ethical leadership has a long history in the leadership literature. As such, it is not a theory of leadership but a recognition of some of the issues that arise in leadership situations, and the importance of doing the right thing, not just doing things right (Ciulla, 2004). Writing in this area has examined how leadership theory and practice could be used to build a more caring and just society

(Ciulla, 1996), albeit fighting shy of resolving the question of what constitutes a 'good' set of moral values, or who gets to decide. Recent scholarship has seen a re-emergence of the moral/ethical aspects of leadership as a focus, but it is commonly seen as having its origins (in modern, organizational contexts, at least) in Burns' (1978: 4) conception of 'transforming' leadership as 'a relationship of mutual stimulation and elevation that converts followers into leaders and may convert leaders into moral agents'. As subsequently developed by Bass and Avolio (1994: 3):

> the goal of transformational leadership is to "transform" people and organizations in a literal sense – to change them in heart and mind; enlarge vision, insight and understanding; clarify purposes; make behaviour congruent with beliefs, principles or values; and bring about changes that are permanent, self-perpetuating, and momentum-building.

Burns sought to appeal to the moral values of followers in an attempt to raise their consciousness about ethical issues and to mobilize their energy and resources to reform societal institutions. In organizational contexts, this translates into building on the individual's need for meaning in order to transcend the day-to-day trials of organizational life. It was a fundamental argument of Burns' work that transforming leadership is a process that changes leaders and followers, and that through this process of seeking the highest levels of morality both parties consider 'not only what is good for themselves, but also what will benefit larger collectivities such as their organization, community, and nation' (Yukl, 2006: 419).

Another mainstream leadership theory that has attempted to incorporate an ethical component into its operationalization is authentic leadership (AL) (Iszatt-White and Kempster, 2019), which has been described as:

> a pattern of leader behaviour that draws upon and promotes both positive psychological capacities and a positive ethical climate, to foster greater self-awareness, an internalised moral perspective, balanced processing of information, and relational transparency on the part of leaders working with followers, fostering positive self-development. (Walumbwa et al., 2008: 94)

Deriving from idealized normative and functionalist aims of delineating a style of leadership capable of producing measurable organizational outcomes (Avolio et al., 2004; Gardner and Schermerhorn, 2004), authentic leaders are said to be 'transparent about their intentions and strive to maintain a seamless link between espoused values, behaviours and actions' (Luthans and Avolio, 2003: 242). This positioning carries with it the implication that their 'espoused values' are ethically positive. Later and more critical conceptualizations of AL, often deriving from existentialist (Algera and Lips-Wiersma, 2012;

Lawler and Ashman, 2012) or psychoanalytic (Costas and Taheri, 2012; Ford and Harding, 2011) traditions, are grounded in a more complex, political and contested understanding of authenticity. As such, they problematize both the supposed moral underpinnings of the AL construct and the notion of a 'self' to which an authentic leader can be 'true' (Ladkin and Taylor, 2010). Equally problematic is the fundamental paradox (Iszatt-White et al., 2021) exposed by examining AL through the lens of emotional labour (EL): that is, that the *in*authenticity of performing EL is accepted by practising leaders as an integral part of presenting themselves as authentic leaders. The problem here – as with other 'positive' (Avolio and Gardner, 2005) forms of leadership for which it is claimed to be the root construct – is that the ethical components of AL are simultaneously under-specified and contradictory.

Much has been written in recent years concerning the need for responsible leadership to move us 'from value to values, from shareholders to stake-holders, and from balance sheets to balanced development' (Kofi Annan, 14 October 2002, cited in Kempster and Carroll, 2016, frontmatter). Thomas Pless, a founding author within the responsible movement, defined responsible leadership as:

> a values-based and thoroughly ethical principles-driven relationship between leaders and stakeholders who are connected through a shared sense of meaning and purpose through which they raise one another to higher levels of motivation and commitment for achieving sustainable values creation and social change. (Pless, 2007: 438)

Enactment of responsible leadership is said to require a change in mindset by the leader, in order to incorporate a much broader view of the stakeholders to whom they are answerable and the 'others' with whom the responsible leader should be concerned (Pless and Maak, 2011). In positioning responsible leadership against the existing leadership literature, responsible leadership suffers from being portrayed as a paragon of all that is best in transformational (Avolio et al., 1991), authentic (Avolio and Gardner, 2005), servant (Greenleaf, 1977; Russell and Stone, 2002), ethical (Brown and Trevino; 2006; Ciulla, 2004) and charismatic (Conger and Kanungo, 1987) leadership: an unwieldy burden for any theorization of leadership to bear, and reminiscent of a return to the outdated 'great man' theory.

Recent attempts to move the study of responsible leadership forward have included the idea of replacing the 'essentialist self' with the 'poetic self' (Freeman and Auster, 2011) as a project for seeking to live authentically, seen as an important component of responsible leadership. Whilst this proposal is interesting, it draws attention to what Hartman (1988) refers to as the 'problem of authenticity', namely that we can get caught between not knowing our values and not knowing whether our values are realizable through action. Freeman and Auster (2011) suggest our values rest on our ability to choose, and that it is through the conscious realization of our choices in a particular project that the real meaning of authenticity lies. In this context, values are seen as inherently relational, with the 'poetic self' existing at the intersection of our values, our past, our set of connections to others and our aspirations. Whilst this extension of the responsible leadership construct offers an interesting parallel to ideas of authentic leadership, it appears to conflate ethics with authenticity and to ignore both socially constructed and attributional approaches. In another attempt to move the construct forward, Cameron (2011) offered a fourth definition (where definitions one and two are recognizable as based on economic accountability and definition three is the now widely accepted stakeholder theory approach) in terms of the ability/inclination to act appropriately or virtuously. In this context, virtuousness is contrasted with ethics in that it is said to be more unchanging and hence to offer the only 'fixed point' in leader decision making.

In addition to defining more closely what we mean by 'responsible' it has also been suggested that we may need a paradigm shift in our conceptualization of leadership (Du Toit and Woermann, 2012) and a requirement for leaders to re-inscribe their understanding of themselves in this role. Du Toit and Woermann draw on Hawken's (1993) insistence on the need for a 'restorative economy' – and hence restorative leadership – if business is to reinvent itself in response to the current ecological crisis. Within this new paradigm, the previous alignment of responsible leadership with transformational leadership is critiqued as coming from an atomistic rather than a systemic viewpoint, and Western's (2010) 'ecoleadership' is proposed as an alternative to the more established Messianic models. Restorative leadership is thus much closer to forms of distributed leadership (Gronn, 2003) in its embeddedness and fluidity, rather than a reliance on positional power and authority.

There is considerable overlap between the principles and intentions of responsible leadership and sustainable leadership. The latter has as its central proponents the body of work by Avery and Bergsteiner (2010, 2011a, 2011b), which proposes 'honeybee' leadership as an alternative to the prevailing shareholder-first 'locust' model and suggests that – rather than requiring a sacrifice in performance to achieve sustainability – this alternative approach can lead to higher performance and resilience for organizations which adopt it. Drawing on their nature-based metaphor, they (2011b) identify 23 principles that differentiate sustainable or 'honeybee' practices from shareholder-first or 'locust' leadership, and arrange them in a pyramid of practices (to be introduced over time) and performance outcomes. Placing innovation, quality and staff engagement at the heart of this framework, they contend that sustainable practices have the capacity to produce positive outcomes in relation to brand

and reputation, customer satisfaction, operational finances and long-term value for both shareholders and other stakeholders. Drawing on the case of Wal-Mart as an early adopter of this approach (2011a), they propose self-interest as a potentially stronger motivator for the shift to sustainable practices than the threat of pressure from major stakeholders or government regulation.

Attempts to steer attention towards the higher order goals that leadership may be utilized to achieve, rather than prescriptions for how to do it, go back a long way. An early attempt was Greenleaf's (1977) servant leadership, based on the idea that leaders should do what they do to serve others rather than for their own glory. Russell and Stone (2002: 150) stated that the 'prime motivation for leadership should be the desire to serve ... Self-interest should not motivate servant leadership: rather it should ascend to a higher plane of motivation that focuses on the needs of others.' They suggest that the functional attributes of the servant leader include honesty, integrity, trust, service and empowerment and that accompanying attributes include stewardship, influence, persuasion and teaching. Thus, servant leadership involves 'standing for what is good and right even when it is not in the financial interest of the organization' (Yukl, 2006: 420). It is interesting to note that stewardship appeared as an accompanying attribute of servant leadership, but not a central requirement. Also addressing the wider responsibilities of business activities, Bolden (2011) links the notion of leading responsibly to issues of sustainability and suggests an agenda for leadership that requires leaders to instil a sense of responsibility for the environment into followers, and to thereby challenge existing business models based solely on generating profit for shareholders. This form of leadership looks beyond wealth creation to consider the needs of a wide range of stakeholders and to balance return on capital with a wider range of possible costs and benefits to be derived from business activity.

Another strand of writing within this genre espouses the notion of purpose or calling as a motivation for leadership. Whilst noting that purpose is arguably axiomatic within leadership discourses that emphasize vision and mission, Kempster et al. (2011) problematize the manifestation of purpose in everyday organizational leadership practices through the work of the moral philosopher Alasdair MacIntyre and his notions of purpose as 'internal goods' associated with well-being that are central to a good human life. MacIntyre (2004) argues that, following the mis-directed good intentions of the Enlightenment, we are now living in a 'post-virtuous era', in which we have lost 'the binding discourse of ethical practice in our dealings with others' (Kempster et al., 2011: 322) – along with our traditional anchors (including religion) to the importance of striving for internal goods – and are subject to increasing pressure to strive for 'external goods'. MacIntyre sees managers as organizational agents for extending this orientation towards external goods and, as such, suggests they are poor moral representatives for the institutions in which they work.

Kempster et al. (2011) build on this position to suggest that societal purposes will be entirely driven out of the discourses within organizations unless addressed through conscious intervention encapsulated within 'leadership as purpose'. It is their aim to steer leadership studies towards a better balance between external and internal goods and corporate and social purposes. As a starting point, they note that leaders as 'managers of meaning' (Smircich and Morgan, 1982) have tended to focus on shaping meaning for employees around existing corporate goals, rather than shifting corporate goals towards broader meaning-related activities and ends. They propose redressing this balance by combining the ideas of MacIntyre and Smircich and Morgan:

> If Smircich and Morgan's (1982) notion that the primary task of leadership is making sense of the flow of organizational experience is connected to MacIntyre's (1997, 2004) philosophy that incorporates virtues, "telos" and "internal goods", we can construct a normative leadership process that seeks to manage the meaning of follower experiences towards sustaining virtues to develop internal goods of personal excellence in order to achieve telos – a good for humans. (Kempster et al., 2011: 325)

They argue that purpose requires greater attention if it is to become manifest in both the corporate and the societal orientations of leaders in organizations, rather than in one to the exclusion of the other. Redressing the balance in this way will require 'personal moral agency' by managers to challenge the purposes of corporate employers: this presupposes the 'right' moral values are already held by managers and leaders. Whilst Kempster and colleagues have done much to clothe leadership for purpose in the trappings of practical reality, this strand of leadership writing more generally is still long on conceptual pronouncements on what leadership should be for, but short on empirical examination of how this translates into practice. As the next section will propose, arguably, the former should be the work of ethicists and philosophers, whilst the latter should be the domain of leadership scholars.

LEADERSHIP RESEARCH: A NOTE ON ADVOCACY VERSUS INQUIRY

As presaged by the preceding section, there follows a brief note on the shift from inquiry to advocacy in leadership scholarship and why this might be problematic. The aim here is not to suggest that leadership scholars should not be aspirational in their focus, or that there is no connection between what leadership is for and how we enact it in practice. Rather, it is to suggest that the shift from inquiry (= how to do leadership better = research) to advocacy (= promulgation of potentially 'un-researchable' or un-operationalizable, aspirational forms of leadership that delineate what we lead for = philosophy) may be just the latest in the continuing travails of leadership as an 'empty signifier' (Kelly, 2014). Kelly's seminal article, in which he posited 'the potential for a negative ontology of leadership; one in which absence, ideological practices and the operation of empty signifiers form the basis for empirical investigation and critical reflection' (2014: 905), stands as a powerful reminder of the dangers of advocating aspirational forms of leadership without grounding them in empirical inquiry. I therefore draw on his argument at some length as an underpinning of my concerns for the current state of leadership scholarship – alas, these concerns have only strengthened in the decade since Kelly's much-cited paper first appeared.

There are three core elements to Kelly's case, relating to the proposal of a negative ontology for leadership as a construct, the implications of its existence as an 'empty signifier' reliant on ideological rather than ontological underpinnings for its 'reality', and the importance of its 'mythical' expression for much of its meaning and power. Kelly's point of departure is the premise that leadership has no intrinsic ontological foundation and is thus dependent on 'second-order', epistemological groundings for its meanings, which are arrived at post hoc. This is equally problematic whether these meanings are framed in terms of leaders, leadership or the outcomes which either of these can produce. This suggests the idea of a 'negative ontology' of leadership such that 'leadership always seems to exist elsewhere, out of sight and out of language' (2014: 914). To borrow from Bennis and Nanus's (1985: 19) delightful simile, 'leadership is like the Abominable Snowman, whose footprints are everywhere but who is nowhere to be seen'.

Given this negative ontology – or ontology of lack – leadership stands as an 'empty signifier': a term that can be filled up with a range of meanings, either by participants in leader–follower relationships and situations, or by researchers seeking to define and codify it. According to Kelly, 'the very purpose of [leadership as a signifier] is not to provide a single meaning, but to create a space through which possible meanings can be negotiated and navigated' (2014: 914). In the context of leadership as a research discipline, he goes on to suggest that it is open to the researcher to decide what substitutes or proxies for leadership (practices, processes, etc.) will provide the most suitable vehicles for representing the negative space left by the empty signifier. At the same time, he argues that it is insufficient to simply draw attention to the fact of leadership as an empty signifier: rather, it is important to identify and highlight the 'work and politics that are performed in [its] name' (2014: 915).

In so saying, he makes the case that whilst 'leadership' is an empty term, this emptiness is 'not without effect or consequence', but instead 'provides a space of productive fantasy through which hopes for a better future or a better world can be expressed, but perhaps never realized' (Kelly, 2014: 915–16). Here Kelly draws on the work of Barthes (1993) to explore the role of myth and myth-making in the power and purpose of the leadership signifier. Using the famous tenet that 'managers are people who do things right and leaders are people who do the right thing' (Bennis and Nanus, 1985: 21), he explicates the way in which mythical chains of signification, moving from 'the first order sign system of "a manager" (signifier) > "managing" (signified) = "doing things right" (sign)' can be utilized to 'produce the mythical connection between morality and leadership; a connection based on the production of an empty signifier that gains force and authority as mythical speech with every reiteration' (2014: 917). It is this interplay between empty signifier and mythical speech, he argues, that underpins the ideological foundations of leadership by giving it the appearance of an ontological reality.

This ideological connection is the real heart of Kelly's argument. He proposes that the 'replacement of truth and fact with the need for beliefs that fit with the socio-political and economic demands of the day' (2014: 913) is what gives the construct substance and keeps researchers and practitioners alike tied to the never-ending task of understanding and/or embodying it. He also suggests that it is this ideological element that explains the recent growth in interest in aspirational forms of leadership as a reflection of the need to address the global challenges we now find ourselves facing. Pulling all of these strands of argument together, for Kelly:

> This is the power of leadership – not its ontological reality as personality, relation, practice or process – but its ideological function to organize, direct, deflect, categorize, centralize, marginalize, inspire, control, liberate, improve, stimulate, seduce, transform, stabilize, threaten, protect and reassure. There is no tension or contradiction in leadership's ability to speak to any and all of these aspirations since it has no content of its own that might cause such antagonism. Through the adoption of a negative ontology we might say that leadership does not deal in content or substance, but in the organization, containment and reproduction of desire. (2014: 912)

So how does this bear on the question of advocacy versus inquiry? For me, the advocating of a range of aspirational forms of leadership is a prime example of the ideological at work. In an echo of Kelly's decade-old concerns, these approaches have taken the empty signifier of leadership and filled it up with whatever seemed politically or socially necessary to address the needs of the day in ideological terms rather than to fill it with genuine 'ontologically' grounded meaning. This is not to suggest that this is a problem in and of itself: we still need 'leadership' – or whatever signifier we choose to replace it with – to fulfil an inspirational (or aspirational?) purpose, as well as a practical or informative one. But we do need to be aware of this inquiry/advocacy gap, and to strive to better ground our aspirations in process and practice – in doing and accomplishing; the how as well as the what.

LEADERSHIP: A DEBASED CURRENCY?

There are other respects in which the underpinnings of the leadership construct are problematic in the context of the 21st century. The case can also be made that the positive intentions of the Enlightenment – together with its unintended capitalist, market-economy consequences – have now passed their sell-by date and are contributing to rather than addressing the global challenges to which they helped to contribute in the first place. If this is the case, then it will be important to move beyond the capitalist baggage of profit and progress that stemmed from Enlightenment thinking if we are to have a chance of resolving these challenges.

The term 'Enlightenment' emerged in English in the later part of the 19th century, with particular reference to French philosophy, as the equivalent of the French term 'Lumières' (used first by Dubos in 1733 and already well established by 1751). In 1783, Jewish philosopher Moses Mendelssohn referred to Enlightenment as a process by which man was educated in the use of reason, whilst for Immanuel Kant (1798) it represented 'man's release from his self-incurred tutelage', this tutelage being 'man's inability to make use of his understanding without direction from another'. Thus, it was seen as a final coming of age: the emancipation of the human consciousness from an immature state of ignorance, in which it was subjugated by religion and monarchy. According to historian Roy Porter (2000), the liberation of the human mind from a dogmatic state of ignorance, founded on the power of religion, is the epitome of what the Age of Enlightenment was trying to capture. This radical shift away from faith-based knowledge and understanding was a response to the preceding century of religious conflict in Europe, and aimed to reform faith back to its generally non-confrontational roots and limit the capacity for religious controversy to spill over into politics and warfare whilst still maintaining a true faith in God. Thus, Enlightenment scholars – such as Spinoza and Mendelssohn – sought to curtail the political power of organized religion and thereby prevent another age of intolerant religious war. In this vein, the period produced novel ideas about religion such as Deism and Atheism, and the promulgation of 'Radical Enlightenment' as a complete separation of Church and State – an idea often credited to English philosopher John Locke. Locke's (1695) rationale for this new principle of the social contract between State and Church rested on the premise that government lacked authority in the realm of individual conscience and that instead there existed a natural right to the liberty of conscience, which must therefore remain protected from any government intervention. Views on religious tolerance and the importance of individual conscience became particularly influential in the American colonies and the drafting of the United States Constitution, where Thomas Jefferson called for a 'wall of separation between church and state'.

Not surprisingly, science came to play a leading role in Enlightenment discourse and thought. Much of what is incorporated in the 'scientific method' (the nature of knowledge, evidence, experience and causation) and some modern attitudes towards the relationship between science and religion were developed by David Hume and Adam Smith during this period, with a particular value being placed on empiricism and rational thought. Many Enlightenment writers and thinkers had backgrounds in the sciences and associated scientific advancement with the overthrow of religion and traditional authority in favour of the development of free speech and thought. The result was tremendous scientific progress during the Enlightenment period, including the discovery of carbon dioxide (fixed air) by the chemist Joseph Black, the argument for deep time by the geologist James Hutton, the invention of the steam engine by James Watt, the experiments of Lavoisier which led to the first modern chemical plant in Paris, and the inventions of the Montgolfier Brothers which led to the first manned flight in 1783. A 'science of man', developed by Hume and other Scottish Enlightenment thinkers, merged a scientific study of how humans behaved in ancient and primitive cultures with a strong awareness of the determining forces of modernity. Modern sociology largely originated from this movement, and Hume's philosophical concepts would also be the basis of classical liberalism. Adam Smith published *The Wealth of Nations*, often considered the first work on modern economics, in 1776. Cesare Beccaria, a jurist and one of the great Enlightenment writers, became famous for his masterpiece *Of Crimes and Punishments* (1764), which was later translated into 22 languages, forming the basis of modern jurisprudence. And prominent intellectual Francesco Mario Pagano wrote important studies such as *Political Essays* (1783) and *Considerations on the Criminal Trial* (1787), which established him as an international authority on criminal law.

There is no doubt that these were all seminal advances in human knowledge and understanding, and that they formed the basis for great steps forward in all aspects of life and society. But they also brought with them less welcome consequences, some of which we have only recognized and acknowledged in recent decades. Dhawan (2014) observes that whilst the exercise of reason deriving from Enlightenment perspectives has been productive of individual emancipation from religious tyranny and the growth of societal democracy and freedom, it has also led to colonialism, imperialism, slavery and crimes against humanity, through the same much-celebrated 'reasoning'. Enlightenment rationality is said to be deeply embedded in the idea of Empire, whose mission involved political subjugation of those it claimed to empower and civilize (Banerjee and Arjaliès, 2021). Thus, the historical narratives through which the European colonial project has been disseminated and reified have been those of 'a liberating and progressive force' (Banerjee and Arjaliès, 2021: 2), whilst the experiences and perspectives of those Indigenous populations on the receiving end have until recently been almost wholly suppressed. Stories of genocide, colonial domination, imported disease, cultural suppression and spiritual subjugation (Dhawan, 2014; Goldberg, 1993) forced upon Indigenous peoples around the globe – India, Africa, the Americas, Australasia – have received barely a mention in our history books and even less in our collective consciences.

At the same time – and of equal significance in the developing narratives around sustainability and global grand challenges – it is argued (Merchant, 1980; Ophuls, 1997) by ecologists that the Enlightenment ideals of progress and development, and the development of a political economy privileging endless growth to which they have given rise, have also had a significant role to play in the degradation of the natural environment. Banerjee and Arjaliès (2021) argue that the human–nature dualism – the notion that humans can control and utilize nature and natural resources for their own purposes – which was a by-product of Enlightenment thinking is primarily responsible for the ecological crisis we face today, but that this alternative to the largely European Enlightenment narrative of progress and reason has been all but obliterated by the Western hegemony which resulted from it. They are unequivocal on this issue:

> The climate emergency facing humanity is a direct outcome of economic and political arrangements that view the natural world as a resource to be exploited only for economic gain while marginalizing alternate worldviews that regard humans as custodians of the planet. (2021: 2)

Similarly Mikhail (2016, cited in Banerjee and Arjaliès, 2021: 5) lays 'species extinction, greenhouse gas emissions, climate change, pollution, soil erosion and melting ice caps' at the door of the Enlightenment, as integral parts of the transformation from pre-modern to modern that has brought us to the Anthropocene.

This notion of the Anthropocene – the current geological epoch in which human activity has been the dominant influence on climate and the environment – is now broadly accepted as the dominant framework for making sense of the modern age, both in terms of the ecological changes taking place and in relation to the role of humans in bringing them about. When human influence on Earth's ecology came to dominate other factors is still much debated, however, with dates ranging from as early as 8,000 years ago when farming and agriculture became widespread (Ruddiman, 2003) to as recently as 1945, when the Earth's geological strata were permanently marked through radiation arising from nuclear fallout (Banerjee and Arjaliès, 2021: 4). Other proposals include the peak of the Industrial Revolution (circa 1800) (Steffen et al., 2011); the invention of the steam engine in the late 18th century, which resulted in growing concentrations of carbon dioxide and methane (Crutzen, 2016) in the atmosphere; and the fossil-fuel-driven economic expansion of the post-war years, starting around 1950 and labelled the 'Great Acceleration' (Steffen et al., 2011). Whilst a case can be made for any or all of these dates as the start of the Anthropocene, it is its association with Enlightenment rationality – through the mechanism of capitalism – that is at the heart of my argument here. Once again, Banerjee and Arjaliès (2021: 5), drawing on earlier work by Ergene, Banerjee and Hoffman (2020), sum the position up both succinctly and starkly:

> If, as Marx demonstrated, alienation of labour from the means of production was a hallmark of modernity, then alienation of nature from humanity marks the Anthropocene. The mastery of nature, a critical Enlightenment narrative, fulfils its destiny in the Anthropocene, where humans are now the most potent force that shapes nature. ... The Anthropocene is the outcome of a political process which sustains a political economy that privileges wealth creation over ecological welfare. (2021: 5)

Inherent in this position is the understanding that human activities have the capacity to – and do, in fact – drive changes in Earth's ecosystems, and that consequently the dichotomy between humans and nature – which underpins Enlightenment rationality through its most potent foot soldier, science – is no longer tenable (Oldfield et al., 2014). Banerjee and Arjaliès (2021: 1) would also argue that what they call 'recent Western imaginaries like the Anthropocene and Gaia proposed to overcome the separation of nature from culture' are, in practice, ineffective, in that they are themselves 'based on exclusions that reflect Enlightenment rationality and legacies of colonialism' (2021: 1).

If science is a foot soldier of the Enlightenment, then leadership is a hand-maiden of capitalism. Clearly, not all leadership is exercised in the pursuit of capitalist goals, but the very notion of both organizational and political leadership in the Western world has, for many decades, been powerfully associated with progress in the form of economic growth and shareholder profits. It has been the remit of the organizational leader to ensure the meeting of these goals for their employer, and it has been the remit of political leaders to create and sustain an environment in which organizations can innovate, manufacture, supply, export and otherwise undertake all such activities as tend to the satisfaction of the growth and profit motivations for which they were formed. If, therefore, the advent of the Anthropocene requires us to question the principles upon which we have organized our Western society, and the aims towards which we have aspired, then it surely requires us to question the role of leadership as its instrument. If the ideals of progress and growth have been elements of the 'baggage' we have loaded upon leadership as a signifier (Kelly, 2014) then it can be argued that the signifier itself is no longer fit for purpose, along with the purposes to which it has predominantly been put.

This is not to say that either the construct of leadership or its daily enactment are inherently or necessarily bad or wrong: I am not proposing the same essential connection that Banerjee and Arjaliès (2021) made between the Enlightenment and capitalism. But I am suggesting that the increasing 'romanticization' of leadership in both academia and the media (Meindl et al., 1985) makes it hard to determine what outcomes can truly be laid at leadership's door and what cannot. This ambiguity, I would argue, suggests that leadership – or, at least, the leadership construct – stands as a debased currency for our current hopes and future aspirations. Better to abandon it and build a new and more credible edifice – one that aligns with our growing understanding of the Anthropocene and the vital importance of redressing the balance in human–nature relations – than to load it with even more baggage in trying to make it fit for purpose in the modern world.

STEWARDSHIP: A CONCEPT FOR ALL SEASONS?

In their seminal work on accounting in the Anthropocene, Bebbington and Rubin (2022) draw attention to the fact that the concept of stewardship has historically underpinned the practice of financial accounting. The process of preparing and auditing financial accounts has as its *raison d'être* the professional custodianship of the financial probity of the organization: it considers the financial resources of the company as held in trust for shareholders and seeks to ensure that these resources are used appropriately and accounted for transparently, thus ensuring the ongoing viability of the company through the continued commitment of its investors. The first duty of any commercial organization must be to sustain itself as a going concern, with this only being possible through the responsible management of its resources and the maintenance of its ability to attract new resources as they continue to operate. Until relatively recently, this duty has been perceived within the closed loop of business owners (shareholders, lenders and other creditors) and the business itself, with business success being seen as a justification in and of itself.

But as Bebbington and Rubin (2022: 582) go on to observe, accounting for financial resources only is no longer sufficient in the Anthropocene, when:

> human actions drive Earth systems functioning, generating effects (for example) on the climate system as well as on the diversity of living creatures. Given these effects, an enlarged understanding of stewardship emerges that focuses on corporate purpose that takes account of wider than financial ambitions and effects as well as on governance processes that can support a broader perspective. (2022: 582)

Underpinning this shift from a purely financial focus to a broader purpose-driven focus is similar to the shift from accounting to accountability. Corporations are increasingly required to hold themselves accountable, not just to their shareholders but to a wide range of stakeholders who may be impacted (positively or negatively) by the organization's operations and activities. Whilst still expected to generate a profit for their shareholders, they are (rightfully) under pressure to do so in a way that is sustainable for employees, communities, wider society and the planet. The widespread currency of the UN Sustainable Development Goals, with their focus on both environmental and societal issues, is a measure of the growing pressure on organizations to take this broader conception of their stewardship duties seriously. The definition of a steward drawn from Maak and Pless (2006) at the start of this chapter – relating to the holding in trust of social, moral and environmental values and resources, and the responsibility for protecting and enriching them for future generations – may no longer appear as the 'pie in the sky' idealism it might once have been dismissed as.

The embeddedness of ideas of stewardship in accounting principles, which stand as a fundamental framework for business operation, is a powerful reason for paying it more attention in both the academic and practical arenas. But Bebbington and Rubin (2022: 582) suggest another when they refer to the importance of 'achieving stewardship for "wicked problems" that emerge from complex adaptive systems'. 'Wicked problems' (Rittell and Webber, 1973) was the phrase utilized by Grint (2005) to delineate those situations that required leadership to resolve them rather than just management. Thus, the connection between leadership and stewardship receives further support.

On this basis, it may perhaps seem that we can graduate to utilizing the concept of stewardship – whether as a qualifier or a substitute – in our leadership thinking without further discussion. But this may be somewhat precipitate: it is easy to assume we know what it means to be a steward, without really getting to grips with its full dimensions and connotations. Is it merely accountability for something (as in the sense of accounting), or does its remit extend to actively holding that something in trust in some way? And if so, for what and to whom? To attempt to answer these questions in the context of leadership – either as a potential substitute or as 'scaffolding' for a better understanding and application of aspirational forms of leadership – this book draws on the rich history of stewardship across a range of research domains to explore what can be usefully – and justifiably – applied to leadership issues, from both academic and practitioner perspectives.

CONCLUSION

I now conclude with a brief overview of the chapters which follow. Having set the scene for why I believe a focus on stewardship is both timely and apposite, Chapter 2 goes backward before going forward: that is, it discusses in more detail 'What's wrong with the Enlightenment?' Specifically, it expands on both historical and recent understandings of the Enlightenment, and its role in Western history; further critiques the focus on progress and profit that modern society has taken as a given for the last hundred years; and explores the role played by leadership in the Enlightenment project.

Chapter 3 then gets to the heart of what stewardship might mean for management and leadership, by developing a core understanding drawn from an integrative review of the literatures across five domains of research. In doing so, it considers both conceptual and empirical research and draws together some key themes within this interdisciplinary body of knowledge that can inform leadership thinking for the future. Chapter 4 takes this discussion further by exploring three core tensions which emerge from the extant stewardship literature, both within and across research domains. These relate to whether core understandings of stewardship have, to date, been backward-looking or forward-looking, whether they have been built on governance frameworks or voluntary action, and whether their primary aim has been the preservation of an existing situation or resource or the initiation of change.

Up to this point, our purpose has been one of integrating and synthesizing what we currently know about stewardship, both the instructive and the challenging. Chapter 5 draws on relational ontologies – both Western and Indigenous – to shift the focus forward to a consideration of how stewardship might inform future leadership. In particular, it explicates the foundational underpinning of these ontologies in a profound connection between humans and nature, and explores the implications of this connection as a counterpoint to the human–nature dualism within modern society. These ideas stand as touchpoints for the final two chapters – which drive the ideas presented thus far into the practical realm of corporate responsibility and propose a future research agenda respectively.

Chapter 6 – the lead author of which is Professor Jan Bebbington of the Pentland Centre for Sustainability in Business – looks at corporate biosphere stewardship and examines what it would entail if corporations were to become active stewards of the biosphere. Drawing from a science-based literature, Jan will set out the requirements that are argued to underpin corporate biosphere stewardship and what organizational science brings to its conception – with a particular focus on the pivotal role of leadership. The chapter culminates with an empirically grounded exploration of the role of 'keystone actors' –

organizations which create disproportionately larger effects by virtue of their size – and the implications for the different leadership capabilities required within these organizations.

The final chapter – Chapter 7 – draws together the threads of the various arguments and perspectives discussed throughout the book and sets out a future research agenda. In doing so, it touches on three perspectives: (1) stewardship *as* leadership – stewardship as a new 'signifier' for our leadership aspirations; (2) stewardship *in* leadership – countering post-Enlightenment capitalism with trusteeship as part of the leader's remit; and (3) stewardship *of* leadership – applying 'reduce, reuse, recycle' to leadership scholarship to refocus the construct. The chapter – and book – concludes with some thoughts on the challenges involved in embedding notions of stewardship in both academic scholarship and practitioner and policy maker agendas.

2.   What's wrong with the Enlightenment?

INTRODUCTION

In the run-up to writing this chapter – and indeed, the entire book – I had what I thought was a reasonable understanding of what people mean when they talk about 'the Enlightenment'. I had covered it in about four PowerPoint slides when introducing the philosophy of the social sciences to my doctoral students, and accepted the popular narrative of 'science over religion' with which it is often summed up. That is to say that I started out with all the common, modern misperceptions about what the Enlightenment was and what it did. This being the case, I had to 'read up' on this topic specifically for this chapter – a journey which proved more fascinating and more complex than I could have imagined in advance. As my sense of how our modern understanding of the Enlightenment emerged, and how this differed from the understandings of those who were part of the movement at the time, so too did the need for a different framing of this chapter from the one I had originally planned – a framing in which an understanding of 'the Enlightenment' was taken as a given. The chapter thus begins with a more substantive introduction to Enlightenment ideas and their history as a necessary precursor to the argument in relation to leadership that it is the purpose of this chapter to make. In crafting this framing, I have been unashamedly selective in my sources, drawing heavily on accounts/perspectives that I found resonant/appealing rather than developing an 'academic' synthesis of the literature. My thanks (for their lucid and compelling perspectives) and apologies (if I have misinterpreted or misrepresented them) go to the authors I have thus drawn upon. In making these selections, I have leant heavily towards the historicization of the Enlightenment rather than engaging with the still ongoing philosophical debates which this term continues to generate (e.g. Baker and Reill, 2001; Garrard, 2006).

Based on this framing, the real heart of the chapter revolves around the ability of 'leadership' as a construct to support us in tackling the world's problems, as captured by the UN Sustainable Development Goals and as – at least in part – deriving from the working out of some of the core themes of Enlightenment thinking. The suggestion by Banerjee and Arjaliès (2021) that

Enlightenment thinking – including leadership's harnessing of the human–nature dualism to claim control over resources and production capabilities in the name of shareholders – is unlikely to be a sound basis for resolving the very ecological problems to which it has historically contributed appears increasingly salient as humanity struggles to address the consequences of 200 years of 'progress' which the Enlightenment kick-started. Instead, the narrative of 'progress' – an unintended offshoot of Enlightenment's goal of human betterment that has become inextricably linked to capitalism – has resulted in a major rift between humans and the most fundamental 'stakeholder' in their activities, namely planet Earth. After discussing the core Enlightenment themes of human betterment, progress and the political economy, and their consequences in terms of economic growth as a 'cure all' for society's ills, inequality and colonialism, the chapter then homes in on the role of leadership. In particular, it asks whether leadership is part of the problem or part of the solution. The chapter concludes with an attempt to 'put Enlightenment back in its box' as a precursor to considering other wisdoms that may serve us better for the future.

THE ENLIGHTENMENT AS INTELLECTUAL MOVEMENT AND HISTORICAL CONSTRUCTION

There is a sense in which there can be said to be two separate 'Enlightenments' – the philosophical movement as it was enacted and understood at the time, and the ways in which it has been reconstructed by historians since. The former was a largely European phenomenon, undertaken by a relatively small group of philosophical writers, and stemming from nuanced perspectives on the issues of the day. Its key themes related to the relationship between reason and religion, a concern that the 'betterment' of the human condition on Earth should take precedence over potential benefits in heaven of living a 'good' life on Earth, and the rise of 'political economy' as a mechanism to bring about material progress. The reconstruction of these ideas by historians, and more recent philosophical thinkers, has resulted in many misconceptions and 'glosses' in relation to these early ideas. The result is a perception of Enlightenment as being in conflict with religion, as being (until very recently) entirely positive in its effects, and as being more cohesive and more geographically widespread than it actually was. This rewriting of the Enlightenment movement – and its seeming ability to change to suit the needs of the time – have perhaps resulted in its becoming another 'hembig' (Alvesson and Sandberg, 2020), but arguably a hembig that has reached the end of its road.

In its original understanding, the Enlightenment was an 18th-century intellectual movement that held out the prospect of a new, and explicitly modern, understanding of the place of humans in the world, and sought to lay the foundations of a radical improvement in the human condition (Robertson, 2015). As such, it was a philosophical idea as much as an historical phenomenon. The English word 'enlightenment', by which the movement came to be known, was a translation of the French word '*lumières*' and the German word '*Aufklärung*' and reflects the three main centres of intellectual activity within the movement, namely Scotland, Paris and a small number of German-speaking cities, including Berlin, Göttingen and Königsberg. The common idea of 'light' had strong religious connotations at the time, but also reached back to, for example, Plato's thesis of 'light [as] knowledge of the true, which we acquire as we leave the caves whose walls of prejudice and ignorance have obscured our vision' (Robertson, 2015: 2). In this context, therefore, the idea of light signified the development of human understanding from its genesis in the senses to its use of reflection and reason. French mathematician Jean D'Alembert depicted this progression in human understanding as a 'genealogy', drawing on 'modern' philosophers such as Bacon, Newton and Locke (as opposed to their 'ancient' Greek and Roman counterparts) to propose a 'tree of knowledge'. A similar line of thought in circulation at the time emerged from Étienne de Condillac's work on language as the vehicle by which senses and emotions were transformed into higher mental faculties. He believed that the structure of language reflects the structure of thought, and compared ideas to the sounds of a harpsichord. Other ideas contributing to this perspective included Benedict Spinoza's materialism and Gottfried Leibniz's rationalism, whilst evidence of the progression of human understanding during this period included the Scientific Revolution of the previous century – a term used to refer to advances in several branches of 'natural philosophy' – and David Hume's attempts to elaborate a new 'science of man'.

By the middle of the 18th century, the idea of 'enlightenment' was more strongly associated with the intellectual movement than it was with religion. Leading Jewish philosopher Moses Mendelssohn regarded it as 'the indispensable handmaid of culture and education' (Robertson, 2015: 6), whilst for Kant – in perhaps the most well-known response to the question 'What is Enlightenment?' – it stood as the 'freedom to make public use of one's reason with the goal of liberating mankind from its self-imposed immaturity' (Robertson, 2015: 7). It is this positioning of reason as the counterpoint to religious faith – and more importantly the power of the institutions of religion – that is often taken as characterizing the Enlightenment as being anti-religion, and has led to the simplification of the movement into 'science versus religion', but this is an unjustified simplification and fails to recognize both the nuances of Kant's stance and the many voices which contested his definition. Such simplifications also fail to recognize the interest of Enlightenment thinkers in broader issues of literature, education and culture – that is, not just religion – and the variety of concerns and contexts that they brought to their writing.

As already noted, the popular, modern conception of the Enlightenment is that it was 'anti-religion', and that it advocated science over faith as the true source of knowledge. As Bartlett (2001: 1) summarized it, 'the Garden of Eden gave way to the State of Nature as the true portrait of our original condition, the obedient love of God to the fear of violent death as our deepest passion'. The supposed religious hostility of Enlightenment thinkers is thus widely regarded as the catalyst for the 'secularization' of society and the resultant shift from religious observation as a necessary dimension of social life to its more limited role as a matter of choice. Whilst there is an element of truth in this portrayal, it is a gross over-simplification and one which fails to do justice to both the aims and the complexity of Enlightenment thinking. In fact, Enlightenment thinking can be associated with a wide spectrum of attitudes towards religion, and only 'radical Enlightenment' should be identified with a radical critique of the rationality and coherence of religious belief (Robertson, 2015). More broadly, Enlightenment's engagement with religion represented a consolidation of a number of existing lines of enquiry and argument – in particular, those that adopted a historical approach to religion – combined with a practical concern to prevent the continuation of the religious wars that had been plaguing their nations in the recent – and not so recent – past. This historical perspective was now set within a new reluctance to sacrifice the possibilities of life here on Earth to whatever prospects might be held out by the Church on behalf of life in the world to come.

Enlightenment engagement with questions of religion began with historical enquiry into the nature of religion itself. Concerning itself with the Abrahamic faiths, it took as a point of departure their nature as 'revealed' religions in which the core tenets of the faith were set out in key texts, and in particular the Christian Bible. Alongside this was the consideration of the 'law of nature' or 'natural religion', which came with the understanding that scientific discoveries reinforced – rather than challenged – religious faith through enhancing human understanding of the miracle of God's design of nature. From this point of departure, Enlightenment scholars undertook an historical reassessment of the Bible as a source of revelation, in particular raising questions over the stability and interpretation of the text. Key weaknesses were highlighted in relation to its authorship, translation and chronology, and the implications of these weaknesses for its claim to revealing the word of God and hence the tenets of a Godly life. The conclusion to these deliberations was the understanding of the Bible as key to the moral and political foundations of *this* world, rather than the next (Robertson, 2015). This in turn led to the questioning of the necessity for religion per se, and the emergence of the radical 'free thinking' movement. As an adjunct to the perceived 'demotion' of faith as a fundamental of human life, Hume (1757/2007) suggested that whilst the polytheism that had preceded Christianity was mere superstition, Christian monotheism – whilst a natural progression in human thought – was little better in that it tended towards fanaticism. In an alternative interpretation of the role of religion in society, French philosopher Nicolas-Antoine Boulanger focused on the development of commemorative, funerary and liturgical religious ceremonies as responses to catastrophe – as exemplified by the Flood – and the insight they provided into human nature. More broadly, in his *Political Essays* (1783) Italian jurist, thinker and author Francesco Pagano offered an account of the course of human history which can be seen as most fully realizing the potential of historical perspectives of religion for society through the connection it makes between this history and the notion of 'progress'. This latter can be argued to be the 'defining concern of Enlightenment thought' (Robertson, 2015: 34).

A second strand of Enlightenment concern with religion related to religious tolerance. Whilst this idea significantly pre-dated the 18th century, the long history of civil and international wars stemming from religious tension led some Enlightenment writers to argue for the superiority of civil peace over confessional uniformity. Different mechanisms and bases were proposed for enacting this priority. For Thomas Hobbes, the overriding principle of a sovereign's power was to determine the common form of worship to be adopted across their realm, in the interests of civil peace. By contrast, John Locke maintained that the law of nature obliges people to worship God in religious communities of their own choosing, over which civil authority – including sovereign authority – has no legitimate jurisdiction. Still others built on Spinoza's metaphysics – and the argument that since God is identified with nature, the freer and fuller the investigation of nature the closer the individual would come to God – to propose the fullest possible liberty to think and to pursue an understanding of God, including freedom of worship, compatible with the peace of society. For Voltaire, religious tolerance was a matter of manners rather than conscience, and stemmed from the greater degree of respect for others which resulted from an enhanced understanding of human behaviour: this, in turn, stemmed from the exercise of reason as a route towards enlightenment. Perhaps the culmination of this strand of Enlightenment concern emerged in the British American colonies where amongst the truths held to be self-evident in their Declaration of Independence (1776) were the inalienable rights of life, liberty – including religious liberty – and the pursuit of happiness.

The third front on which Enlightenment thinkers engaged with religion concerned the political relationship between the sacred and the civil, and the role of civil authorities in ensuring that 'claims of grace' should not continue to endanger civil peace through the enactment of measures to prevent further religious wars (Robertson, 2015). As with religious tolerance, this was a concern that pre-dated the Enlightenment itself, but the late 17th century provided a new context in which to rehearse the existing arguments and to develop new ones. A central manifestation of this strand of thinking took the form of new 'civil' histories of the states of Europe, the most well-known of these treatises being Edward Gibbon's (1776–1789) six-volume *The History of the Decline and Fall of the Roman Empire*. Whilst much of Gibbon's reasoning, and in particular his attribution of the fall of the Roman Empire to the advent of Christianity, has since fallen out of favour it has also been claimed as representing the best of Enlightenment engagement with religion (Robertson, 2015) and as aiming to do justice to both civil and sacred history. Whilst this claim might represent Gibbon's ambition rather than his achievement, *Decline and Fall* did demonstrate the impossibility of writing either a purely civil or a purely sacred history of the relationship between Church and state and the value of eliding the distinction between a natural law of morality and salvation by divine grace.

Overall, then, the Enlightenment was not simply and wholly critical of religion, nor was it desirous of replacing faith with reason and science. Rather, it contributed to the understanding of religious doctrine and practice, and set out a new thesis concerning the balance between religious and secular concerns and between the peace of society and freedom of belief. Thus, to return to the opening premiss of this discussion, whilst the Enlightenment certainly contributed to the longer-term process of secularization, it was not the cataclysmic cause of this shift through a wholesale attack on religion. What it did do – through sceptical, historical enquiry – was to shift the focus away from the promise of an afterlife and towards the desire for a good life in the here-and-now, and shine a light on the way in which religious teaching had actually served to provide a blueprint for this earthly end as much as it had set out the path for entry into heaven.

Alongside its contemporaneous association with secularization, the Enlightenment is also frequently understood in relation to its supposed political consequences, and in particular the French Revolution. More recent interpretations have shifted the focus onto its social and cultural impact, and onto exploring the mechanisms through which a relatively small number of 'Men of Letters' were able to have such far-reaching impact on public opinion and public life. The emergence of a 'public sphere' of life – separate from Church and State – and the 'institutions of sociability' (Robertson, 2015) of which this public sphere came to consist in the 18th century played an important role in the movement's success. The proliferation of coffee houses, masonic lodges and social 'salons' all offered spaces where the general public could meet to talk about ideas, free of the constraints of religious ceremony or civil formality. At the same time, the expansion of the printing industry – driven by increases in scale and accessibility and decreases in cost – offered the public more ideas on which to exercise their thoughts and conversations. Review journals brought knowledge of books and their content to people who would not otherwise have had access to them, thus further expanding the reach of

Enlightenment ideas and their authors' status. The advent of copyright laws – and the independent income this generated for authors, leaving them free of the constraints of patronage – was also instrumental in generating the intellectual independence which drove, or at least facilitated, the Enlightenment movement. Enlightenment thinking was also embedded in the structure of society through the founding of academic chairs in some universities – Halle, Königsberg, Göttingen, Glasgow and Edinburgh, for example – where those who would go on to become government ministers and officials might go to be educated. In Britain, where the Enlightenment was a largely Scottish affair, both Oxford and Cambridge remained 'unreconstructed'. More directly shaping public opinion were the informal societies – for example, the Society of Improvers in the Knowledge of Agriculture, formed in Scotland in 1723 – through which ideas based on reason and rational knowledge were disseminated into the daily lives of ordinary people.

The historical (re)construction of the Enlightenment began to surface in the early 20th century, as scholars sought to explicate the intellectual origins of the religious wars and civil revolutions of the period. The process of historical construction gained momentum following World War II in an attempt to frame Enlightenment thinking as a better basis for articulating a sense of past nobility than the extreme nationalism and racial doctrines of the recently endured war. That it was historians as well as philosophers who undertook this endeavour perhaps explains the ever-increasing topical breadth and geographical scope that has been frequently attributed to the, at the time, relatively localized and focused movement. The modern, popular notion of the Enlightenment owes much to its establishment as an academic discipline in the 1950s and 1960s and the consequent identification of Enlightenment themes with broad, European philosophical ideas that were then emerging. This expanded and elaborated reconstruction, which morphed according to the needs of the time, also took widespread root in the public consciousness as an emblem of modern humanity and society. In this way, the Enlightenment expanded geographically, socially and intellectually to go from being a movement centred in a small number of cities across Europe, focusing on a relatively narrow set of ideas, to being a global concept that infiltrates every aspect of intellectual activity. As suggested by historian John Pocock, Enlightenment went from being a single, cohesive discourse to being a 'family' of discourses – after Wittgenstein's theory of languages – and it is through this notion of family resemblance that it has been able to expand and shift to fit the changing interests of both modern scholarship and societal concern (Robertson, 2015).

Not surprisingly, given the changing circumstances in which historians have sought to utilize the Enlightenment to serve their current needs, and the different framings of 'human betterment' that these needs have reflected, the Enlightenment has had a contested history since interest in it first arose. Most

recently, the positive gloss that Enlightenment-driven 'progress' had historically worn has begun to wear off, and the downsides of *material* betterment
have come to the fore. It is to this journey from progress to the Anthropocene
that we now turn.

CONSEQUENCES OF ENLIGHTENMENT THINKING: 'PROGRESS', THE MARKET ECONOMY AND THE ANTHROPOCENE

As already indicated, the Enlightenment heralded a shift in focus from the
life to come to life on Earth. Manifested in a striving for the betterment of the
human condition, this core theme came with a number of consequences, both
moral and practical. Moral considerations revolved around the need to balance
a religious duty to promote the good of others with the believed supremacy of
the selfish passions, and the role of the state in promoting and maintaining this
balance. More practical were the implications of delivering human betterment,
particularly in the form of material well-being. This kind of 'progress' required
growth in the material goods available, as well as increased income with which
to purchase them. It required a greater focus on what became known as 'political economy' – what we would call the discipline of economics – to manage
the market economy which resulted. And it resulted in some acknowledged
but less positive outcomes – an increase in inequality, for example – that have
ultimately led us to the current dilemmas of the Anthropocene.

The notion of human betterment – perhaps the *raison d'être* of the
Enlightenment – was grounded in the prospect of greater good and the
mitigation of much suffering: the alleviation of hunger and an increase in
the accessibility of the 'necessities and conveniences' of life for all ranks
in society (Robertson, 2015: 50). Proposed by Scottish economist Adam
Smith, it was seen as encompassing more than just material goods, however.
Betterment could also be understood in terms of status – although this could
be achieved, at least in part, through the acquisition of material wealth. There
was, for Smith, an acknowledged moral ambivalence in relation to the desire
for betterment, and he explicitly recognized that it had the potential to exacer-
bate the existing inequalities in society. Rousseau's critique of the moral and
political consequences of individual betterment at the expense of others was
particularly strident, and stands as a key writing of the Enlightenment period.

The notion of 'society' as a precursor to betterment was a key concept in the
Enlightenment's inquiry into moral philosophy, history and political economy
in the 18th century. Understanding how and why humans became sociable,
developed social institutions and – to some degree at least – overcame the
selfish striving for personal survival and advancement that we inherited from
our animal ancestors formed the subject matter of much philosophical and

historical writing of the period. German philosopher Samuel Pufendorf suggested that humans were obliged to be social with one another both by the laws of nature and by God's command. At the same time, he acknowledged that our natural state was one of unsociability, where our passions and individual desire took precedence over any concern we might have for others. It was, he said, because of these competing drivers of behaviour that humans need others to govern them, and to moderate the effects of their natural passions. In this context, the driver for sociability, and for overcoming mutual suspicion and selfish desire, was utility rather than virtue. The so-called 'problem of sociability' (Robertson, 2015: 53) was first resolved historically, through an understanding of the laws of nature and how best to survive within them. This in turn led to the development of societal institutions which served the collective good and, ultimately, institutions of state designed to enact the same solutions at a national and international level.

In a similar vein to Pufendorf, Thomasius focused on the role of 'decorum' and the rules of society in taming, or at least managing, the passions. At a national level, he saw the ultimate purpose of the state as being the containment of religious passions, and hence the prevention of civil and international wars of religion. In contrast, whilst Pufendorf and Thomasius saw this kind of sociability as being historically acquired, English philosopher John Locke contended that under God's command we are under direct obligation to seek the good of others as well as ourselves: that is, we do not have to acquire this through a process of civilization. Blaise Pascal, in his *Lettres Provinciales* (1657), drew on Augustinian theology to suggest that it was, in fact, self-interest that somehow brought and kept humans together. This thesis coincided with a new interest in Epicurism, the notion that we should aim for what is useful and agreeable rather than striving for the moral excellence of Stoicism as the soundest basis for living sociably together. In a satire on the hypocrisy of attempting to reform society through the imposition of moral restraint, social commentator Bernard Mandeville (1714) offered an unusual analysis – which he claimed was philosophical as well as satirical – on the workings of sociability in 18th-century London as an exemplar of the 'modern' city. In it, he accepted that human passions could only be tamed by the institution of a state-imposed system of justice, but maintained that in a city like London such systems still left significant scope for the passions to be indulged in harmless – or at least legal – ways. His own particular interest was in luxury goods – particularly women's fashions – and their acquisition and display as indicators of social status. Through the desire to emulate those from a higher social status than oneself, women of all social classes contributed to the 'emotional structure of "luxury"' (Outram, 2019: 55) which in turn underpinned its economic importance. Despite suggesting that women and their love of fashion caused a 'disjunction between consumerism and virtue' (1723: 236),

Mandeville also claimed there were significant economic benefits to this type of luxury consumption, in that it promoted a degree of wealth-distribution and enhanced self-esteem that outweighed any moral downsides. At the same time, the consumption of luxury – and other – goods served to create employment, encourage commerce and promote diversity of expression. As such, Mandeville saw London as an excellent representation of human betterment, notwithstanding the absence of any moral justification for the behaviour he celebrated.

Whilst Smith saw sympathy with the motives and circumstances of others as an important – though not necessarily sufficient – basis for moral philosophy and the requirement to consider the good of others, Kant refuted the derivation of principles from the historical observation of social behaviour which this implied. His notion of 'moral autonomy', which is synonymous with Enlightenment thinking and one of the most well-known statements of Enlightenment aims, rests rather on a priori formulations grounded in reason. On this basis, moral values and principles should be universally applicable and must stand independent of both Church and State. As Robertson (2015) notes, however, this notion of a priori ethics did not resolve the problem of sociability; reformulating the intractability of this problem as 'unsocial sociability', Kant acknowledged both the resilience of human passions and the inadequacy of institutions of justice and government in countering them.

At a more practical level, 'society' in the 18th century emerged through a number of innovations that changed how individuals interacted, and the rights and duties they held with respect to each other. The legal right to hold land as property was foundational to the accumulation of wealth and status. The invention of paper money (first issued by the Bank of England in 1694) contributed to this ability to accumulate wealth, as well as to the facilitation of trade in goods and services. Both of these innovations were grounded in and reliant upon the institutions of government and an effective legal system that enabled individuals to rely upon the terms of trade or the maintenance of property rights within a well-governed and 'civil' society. At the same time, the shift from rural to city dwelling for many – including those who were reaping the rewards of land ownership – and the increased productivity arising from the 'division of labour' which it brought about (Outram, 2019) promoted the production of more goods upon which they could spend their money and the increase in leisure time (for some) to enjoy the kind of social opportunities (coffee houses, 'salons', masonic lodges and the consumption of ideas in print) already discussed above.

The turn to history associated with the Enlightenment was a manifestation of the belief that political events should be understood within the framework of the society in which they took place. For this reason, historical accounts often focused on the structure of ranks within society and the manners of people at different levels, as well as contextualizing these within the constraints arising from different geographical locations, climatic conditions and means of economic subsistence. These considerations resulted in a re-conception of history as a dynamic process rather than a static record of events. Inherent in this dynamic process was the notion of 'progress' – another cornerstone of Enlightenment thinking. Thus, the early evolution of society progressed through the formation of communities, the cultivation of the Earth and the potential to possess property and land, all of which were understood as preconditions for later forms of economic progress. The notion of progress came to be captured by the shaping of proposed 'stages' in human and societal development. So, for example, Ferguson (1767) proposed that barbarian societies were distinguished from mere savages by their acceptance of property rights, but 'polished society' and 'commercial nations' required the acceptance of the personal rights of the individual. This, in turn, required that the individual accepted the subordination of their position within a secure social and political hierarchy. An alternative classification of the stages of societal development (Robertson, 2015) relied on the prevailing modes of subsistence, moving from hunting to pastoral, to agricultural, to commercial.

Whilst these stage-based models enabled historians – and their audiences – to think in terms of the progress of society overall, it was also acknowledged that progress was not uniform in its effects and degree and that a 'racial hierarchy' (Robertson, 2015: 62) resulted that saw white Europeans occupying privileged places at the summit of the hierarchy whilst black Africans were relegated to the bottom. The reality of this inequality – and its manifestations in colonialism and the legacy of the slave trade – is everywhere around us in the 21st century, but was not universally acknowledged by Enlightenment thinkers. Hence, for example, Adam Smith's (1776) classic exposition of the 'natural progress of opulence' in *The Wealth of Nations* – in which 'the rising tide lifts all boats' (Outram, 2019: 46) – significantly underplayed the potential for some 'boats' to be held under by the oppressive activities or unequal opportunities of others. The absence of ethical and specifically teleological motivations in much Enlightenment thinking – grounded rather in reason than in altruism – resulted in a similar absence of the idea of purposive development as a cause of progression from one stage to another. There was thus no assumption that progress between stages was automatic, or that the institutions of society – with their restraining effects on the selfish passions – would intervene to promote its increased likelihood.

Rather, 'progress' was seen as the result of individuals exercising their free will on the back of the crucial human quality of 'perfectibility' – the capacity to change and to improve their original condition – and their selfish desire to do so. On this argument, the consequence of the acceptance of property was encouragement of the human desire to distinguish oneself from others by increasing one's own status, which in turn led to inevitable inequalities. The previously unimaginable availability of goods – including inessential luxury goods – resulting from the material rewards of ownership and innovation likewise led to corruption. It was the irreducible existence of the potential for selfish acts of free will that gave rise to this potential for corruption alongside the potential for improvement. Smith's argument of benefits for all seemed blind to this detrimental outcome of what he termed the 'invisible hand' of political economy, an idea that became a central discourse of the Enlightenment. This 'invisible hand' saw only the employment created by the desire for status, not the often appalling working conditions and inadequate wages that went with it. It saw the wealthy 'divid[ing] with the poor the produce of all the[] improvements' arising from their attempts at 'the gratification of their own vain and insatiable desires', completely ignoring the lack of moral progress which was so often manifest in the industrial and commercial practices of the day. For Smith, the transformative power of commerce was measured solely in material wealth, defined as per capita income across the nation as a whole, and progress was the ability of a society to keep this per capita income increasing. This commercial progress should be conducted as fully and freely as was compatible with the peace and defence of the nation. Thus, growth – the inevitable bedfellow of progress – became another brick in the wall of human betterment in this world rather than the next, and a legacy for which we are still paying today. And whilst no variant of Enlightenment promised endless growth (Robertson, 2015), the absence of an 'exit strategy' – a moral basis or practical mechanism for halting the production and consumption juggernaut – has arguably resulted in the global problems of the Anthropocene as a direct descendant of Enlightenment's betterment project.

The attainment of human betterment through progress and growth brought with it the development of a market economy – dependent on production and trade rather than individual subsistence – and the invention of 'political economy' as a body of understanding and an academic discipline. Emerging between the end of the 17th century and the French Revolution in 1789 (Outram, 2019), political economy – what we would today refer to as economics – concerned itself with such issues as production, consumption, trade, and financial issues such as currency and borrowing. The term is reflective of the deeply political origins of the writers' perspectives on these issues and their basis in political theory rather than economics per se. The scope of the subject, in relation to concerns of international rather than localized trade, the growing momentum of widespread industrialization and the role of the state in controlling vital commodities such as grain, was also reflective of the activities of empire building which accompanied it. Thus, the growth of political economy as a separate intellectual discipline was strongly shaped by the practical European concerns of the 18th century, together with their knock-on effects. Spanish, Portuguese, Dutch, French and British colonial territories gave access to new and exotic goods, at the same time as generating colonial conflicts and European wars. The huge cost of these wars, and the debts which resulted, led first to economic crisis and then to financial innovations that reshaped both domestic and international economies. The founding of national banks – the Bank of England was founded in 1694 – and the invention of paper money gave rise to national debt rather than royal debt as the linchpin of the credit needed to support economic expansion, and as an alternative to taxation as a source of funding for further global ambition.

At the same time, the measure of a successful state came to revolve around economic matters rather than purely territorial ones – or around its ability to enforce confessional uniformity on foreign territories. International competition became of prime importance and economic ideologies – such as mercantilism as a 'zero-sum game' – became inextricably linked with ideas of progress and growth. Under the auspices of colonialism, most countries – including England – that possessed colonial territories insisted that they ship back raw materials to the 'mother country' and bought finished goods from them, thus making it all but impossible for them to develop industries of their own.

This, together with the slave trade which supported much colonial, mercantile activity, was the source of growing resentment and a number of backlashes. Some colonies managed to develop successful local economies despite their colonial overlords, whilst the American revolution of 1776 saw the British colonies in North America throw off their yoke entirely. Underlying all of these colonial adventures – and another source of resentment – was the ambiguity surrounding the espoused motives of the 'civilizing mission' (Outram, 2019: 49) of colonialism to bring about the religious conversion of the Indigenous peoples who fell under their rule, versus the perceived actual motive of commercial dominance and exploitation these peoples experienced at the hands of the settlers. Similarly, the progressive ideals expressed in Enlightenment projects of colonialization were frequently translated into expedient processes of settlement with clearly capitalist intent (Brand, 2017) at the same time that both the capitalist narrative and that of the experience of the Indigenous populations thus settled were largely suppressed. This ambiguity was further clouded by the existence of nearly sovereign commercial companies, such as the East India Company. This company, granted the rights to autonomous government of its territorial acquisitions, to mint money, to command fortresses and troops, to form alliances, to make war and peace, and to exercise both civil and criminal jurisdiction over its possessions in the Indies by Charles II (Chisholm, 1911), was an almost 'absolute' institution (Outram, 2019) due to the vast distance between its operations on the ground and its legal and financial operations back in London. As noted by Diderot, the moral iniquities which this system allowed to persist in the colonies were in no way for the 'happiness of mankind' (cited in Outram, 2019). Interestingly, Adam Smith stood as an opponent to both mercantilism and colonialism (Outram, 2019), whilst more recently, the argument has been made (Duara, 2021: 610) that the 'nation form is the "epistemic engine" driving the global circulatory and doxic Enlightenment ideal of the conquest of nature and the perpetual growth that sustains the runaway technosphere'. Thus, all the crises of the current and last century – financial, economic, epidemic and climatological – can arguably be attributed to the cascading effects of the pursuit of national interests and the ownership of national territory and its associated resources.

Another fundamental aspect of progress and growth was the need to command the natural resources with which to produce goods. As already noted, this was an underpinning rationale for colonialism, but was also a concern of non-colonial states such as Germany. For them, a key economic ideology of the period was Cameralism (Outram, 2019: 52), derived from the German word '*Kammer*' (treasury), and perhaps the oldest and longest-lasting of the disciplines created under the heading of political economy (Outram, 2019). This ideology focused explicitly on the perspective of the ruling elite and their ability to find, measure and exploit natural resources through the mechanism of new bureaucracies. Concerned in particular with the large-scale exploitation of minerals, timber and agricultural land, they drew power from their ability to control these and other resources to the detriment of small-holders and peasants who could not compete with them. They were aided in this endeavour by entrepreneurs and inventors who sold schemes which promised to enhance the ability of purchasers to access valuable raw materials. These schemes ranged from new water pumps and new ways of rearing cattle to new systems for drilling soldiers or new ways of teaching in the universities in which future bureaucrats were educated (Outram, 2019: 53). Despite this clearly exploitative stance towards the Earth's resources, Cameralists still claimed a deeply religious underpinning for their ideology, in which they 'remembered the biblical injunction that the natural world was created by God for man, and that man should be its steward as well as its exploiter' (Outram, 2019: 53).

All of these activities were built on the implicit foundation of nature as a resource for humans to utilize and consume at their will, and the resultant human–nature bifurcation (Walsh et al., 2021). Deeply embedded in Western epistemologies arising from the Enlightenment and the Scientific Revolution which followed, this bifurcation has been claimed as 'largely responsible for creating profound divisions and patterns of exploitation between humans and nonhumans' (Walsh et al., 2021: 77) and producing the 'philosophy of empiricism that shaped the development of science, technology, and industry throughout the modern period'. The result, arguably, is the Anthropocene: 'the proposed geological epoch in which human activities outstrip glaciers in changing the face of the Earth' (Tsing, 2016). Drawing on the shared genealogy of *Anthropo*cene and *anthropo*logy in 'Enlightenment Man' (2016: 3) Tsing argues that the notion of the Anthropocene 'refuses the heroism of Man's struggle against His great antagonist Nature and reveals the terrors of the planet-wide destruction'. For her, the bifurcation between humans and nature produces 'ecologies of alienation' (Tsing, 2016: 13) through which 'living things are transformed into resources – future assets – by removing them from their life worlds' and making them into 'machines of replication'. In this way, 'progress' is enacted through 'production', and ultimately leads to crisis. As an anthropologist, Tsing's sense of crisis encapsulates the 'virulent magic and maleficence of the colonial embrace' (2016: 8) through which rich resources were acquired and cheap labour was ensnared, such that '[f]rom its inception, then, modernity has been layered with the histories of the colonized and the excluded' (2106: 10–11). Whilst she goes on to explore the 'patchy-ness' of the repercussions of the Anthropocene, and the importance of grounding our understanding of these repercussions parochially as well as globally, she nonetheless argues against the potential of a 'good Anthropocene' in which the application of capitalism and technology will fix the problems that have so far been created. As she powerfully concludes:

> Man will be in charge of supervising Himself. But the master's tools will never dismantle the master's house. If new forms of human and non-human death arise in ecologies of alienation, more alienation will only exacerbate the problem. (Tsing, 2016: 13)

Whilst Tsing draws on climate change, the extinction crisis and radioactive pollution as examples of the human legacy to planet Earth, we are increasingly recognizing the whole gamut of the UN's Sustainable Development Goals, both human and environmental, as standing in the shadow of Enlightenment-driven 'progress'. As noted in Chapter 1, there is hope that this recognition will over time trigger a fundamental shift away from the historical focus on growth fuelled by consumerism, at the same time as challenging the ability of Enlightenment-based thinking to solve global issues created by that same Enlightenment thinking (Banerjee and Arjaliès, 2021). At the same time, the question has rightly been asked as to whether the post-Enlightenment lesson concerning the limits to our ability to control nature – and the future – to suit our own agenda has, in fact, been learnt (Horlick-Jones, 2013). In the context of risk analysis as a product of Enlightenment thinking and a perceived mechanism for delivering the 'ultimate Enlightenment fantasy: to provide successive generations with the capacity to progressively control the world more effectively' (2013: 489), Horlick-Jones highlights the potential for risk analysis to be a source of future risks by 'sweeping them under the carpet' and instead indulging in 'fantasies [of innovation and control] characteristic of the worst romantic excesses of Enlightenment thinking' (2013: 490). This argument is strongly resonant of both our assumption that 'more of the same' can get us out of the problems historically generated by an insatiable desire for progress and growth, and much of the world's current response to the impending climate change crisis.

'ENLIGHTENED' LEADERSHIP: PART OF THE PROBLEM OR PART OF THE SOLUTION?

Whilst the notion of political leadership has been a subject of study from time immemorial – Aristotle was trying to understand leadership in a political context over 2,300 years ago – organizational leadership can arguably be understood as a child of the Enlightenment. In the late 19th and early 20th centuries, growth in demand for goods and services by a more affluent population (in the Western world, at least) led to a move away from craft-based production in favour of more mechanized methods capable of producing in greater quantities. Small craft shops gave way to larger factories – originally 'manufactories'– and the era of the deskilled production worker began. The core ideas of 'scientific management' which followed were developed by Frederick Winslow Taylor in the 1880s and 1890s, and were first published in his monograph *Shop Management* in 1903 and later expanded in *The Principles of Scientific Management*, published in 1911. As a foreman at the Midvale Steel Works in Philadelphia, Pennsylvania, Taylor noticed the natural differences in productivity between workers, which he attributed to differences in talent, intelligence or motivation. In attempting to formalize these observations, he was one of the first people to apply scientific methods to the problems of production and manufacturing, devising a systematic method of analysing and synthesizing work processes that would enable him to develop 'best practices' that could then be generalized to other factories. He believed that working practices based on standardization would produce better-quality outputs and more efficient production than the old craft-related 'rules of thumb' which he still saw operating around him. Based on careful study of how specific work tasks were accomplished most effectively, he implemented detailed step-by-step procedures – the bedrock of 'scientific management' – that were contingent on a high level of managerial control over employee work practices. Thus, the early remit of management was to control and administer 'unwilling' workers, with the emphasis very firmly on efficient production and task completion. Whilst Taylor had observed that some workers were more motivated than others, he did not suggest that managers should try to motivate them, but only to monitor their work rate. These ideas were the early origins of 'Fordism' and the development of mass production lines that moved at a certain pace and required workers to keep up. By 'management' here, we are talking about little more than 'supervision' – and large organizations had 'owners' rather than 'leaders'. These were the people who invested the capital and extracted the profits, and saw their workers as just another resource in the production process.

Henri Fayol, a contemporary of Taylor's though not a colleague, developed a general theory of business administration independent of scientific management – often known as Fayolism – which became one of the most influential contributions to modern concepts of management. As defined by Fayol, business administration consists of the performance or management of business operations and thus the making or implementing of major decisions within an organization. In this context, 'administration' refers to the all-encompassing process of organizing people and resources efficiently so as to direct activities towards common goals and objectives. As such, and in contrast with Taylor's more supervisory version, it is clearly recognizable as 'management' as we know it today. Fayol's was one of the first comprehensive statements of a general theory of management, proposing six primary management functions, namely: forecasting, planning, organizing, commanding, co-ordinating and controlling. Reducing these functions to four, Daft (2003) covered much the same ground at the same time as consolidating commanding and co-ordinating into the more recognizable 'leading'.

From these progress-inspired roots, the notion of organizational leadership developed through a series of stages, each of which brought the construct closer to something we would recognize today. And each new perspective grew from the failings of its predecessor to explain what was happening in organizations and to provide the scaffolding for leadership that would deliver the required results of shareholders (increasingly the successors to direct owners as the dominant stakeholders in the industrial enterprise). At the same time, the supposed distinction between leadership and management was also debated and defined. So, for example, Kotter claimed that:

> Management is about coping with complexity. Its practices and procedures are largely a response to one of the most significant developments of the twentieth century: the emergence of large organisations. … Leadership, by contrast, is about coping with change. Part of the reason it has become so important in recent years is that the business world has become more competitive and more volatile. (Kotter, 2001: 86)

He thus attributes the rise of leadership in an organizational context to the change of pace and growth of uncertainty to be observed there. Early industrialists were focused on producing and selling goods in a relatively unchanging environment and with relatively little competition. Good management – to produce and sell products efficiently – was sufficient here. The advent of more competition between manufacturers, more demand from customers for novelty and innovation, and – most recently – the development of a 'global market' have resulted in the need for businesses to be in a constant state of change, bringing workers along with them. This has required leadership both to drive it and to deal with its consequences. From this we can see how the notion of leadership has been inextricably bound up with the capitalist, progress-driven project which grew out of the Enlightenment's desire to promote betterment of the human condition. The problem has been that it does not seem to matter whether we consider early trait-based theories (Carlyle, 1846; Kirkpatrick and Locke, 1991), subsequent behavioural (Blake and Mouton, 1981) and contingency (Hersey and Blanchard, 1982) theories, or more recent post-heroic (Badaracco, 2002; Pearce and Conger, 2003) and relational (Uhl-Bien, 2006) approaches to leadership, their usage has been largely the 'betterment' of shareholders, rather than wider stakeholders or the state of nature. Whilst the 21st century has seen more 'aspirational' forms of leadership – ethical (Ciulla, 2004), responsible (Pless and Maak, 2011) and sustainable (Avery and Bergsteiner, 2010) leadership have already been mentioned in Chapter 1 – seeking to shift attention 'from value to values, from shareholders to stakeholders, and from balance sheets to balanced development' (Kofi Annan, 14 October 2002, cited in Kempster and Carroll, 2016, frontmatter), it is questionable whether yet another form of leadership has the ability to stop the Anthropocene juggernaut in its tracks. The 'romanticization' of leadership (Meindl et al., 1985) by both academia and the media has resulted in its perception as being at the source of all organizational outcomes – both good and bad – at the same time as those outcomes have been almost universally formulated in terms of growth and profits. This inextricable association with the interests of shareholders – rather than wider stakeholders – positions leadership as inescapably the handmaiden of Enlightenment goals: sloughing off this capitalist baggage is always going to be a big ask. It is not leadership per se that is the problem – although this is sometimes the case as well (Conger, 1990) – but the baggage attached to the leadership construct. From this perspective, the new, more aspirational forms of leadership already mentioned merely serve to add an additional sense of burden to the practising leader's shoulders, without necessarily offering concrete strategies for enacting what these theories advocate. Hence it is the proposition of this chapter – and, indeed, the entire book – that we consider a radical reframe: that we start from a new place rather than to trying to deconstruct and reconstruct leadership. The notion of stewardship as a useful vehicle for this reframe is hopefully reasonably intuitive. At the least, if leaving leadership behind is too much of a wrench, we can explore the potential for utilizing stewardship principles as scaffolding for navigating the aspirational forms of leadership that currently claim our attention.

CONCLUSION

Before leaving the subject of the Enlightenment, it is perhaps worth consider-ing postmodern philosophy as a process of rethinking Enlightenment ideals, and the notion of Anti-Enlightenment. As Gasparyan (2016) tells us, the prefix 'anti' in this context can be interpreted in two ways. Thus, Anti-Enlightenment is:

> on the one hand, weeping over the failed Enlightenment, but on the other hand, a rebellion against the Enlightenment, which, though having been accomplished, fell short of hopes and expectations associated with it. (2016: 607)

Drawing on Rousseau, Gasparyan interprets the first position as a call to 'Go back to barbarism!' (2016: 608). This seems like a rather extreme interpre-tation of Rousseau's belief that humans are innately good and that it is only the influence of urban civilization that has brought out their more negative characteristics of pride, jealousy, envy and greed. For Rousseau, human 'per-fectibility' resides in moving some way from the 'primordial state of nature' but not too far. Thus, some degree of material betterment was to be viewed as positive, but taken to excess, it could only be productive of selfishness and evil, with inequalities of wealth, rank and power being the inevitable conse-quence of the civilizing process. As Rousseau puts it in his *Discourse upon the Origin and Foundation of the Inequality among Mankind* (1761, cited in Lovejoy, 1923/1960), the *amour propre* of self-regard which emerged in the later stages of 'civilization' is a:

> factitious feeling arising, only in society, which leads man to think more highly of himself than of any other ... it is this desire for reputation, honours and preferment which devours us all ... this rage to be distinguished, that we own what is best and worst in men – our virtues and our vices, our sciences and our errors, our conquerors and our philosophers – in short, a vast number of evil things and a small number of good.

But the solution to this civil evil is not suggested as a return to barbarianism, but to a more nascent stage of societal development: not the 'infancy' of humanity but its 'youth'. Thus, Rousseau proposed reorganizing society under a new social contract that retains the notion of progress in relation to 'all those powers and achievements which express merely the potency of man's intel-lect' whilst at the same time curbing the exercise of those which resulted in 'an increasing estrangement of men from one another, an intensification of ill-will and mutual fear, culminating in a monstrous epoch of universal conflict and mutual destruction' (Lovejoy, 1923/1960: 36). As Lovejoy goes on to note, these are 'precisely the two processes ... [that have] been going on upon a scale beyond all precedent: immense progress in man's knowledge and in his powers over nature, and, at the same time, a steady increase of rivalries, distrust, hatred and, at last, [the most horrible state of war]' (1923/1960: 36). Anticipating Duara (2021), Lovejoy also notes the extent to which 'amour propre' in its collective form – in pride of race, of nationality, of class – has been at the root of much of the 'evil' arising from this tendency. For the modern world, even a return to humanity's 'youth' may be a step too far: the throwing out of the baby along with the bath water! Nonetheless, as will be considered in Chapter 5, the potential for *tempering* the Western ideals of civilization stemming from rationality and science with the more ancient wisdom and relational ontologies of Indigenous worldviews has much to offer. This reframing of the Enlightenment project may suggest a shift from the 'betterment of the human condition' to the 'betterment' of the Earth ecosystem – including but not exclusively humans – as a more enlightened goal to shoot for. On this reading, the notion of stewardship clearly has a role to play.

The second position – that of the Enlightenment having been accomplished but fallen short of the hopes and expectations it raised – is perhaps a more fundamental criticism in that it challenges as 'dangerous and harmful' (Gasparyan, 2016: 609) the very agenda which Enlightenment thinking set out. From this perspective, the idea of human maturity resting in the 'courage to use your own understanding' (Kant, 1784/1996: 58) is, according to Gasparyan, deeply flawed in terms of the devastating consequences said to derive from trusting to our own minds independent of other sources of guidance. Drawing the distinction between rationality and morality, Gasparyan (2016: 613) concludes that: '[i]f we believe that every time we listen to the voice of our reasoning we hear the voice of our own conscience, we are just outright wrong!'

Under either reading of the postmodern rethinking of Enlightenment ideals, modern society is left with a huge problem to resolve and, arguably, the wrong tools with which to resolve it. Whilst we can only start from where we are, it is perhaps time to put the Enlightenment back in its box and move on. Along with Robertson (2015), this chapter suggests the benefits of reconstructing the Enlightenment as per its original definition and intention – that is, as a 'distinct intellectual movement of the 18th century, dedicated to the better understanding, and thence the practical advancement of the human condition on this Earth' (2015: 13) – with all the limitations that definition includes. On this basis, it is also time to move forward to more enlightened, post-Enlightenment understandings of progress and humanity.

3. Stewardship across different research domains: getting to a core understanding

INTRODUCTION

Having proposed the notion of stewardship as having value as a new perspective for leadership in the 21st century, the question arises, what do we mean by 'stewardship'? Chapter 1 framed a 'steward' as 'someone who understands themselves as a custodian of social, moral and environmental values and resources', trusted with their protection and enrichment, and guided by the question 'What am I passing on to [] future generation[s]?', drawing specifically on Maak and Pless's (2006: 108) work in the field of responsible leadership. We also saw the notion of 'trusteeship' arising from Bebbington and Rubin's (2022) work on accounting in the Anthropocene, in which they draw attention to the fact that the concept of stewardship has historically underpinned the practice of financial accounting, where accountants act as the professional custodians of the financial probity of organizations, holding the financial resources of the company in trust for shareholders. But the aims of these two pre-definitions or points of departure are in many respects very different. The first is concerned with the idea of a broad-based legacy for all, encompassing all the Earth's resources and all the decisions made in relation to their use, whilst the second has the more limited remit of ensuring that resources of a specific organization are used appropriately and accounted for transparently, to secure the ongoing viability of the company for the benefit of its investors. Thus, differences emerge in relation to what is to be held in trust, for whom and to what end.

These differences, and the many more that appear in the literature, all contribute to the rich nuance of what the notion of stewardship may have to offer future leaders, at the same time as requiring significant analysis to synthesize and make sense of them. It is the aim of this chapter to begin this sense-making process, drawing on the widest possible interpretations and applications of the concept of stewardship, and considering how they have informed thinking in leadership research specifically and the social sciences more generally.

Given the complexity of what is being attempted here, some preliminary explanation on the choice of review methodology and its advantages is provided before the review methodology itself is explained. This is followed by a descriptive exploration of the various understandings of stewardship across six research domains, leading the reader towards the 'bricolage' of meanings that we find in the social sciences. The chapter thus focuses on the individual research domains, leaving the synthesis across domains – and the tensions that this highlights – to be discussed in Chapter 4.

REVIEW METHODOLOGY

Torraco (2005: 356) defines the integrative literature review as 'a form of research that reviews, critiques, and synthesizes representative literature on a topic in an integrated way such that new frameworks and perspectives on the topic are generated'. As such it can be understood as a form of primary research in its own right (Hoon and Baluch, 2020), making it distinct amongst literature review approaches. Whilst being 'strongly anchored in a representative description of a field' (Elsbach and Van Knippenberg, 2020: 1277), integrative reviews go beyond this descriptive function by deriving new insights through the critique and synthesis of representative literature and the generation of new theoretical frameworks and perspectives (Cronin and George, 2023; Torraco, 2016). This is achieved by balancing the generative power of the narrative process with systematic processes of integration (Fan et al., 2022). Cronin and George (2023: 173) note that the 'disciplined imagination' required to 'redirect' thinking in a given field in this way can also be useful in synthesizing knowledge across domains.

Whilst a systematic review is seen as the 'gold standard' (Snyder, 2019: 334) of rigour and replicability, it has been noted (Snyder, 2019) that this approach does not lend itself to reviews of broad topic areas – such as stewardship – that have been conceptualized differently within diverse disciplines or domains. As Snyder goes on to note, an integrative review can be a better choice when the aim is to combine perspectives to develop a new theoretical model rather than to review all the articles ever published on a more narrow topic. Similarly, Post et al. (2020: 351) argue that 'advancing theory with review articles requires an integrative and generative approach' in order to 'connect research findings from various disparate sources in original ways' (2020: 352). This is an echo of Torraco's (2016) call for combining integrative and generative processes in 'unlocking the potential for making a theoretical contribution' (2016: 352). As noted by Cronin and George (2023), integrative reviews are ideally suited to processes of sense-making and sense-giving within academic scholarship (Huff, 2008) and to the bringing together of different 'conversations' (Huff, 2008) that are often rooted in different paradigms or communities of practice

(Burrell and Morgan, 1979). All these factors – and in particular the ability to integrate literature across different domains – suggest an integrative review as the ideal approach to bring together perspectives on stewardship from such varied domains as business and management, environmental studies, innovation and technology, and the life sciences and biomedical sciences.

Whilst there are a number of 'best practice' methodology sources for academics intending to conduct a systematic literature review (SLR) (Denyer and Tranfield, 2011; Moher et al., 2009; Tranfield et al., 2003), the methodology is less clearly delineated for integrative reviews. Advice and guidance on undertaking an integrative review do exist (Cronin and George, 2023; Snyder, 2019; Torraco, 2005, 2016), but have not been as definitively codified as for the SLR – there is no 'standard' flow diagram for the paper selection process, for example. In developing the methodology below, the current review draws upon all of the above sources, together with Post et al. (2020). The overall aim of the methodology was to develop new conceptual understandings of stewardship through 'ongoing interactions of reading and writing, sense-making and sense-giving, consumption and production' (Patriotta, 2020: 1275) in order to ensure a quality review that has depth, rigour, replicability and usefulness (Snyder, 2019). It was intended to serve as the springboard from which 'actionable managerial knowledge' (Post et al., 2020: 354) could be generated and, in particular, to set the scene for the discussion of a number of core tensions in relation to leadership-as-stewardship which follow in the next chapter.

The scope and boundaries of the review are drawn from an examination of the Subject Categories utilized by the Web of Science (WoS) database, intended to include the broadest range of application domains likely to yield results that might be of interest in relation to leadership and management. Using WoS research areas to cluster the individual subject categories, six research 'communities of practice' (Lave and Wenger, 1991) were utilized in classifying search results within the review. Taking the adoption of the Sustainable Development Goals by the UN in September 2015 as a proxy for when interest and scholarship in this field began increasing exponentially, and first topped the 300-papers-per-year mark, the time boundaries for the initial search were set at January 2016 to July 2022. The search was performed via WoS, which commonly indexes the highest number of publications associated with management and organization studies. Only full text, peer-reviewed articles, written in English, from journals with a two-year Impact Factor of 1.0 or above were included, with the search being conducted on titles only to keep the number of articles within manageable bounds. This broad-spectrum approach aimed to ensure that the widest possible understanding of stewardship was accessed, and that the leading journals in all relevant domains were incorporated into the review, in line with its integrative intentions. The search terms utilized were 'stewardship' and 'steward*': no synonyms or near alternatives were included in order to retain a strong focus on the core topic. The initial WoS search yielded 3,707 items. Following the elimination of 997 duplicates, articles not in English, books and book chapters, this number was reduced to 2,710 articles. These results were then screened to remove a further 310 articles for which the source journal had a two-year Impact Factor of below 1.0, to leave a total of 2,400.

These articles were then grouped according to their primary WoS research category. There was significant variation in the numbers of articles referencing stewardship in the different domains, from 1,773 in the human life sciences to 10 in the arts and humanities. This disparity required the development of a strategy for selecting a representative sample from each domain, without the need to review all 2,400 papers! Based on a reading of the article abstracts, the greater of five articles or 10 per cent of the total from each category were initially selected for this representative sample, and for detailed analysis within the integrative/generative review process. To be selected for final inclusion in the sample an article needed to meet one or more of the following criteria:

(a) Definitive – exemplifying the understanding of 'stewardship' within the community of practice of which it is a part;
(b) Seminal – exemplifying the origins or historical development of that understanding within the community of practice; or
(c) Topical – illustrating current issues or debates within the community of practice.

Following Cronin and George (2023: 169), the intention was to 'provide a fair representation of the perspectives from each community of practice to ensure balance'. Where this initial sampling was felt to yield a sample that did not do justice to the variety of understandings to be found in a given domain – which, interestingly, was more the case with the very small domains than with the largest – additional papers were introduced into the analysis where this was felt to be add value. The watchword here was nuance rather than rigidity!

As noted by Whetten (1989, cited in Torraco, 2016: 422), '[i]n theoretical research, data analysis is replaced by logic and clear conceptual reasoning as the basis for arguments and explanations'. Analysis thus requires an imaginative 'back and forth' dialectical interrogation between the phenomenal world and the existing literature (Hoon and Baluch, 2020). In undertaking this interrogation, the review paid attention to both the integrative and generative aspects (Post et al., 2020; Torraco, 2016) of the review process. The former, integrative, aspect involved a critical analysis of the existing literature, with the aim of identifying themes and patterns, and hence synthesizing understandings of stewardship within and across the domains under study. The latter, generative, aspect entailed creating new ideas and theories from the review in order to consider what we can learn from this broad-based literature that supports the idea of leadership-as-stewardship as a productive new direction for future research. Some of these ideas will be discussed in the current chapter, whilst others will carry over into the next.

SO WHAT DO WE MEAN BY 'STEWARDSHIP'?

Working with the 2,400 articles turned up by the search, it was first necessary to identify the themes and patterns within the individual domains. This analysis produced some recognizable and resonant understandings of stewardship – understandings that aligned straightforwardly with notions of trusteeship or custodianship – but also some surprises. It also highlighted the ways in which management literature – and the social sciences more broadly – have drawn upon other disciplines in crafting their understanding of stewardship. The resultant bricolage of meanings offers an interesting and nuanced source of inspiration for the discipline of leadership. Whilst it is beyond the scope of this chapter to review extant leadership literature in detail, it will consider some of the resonances – and possible disconnects – between leadership theory and stewardship.

STEWARDSHIP IN THE ARTS AND HUMANITIES

The literature search identified only 10 articles on stewardship with a primary domain classification of arts and humanities (A&H). Journal sources within this domain included such diverse titles as the *British Journal of Politics and International Relations*, the *Journal of Agricultural and Environmental Ethics*, the *Journal of European Public Policy*, the *Journal of Language and Social Psychology*, the *Landscape Journal* and the *Oral History Review*. Papers chosen, and discussed below, reflected this broad-based landscape at the same time as focusing on topics or themes not replicated in other domains. So, for example, a paper discussing how providers' reason-giving for symptom management advice affected perceptions of advice quality and other outcomes in the context of antibiotic stewardship (Foley et al., 2020) was not included because it added to our understanding of reason-giving rather than of antibiotic stewardship – a topic that was covered in depth in a different domain.

Within the A&H domain, there was a prominent focus on global challenges in relation to the target of stewardship activities (Knauß, 2018; Mathevet et al., 2018) together with less prominent concerns around our responsibilities in relation to human testimony representing diverse and inclusive truths (Nunes, 2017). Understandings of stewardship centred largely on the relationship between humans and nature, and the consequent moral obligation towards the next generation in relation to resources and the environment (Knauß, 2018).

The relational ontologies perspective was also present in the collaborative endeavour to enhance the discoverability of different truths in oral histories from a post-colonial perspective (Nunes, 2017). Less prominent was a structural, governance-related perspective present in explorations of human rights issues (Lacatus, 2018) and 'post-superpower' world leadership (Wæver, 2017). In the context of environmental stewardship, Mathevet et al. (2018) offered a typology of stewardship approaches, utilizing the two dimensions of citizen participation and systems thinking. Some of these contributions are discussed in more detail below.

One of the most resonant contributions (in relation to the current project) in A&H was Knauß's (2018) paper on conceptualizing human stewardship in the Anthropocene via an exploration of the 'rights of nature' approach as found in Ecuador, New Zealand and India. With Earth stewardship as its primary focus, the paper considered the impact of giving nature rights in the same way as people have rights. From this perspective, humans are seen as having a responsibility to nature rather than being entitled to treat it as a resource. Giving nature the 'rights, duties and obligations of a living person, in order to preserve and conserve them' (2018: 712), the rights-of-nature approach is suggested as a 'necessary step towards securing the ability of ecosystems to remain healthy and thrive' (2018: 714). Whilst Knauß does not specifically define stewardship, phrases like 'duty to prevent further damage to the Earth' (2018: 706) and 'our common obligation to save the Earth' (2018: 707) give a clear indication of his intended thesis, at the same time as drawing on accepted legal understandings of stewardship in relation to the rights and duties of legal persons that cannot stand for themselves (such as children and artificial persons).

Knauß's case studies include references to an Ecuadorean law (2008, article 10) which states that 'Pachamama (Mother Earth) where life is reproduced and exists, has the right to exist, persist, maintain and regenerate its vital cycles, structure, functions, and its processes of evolution' (2018: 707–708). Based on this premise, the case is made that '[t]he past generations have handed over the "Mother Earth" to us in its pristine glory and we are morally bound to hand over the same Mother Earth to the next generation' (2018: 713). Knauß sees the 'interconnectedness of man and nature' implicit in the rights-of-nature approach, together with the 'holistic narrative' it suggests, as providing a 'catalyst for the growing acceptance of systemic indigenous worldviews'. At the same time, 'giving rights to entities that previously were considered as mere objects' is proposed as 'the most powerful normative tool of Western modernity' (2018: 704).

From a very different perspective, Lacatus (2018) considers regulatory stewardship in the context of human rights networks. Regulatory stewardship is defined as 'the assignment of mutual-monitoring and support responsibilities among intermediaries, with the goal of safeguarding against capture and enhancing performance' (Pegram, 2017: 230). Occurring in regulatory systems with multiple intermediaries, stewardship seeks to explicate concerns about the performance of intermediaries and their influence on regulatory interactions. In this context, Lacatus explores the use of tools from managerial stewardship to facilitate intra-network collaboration and engagement in hierarchical stewardship, to gain access to international networks and take on a leadership role globally and regionally. Interestingly, stewardship, regulation and governance appear to be utilized as virtual synonyms in this paper, as well as being linked to literature on 'orchestration'. Weaker by design and more heavily dependent on voluntary participation, networks of human rights institutions are said to 'rely more heavily on stewardship than individual actors, to safeguard against capture by regulators and other intermediaries' (2018: 815–816).

Different again is the argument (Nunes, 2017) that oral history stewardship, as a mode of digital archival practice, offers a useful entry point into understanding and engaging with critical theory in the humanities. Archival stewardship is defined as 'the development of the encoding standards and database design that allows us to perform our search queries' (2017: 350) in order to 'enhance discoverability' (2017: 356) of previously obscured, hidden or ignored primary sources. The post-custodial approach to primary source materials implied by this argument, in its emphasis on stewardship rather than ownership of collections, represents a significant break from the tradition of archival custody; 'whereas custody connotes physical guardianship, legal responsibility, and a one-time transfer of collections from originator to archive, stewardship connotes an ongoing collaborative relationship in which a repository manages but does not own a community's archives' (2017: 351). This shift in approach recognizes a new direction of archival responsibility, perhaps akin to the emerging corporate focus on stakeholders rather than shareholders. In the archival context, this is articulated by archives scholar Michelle Caswell as 'archives [being] ultimately responsible to the community, and not to an individual donor, a larger parent organization, or an elite board of trustees' (cited in Nunes, 2017: 351).

STEWARDSHIP IN THE HUMAN LIFE SCIENCES

Whilst the human life sciences (HLS) domain was the most numerous category of stewardship-related articles by a significant margin (1,772 articles out of a total of 2,400), it also had the most cohesive perspective on stewardship. This took the form of an almost universal 'technical' definition of stewardship found in the selected sample, dominated by medical literature. Thus, over two-thirds of the sample papers related to the optimization of antimicrobial medicines to achieve the best possible outcomes for individual patients whilst minimizing the development of systemic microbial resistance. Antimicrobial stewardship relates to co-ordinated programmes that promote the appropriate use of anti-microbials (including antibiotics), improve patient outcomes, reduce microbial resistance and decrease the spread of infections caused by multidrug-resistant organisms. Antimicrobial stewardship efforts thus tend to be focused on decreasing unnecessary and inappropriate antibiotic use (either antimicrobial selection, dosing, route or duration), a key driver of antimicrobial resistance. In turn, antibiotic resistance occurs when bacteria develop mutations that make it harder for medicines to destroy them. This happens when antibiotics are over-used, such as for minor infections that your body could fight off on its own. Antibiotic resistance makes some bacterial infections very difficult to treat and more likely to be life-threatening.

Journals within this domain included *Advances in Therapy*, the *American Journal of Clinical Pathology*, the *European Journal of Clinical Microbiology*, *Frontiers in Pharmacology*, *Globalization and Health*, *Infection Control and Hospital Epidemiology*, *International Journal of Quality in Health Care*, *International Journal of Environmental Research*, *International Journal of Medical Informatics*, the *Journal of Antimicrobial Chemotherapy*, the *Journal of Family Medicine and Primary Care* and the *Journal of Patient Safety*. Papers utilizing the 'technical' definition of stewardship outlined above covered a broad geographical spread – from Africa (Brink et al., 2016; Gebreteklc et al., 2020) to America (Anderson et al., 2019), from India (Kumar et al., 2021) to China (Akpan et al., 2020) and from developing countries (Shafiq et al., 2016) to Europe (March-Lopez et al., 2020; Rodari et al., 2020; Tiri et al., 2020). The inclusion of a number of papers (e.g. Goff et al., 2017; Sweileh, 2021) drawing on World Health Organization (WHO) calls for co-ordination of recommen-dations speaks to the global nature of this issue and underpins the ubiquity of the 'optimization' stance within medical literature. Similarly, literature within this domain covered a range of medical conditions and specialisms, such as paediatrics (Gerber et al., 2021; Horikoshi et al., 2018), organ transplants (Wang et al., 2018), tuberculosis (Pattupara et al., 2019), bloodstream (Maeda et al., 2016) and respiratory tract (Ashiru-Oredope et al., 2020) infections, and combat injuries (Barsoumian et al., 2020). A new addition to this pantheon has been research into the effects of Covid-19 on antimicrobial stewardship issues (Rezel-Potts et al., 2021). A third dimension within this literature relates to the medical locations, and related agents, within which antimicrobial stewardship is practised. These includes core sites such as primary care (Avent et al., 2020), intensive care units (Gursoy et al., 2022) and community pharmacies (Atif et al., 2020), and more challenging locations including nursing homes (Tandan et al., 2022), emergency departments (Buehrle et al., 2021) and regional and remote hospitals (Bishop et al., 2019). The common thread throughout all this literature is the notion of optimization as a balancing of risks and benefits, usually through co-ordinated programmes of governance.

The idea of optimizing risks and benefits is also found in the next largest strand within the HLS literature, relating to other forms of optimization within a broadly medical context. These include the use of antibiotics when treating food-producing animals (Acharya et al., 2021; Patel et al., 2020) and by dentists (Ang et al., 2021), as well as the effective selection of laboratory tests (Baird, 2019; Roth et al., 2020) and the rationalization of other medical resources (Jain et al., 2021; Kopar and Lui, 2020). Also within this strand is the importance of gaining patient buy-in to optimization programmes through awareness campaigns in the national press (Rush et al., 2019) and patient engagement activities (Hughes et al., 2020).

A related theme within HLS addresses other approaches to antimicrobial stewardship, in particular monitoring and other forms of governance (Chaparro et al., 2022) aimed at improving decision support in prescribing. Papers discussing diagnostic (Tiseo et al., 2021) and prophylactic (Cengiz et al., 2020; Williams et al., 2018) interventions also align with the broader optimization theme within HLS generally. A small number of papers related to data management topics (Inau et al., 2021) such as health informatics (Cumbraos-Sanchez et al., 2019) and protocols for sharing medical research data (Dijkers, 2019) and were largely ethics-focused. A few papers explored corporate social responsibility in public health (Wei et al., 2021) and other topics connected with broad themes such as Indigenous worldviews and health systems (Chatwood et al., 2017), and a 'whole health economy' (McLeod et al., 2019).

STEWARDSHIP IN NON-MEDICAL LIFE SCIENCES

Not surprisingly, there is a significant overlap between HLS and non-human life sciences (NHLS), with a significant proportion (over one-third) of NHLS papers relating to antibiotic optimization in animals. This strand of writing draws on the same understanding of stewardship as that found in HLS and thus adds no further value to the present review. Beyond this largely 'technical' element, journals in this domain include the *Agronomy Journal, Bioinformatics, Conservation and Society, Conservation Biology, Current Opinion in Environmental Sustainability, Ecology and Society, Energy Policy, Frontiers in Marine Science, Frontiers in Veterinary Science*, the *Journal of Industrial Ecology*, the *Journal of Political Ecology, Land, Restoration Ecology, Sustainability* and *Urban Forestry and Urban Greening*. As suggested by these titles, non-medical research in this domain relates to resource management – and land in particular – with an emphasis on conservation and preservation (Coley et al., 2021), either on a voluntary basis or through programmes of governance. Overall, the understandings of stewardship across this domain focused on the maintenance of a status quo (conservation/preservation) or the near-term balancing of competing forces (optimizing). The focus is on the here and now, and the application of governance mechanisms and protocols for achieving specific goals. The idea of 'regeneration' (Ding and Schuett, 2020), rather than conservation, has recently emerged as a more forward-looking perspective on land and resource management within this domain.

As an example, Coley et al.'s (2021) paper on beliefs about human–nature relationships utilized a hypothetical urban waterway to explore the ways in which people conceptualize the interconnected relationship between humans and nature, and the implications for environmental investment and steward-ship. They identified a number of cognitive biases in how research partici-pants characterized these human–nature relationships, as well as the value of highlighting local (rather than global) benefits of waterway conservation as a means of decreasing relationship asymmetry. Their findings have signifi-cance in deciding how best to engage stakeholders in environmental conserva-tion through understanding how both group-level needs and individually held beliefs contribute to each person's decisions to endorse or reject conservation policies. This paper thus offers an interesting example of the burgeoning con-servation literature.

As an alternative – and relatively new – perspective within this domain, Ding and Schuett (2020) turn their attention to the idea of 'regeneration', rather than conservation, and a more forward-looking and interventionist perspective on land and resource management. Their research asks the question: does generativity play a role in predicting the commitment of volunteers' environ-mental stewardship? In this context, 'generativity' is defined as 'a focus on the next generation', which the authors claim has not been examined in relation to environmental stewardship. Their study examined factors that contribute to the commitment of volunteers for the Texas Parks & Wildlife Department (TPWD) and identified six categories of motivations (helping the environment, project organization, values, learning, career and social), four dimensions of satisfaction (organizational support, project organization, sense of empower-ment and group integration), and two factors of commitment (affective com-mitment and normative commitment). Whilst Ding and Schuett draw attention to the value of their research in enhancing stewardship efforts for agencies and organizations in recruiting and engaging volunteers, it is perhaps more notable for shifting the focus towards – and showing the potential for – generativity as a contributary factor in environmental stewardship.

Rawat's (2017) study of sustainable biodiversity stewardship and inclusive development in South Africa explores the effectiveness of fiscal incentives in encouraging landowners to undertake the considerable cost of biodiversity stewardship programmes. The study found that income tax deductions and property rates exclusions encouraged private landowners to protect local ecosystems, improve water yields, mitigate fire and flood risks, and promote landscape-scale connectivity. These incentives also contributed to broader socio-economic goals aligned with inclusive development by encouraging the inclusion of marginalized or disadvantaged communities and the creation of green jobs. In a similar vein, Sangha (2020) makes the case for both financial and non-financial stewardship schemes, focusing on the importance of supporting Indigenous populations and local communities (IPLCs) in managing the sustainable use of natural resources under their care. Sangha highlights the financial value of existing stewardship practices undertaken by IPLCs as a natural part of their way of life and cultural heritage, and the absence of any support being offered to them for practices from which they receive no personal benefit. As an example, the value of carbon sequestration, biocontrol, and air and water regulation on IPLC-managed lands is estimated at USD 1.16 trillion per year. The paper goes on to propose the need for mechanisms, including respecting IPLCs' rights and access to land and appropriate financial instruments such as Payments for Ecosystem Services (PES), to enable them to continue their important work. Given that PES schemes usually involve a payment to the ES provider by the beneficiary, the IPLC context requires the establishment of a global platform of accountability, with links to both state and regional schemes, through which financial support for Indigenous/local conservation practices can be channelled.

STEWARDSHIP IN THE PHYSICAL SCIENCES

The theme of resource management carries through into the physical sciences (Phys S), with a strong leaning towards grand challenges for both the environment and society. Journals within this domain included *Climate*, the *Journal of Soil and Water Conservation*, *Big Earth Data* and *Nanomaterials*. Whilst this was a relatively small domain – with only 23 articles being returned from the search – it nonetheless includes and reinforces some important themes relating to stewardship. Resource security is a recurring issue in this domain, for example in relation to water-saving irrigation techniques aimed at ensuring natural resources sustainability in food supply networks (Tsolakis et al., 2019). Dealing with the practicalities of resource stewardship, research has addressed the tensions between the development of sustainable hydropower and the concomitant environmental impact (O'Brien et al., 2021), and between the competing rights of shared human heritage and jurisdictional usage agreements in relation to marine biodiversity (Riding, 2018). In relation to farming – and expanding on the theme of financial incentives discussed under NHLS – White et al. (2022) highlight the challenges of bringing farmers on board as stakeholders within agricultural ecosystem services and of designing effective conservation incentive programmes that reflect the tensions between farmers' intrinsic motivations for sustainable land usage and the need for external governance. Thus, despite the small quantity of stewardship-related work in this domain, it nonetheless highlights a number of key understandings of the term. These include risk/benefit management akin to the theme of optimization found in the life sciences, data 'shepherding' similar to the custodianship of digital archives found in A&H and legally binding governance structures also discussed within A&H. Overall, these themes – some of which are discussed in more detail below – can be summarized under the headings of conservation and governance.

The notion of resource security as a pragmatic form of stewardship is picked up by Tsolakis et al. (2019) in relation to the need to meet growing global food demand with state-of-the-art food production technologies to increase farming efficiency and enhance food security. This is a very different perspective on stewardship from the Indigenous worldviews discussed above. Here, the focus is on human well-being – not to the exclusion of planetary well-being, but with the latter as a poor second. As such, Tsolarkis and colleagues seek to utilize automated sensors for water monitoring as a means of combatting the effects of freshwater overexploitation in agriculture, particularly in arid and water-scarce areas. 'Water stewardship' in this context is focused on supporting 'smart farming' and 'precision agriculture' (2019: 1) as a means of ensuring natural resources sustainability in food supply networks: a necessary, if somewhat 'selfish' approach. Similarly focused on the practicalities of resource stewardship, O'Brien et al. (2021) explore the risk/benefit balance between hydropower as a sustainable, renewable energy source and the potential environmental impact (upstream and downstream of the power plant) of utilizing this form of energy. In contrast, however, their perspective on stewardship recognizes the tensions between the growing demand for water-powered energy as part of a renewable energy mix and the importance of benefit-sharing of water resource developments with vulnerable human communities.

Riding (2018) takes this debate a step further by exploring how the international legally binding instrument (ILBI) developed by the UN General Assembly in 2015 (under the UN Convention on the Law of the Sea; UNCLOS) supports the conservation and sustainable use of marine biological diversity in areas beyond national jurisdiction. Specifically, it highlights the tension between the principle of the common heritage of mankind and high seas freedoms embodied in UNCLOS as one of the issues which must be addressed in an international agreement such as that proposed in 2015. Riding argues that 'environmental stewardship may provide the framework for such a sui generis regime', but that it must be 'grounded in international legal principles and act as a balance between competing values, perspectives and interests in the conservation and sustainable use of marine biodiversity beyond national jurisdiction' (2018: 435). For Riding, this constitutes a necessary redefinition of environmental stewardship if it is to deliver a governance framework capable of dealing with conflicting pressure for international decision-making for the conservation and sustainable use of marine biological diversity on the one hand, and the maintenance of existing regional and sectoral frameworks on the other.

Finally, there was also a paper (Papadiamantis et al., 2020) dealing with the stewardship of metadata in nano-safety research. On the back of the emergence of nano-informatics as a key component of nano-technology and nano-safety assessment for the prediction of engineered nanomaterials properties, inter-actions and hazards, the authors highlight the need for the development of minimum reporting standards to ensure access to high-quality, curated data-sets. Recommending the application of FAIR (findable, accessible, interopera-ble and reusable) data principles, the paper also acknowledges the importance of human 'data shepherding' based on clear roles and responsibilities across the complete data lifecycle and a deeper appreciation of what metadata is, and how to capture and index it. This understanding of stewardship has resonance with that found in the technology domain, discussed below.

STEWARDSHIP IN TECHNOLOGY

As suggested in the previous section, in the small but burgeoning literature within the Technology (Tech) research domain, the concern is almost exclu-sively with data management issues. This covers research data, archival and library resources and, in particular, oral histories, with journals including both overtly information/data related titles – such as *Online Information Review* and *Government Information Quarterly* – and more 'applied' users of data technology – such as the *Journal of Sustainable Tourism* or the *Journal of Academic Librarianship*. Perspectives range from perceptions of libraries and their resources as 'guardians of the human spirit' (Hunter and Buchanan, 2021) to practical initiatives to enhance the reusability of research data and maximize research impact (Bloemers and Montesanti, 2020). The core understanding of stewardship in this domain is thus one of security. Echoing the theme of opti-mizing risks and benefits that was prevalent in the domain of medicine, tech-nological research also considers the risks and benefits of inter-organizational 'data ecosystems' (Van Donge et al., 2022) and the resultant dependence of each contributor on the appropriate data stewardship practices of other members of the ecosystem.

Picking up on the FAIR data principles discussed above, Bloemers and Montesanti (2019) offer a framework aimed at supporting funders in driving the transition towards FAIR data management and stewardship practices in research. Their study is driven by the increasing requirement by research funding organizations (RFOs) for grant holders to 'deliver reusable data as an output from their research projects, and to share their data to contribute to future research' (2019: 172). It also recognizes that FAIR principles, new practices for research data management and stewardship, and data management plans are essential elements in creating reusable data and optimizing data sharing. The underlying motivation here is to ensure that public funding is invested efficiently and delivers a good return on the investment through measures which support unrestricted secondary use wherever possible, and wherever ethical and legal obligations permit. As with other strands of writing within this domain, the need to balance security with availability has echoes of the theme of 'optimization' – albeit in relation to different juxtapositions of factors – seen in the management of antibiotics in the life sciences.

In a very different vein, Hunter and Buchanan (2021) consider the role of public libraries in enacting 'responsive stewardship' in times of crisis, using the Covid-19 pandemic and its aftermath as a case in point. Highlighting the role of public libraries in helping under-served and under-represented populations, the paper also notes that these groups of people are the ones that suffer disproportionately when library services are removed or curtailed. In many cases, these services are not reinstated when the crisis is over. In these situations the lifeline they provide – they give examples ranging from unemployed people requiring help with crafting CVs to people requiring access to internet and printing services, and even the location of community gardens in library grounds – is not easily replaced from other sources. The main thesis of Hunter and Buchanan's work is an impassioned call for libraries to advocate for the rights of those patrons who have been disadvantaged by post-Covid measures, and to reinstate libraries, not just as repositories of knowledge and information but as vital sources of community. Drawing parallels with the fate of Winston at the conclusion of George Orwell's *1984* – whose captors refer to him as 'the last man ... the guardian of the human spirit' (Orwell, 2017: 241), they suggest that the '[g]uardianship of spirit and information is now in the hands of libraries' (2021: 859). The crusading tone of this thesis reflects an openly political stance more commonly found in environmental lobbying, whilst the notion of guardianship as a form of stewardship echoes the foundations of holding something in trust with which this book – and this chapter – first started.

STEWARDSHIP IN THE SOCIAL SCIENCES: A BRICOLAGE

The social sciences (Soc S) have been comparative late-comers to the concept of stewardship and have – perhaps for this reason – borrowed from other research domains to create a complex bricolage of meanings and perspectives. Underpinning the complex bricolage is an interdisciplinary approach to bringing together different agendas and perspectives. Examples of this approach include the conjoining of accountancy-based understandings of financial stewardship with Anthropocene understandings of how human actions drive the functioning of Earth systems to develop an enlarged understanding of corporate purpose and governance processes beyond the purely financial (Bebbington and Rubin, 2022), or the importation of Indigenous worldviews into addressing such issues as climate change and sustainable development (Hansen and Antsanen, 2018). Journals within this somewhat sprawling domain cover a wide range of topic areas, including mainstream management (*British Journal of Management, Journal of Business Ethics*), accounting and business administration (*Accounting and Business Research, Public Policy and Administration*), education (*Education Research, Environmental Education Research*), small businesses and entrepreneurship (*Family Business Review, Journal of Small Business and Enterprise Development*), marketing (*Journal of Marketing, Journal of Consumer Policy*), urban living (*Landscape and Urban Planning, Frontiers in Sustainable Cities*) and wider society (*AlterNative – An International Journal of Indigenous Peoples, Society and Natural Resources*).

Of all the research domains covered by the literature review, it is the social sciences that are hardest to synthesize into a single overarching theme, either around what is being stewarded or around the nature of that stewardship. Nonetheless, the 235 papers returned by the search can be said to have a leaning towards perspectives that acknowledge the idea of the Anthropocene – 'the proposed geological epoch in which human activities outstrip glaciers in changing the face of the Earth' (Tsing, 2016) – as a key underpinning of most management and social activities now and in the future. Similarly, the themes which emerge can loosely be framed by the two-pronged strategies of governance and re-education, and by the search for a 'better way' via an emergent interest in Indigenous peoples and their more holistic worldviews. These themes, and the debate between 'carrot' and 'stick' they represent, are discussed below.

The need to reinforce stewardship initiatives through mandatory frameworks, and the differing mechanisms through which this governance might be enacted, is a prominent debate within the social sciences domain. Research has both advocated and evaluated various forms of extrinsic regulation and compliance programmes (Romero and Putz, 2018), voluntary (Lemes et al., 2021) and compulsory (Tey and Brindal, 2021) certification of sustainability standards, and other forms of governance, including economic incentives (Lliso et al., 2020), co-management arrangements (Latta, 2018) and monitoring by institutional investors (Nguyen and Shiu, 2022). Interestingly, the WHO introduced the concept of stewardship in the health sector to clarify the *practical* components of governance (Brinkerhoff et al., 2019) – rather than introducing governance measures to support stewardship initiatives – with a focus on how government actors take responsibility for fulfilling health system functions, ensuring the well-being of the population and equity of access, and co-ordinating interaction between the health service, government and society.

Chan et al. (2019) noted that there are multiple options for accountability, including public reporting, community accountability structures, results-based payment, accreditation and inspection. Bebbington and Rubin (2022) made the connection between accounting and accountability in their work relating to accounting in the Anthropocene. For them stewardship is a concept that has historically underpinned the practice of accounting, albeit focusing almost entirely on the stewardship of financial resources held in trust for shareholders. The advent of the Anthropocene requires a significant shift in both the scope and the beneficiaries of accounting practices, however, with a parallel shift from accounting to accountability. According to Bebbington and Rubin, measures of organizational performance need now to encompass the demands of planetary stewardship and an enlarged understanding of corporate purpose. They propose a 'road map' for governance processes that take into account these wider ambitions, together with answerability to stakeholders rather than just shareholders, and highlight the significant advance in current accounting practice which this shift represents. Finally, they suggest that 'achieving stewardship for "wicked problems" that emerge from complex adaptive systems (with emergent elements and tipping points) might be best addressed by coalitions of organisations collaborating to achieve systems effects' (Bebbington and Rubin, 2022: 582). Notwithstanding the important mind-shift reflected in this focus on corporate governance beyond the purely financial, it is still constrained by the need to balance profitability with contributing to social benefit (Dmytriyev et al., 2021), arising from the 'epistemic blindness' (Banerjee, 2022) deriving from colonial/Western ways of knowing and being and the market economy perspective to which these have historically led.

In another take on the need for system-level effects and how to achieve them, Klettner (2021) focuses on stewardship codes and investor governance. Stewardship codes have emerged in recent decades as a response to the issue of share ownership of listed companies becoming more concentrated in the hands of large institutional investors, and the challenge that this presents to the traditional agency theory view of corporate governance as a mechanism to resolve the separation of ownership and control. The alternative approaches to corporate governance that have emerged all share the notion of investor stewardship as a core underpinning, but interpret this notion in different ways. Klettner considers the question of whether institutional investors should act primarily as stewards of their investee companies (agency theory), of beneficiaries' funds (agency capitalism), of a market/economy (universal ownership) or of society (stakeholder theory), and proposes a typology of stewardship codes as a framework for understanding cross-country variation in investor stewardship policy.

Another key debate within this strand of work relates to the contrasting implications of stewardship theory and agency theory within organizational contexts. In a corporate context, 'agency theory suggests CEOs take advantage of their powerful positions to maximize their personal economic utility, whereas stewardship theory suggests CEOs are motivated through intrinsic rewards and will balance their interests with those of other stakeholders' (Martin and Butler, 2017: 633). To counter this somewhat negative, self-serving view of corporate leaders, attempts have been made to combine the agency theory which underpins it with stewardship theory in a more nuanced understanding of the similarities and differences between these drivers of behaviour (Obermann et al., 2020; Schillemans and Bjurstrom, 2020). Obermann et al. (2020) showed that factors such as psychological ownership were important in bridging the gap between the two perspectives and developing a more expansive understanding of management behaviour. Agency theory has also been contrasted with stewardship theory to explore the relative merits of control/verification versus trust (Schillemans and Bjurstrom, 2020) in the context of semi-autonomous government agencies. Previously treated as competing approaches, Schillemans and Bjurstrom (2020) analyse how they can be combined to produce a more widely satisfactory mechanism for the effective delivery of services based on trust and verification. They go on to develop a survey instrument aimed at measuring this combined approach. These bridging perspectives have resonance with other developments in management research aimed at reflecting a broader range of organizational goals and the shift from business- to society-centric measures of business performance (Wickert, 2021). It also resonates with the idea of corporate social responsibility (CSR) as 'an umbrella term for the debate about the role of business in society and about how the business-society relationship informs the treatment of society's social, ecological, and ethical challenges by businesses' (2021: E2).

As an alternative to governance-based mechanisms, more intrinsic approaches to (re)education (Taylor, 2017), the fostering of pro-environmental attitudes (Hoover, 2021) and the exploration and adoption of alternative, usually Indigenous (Gibson and Warren, 2018; Reo et al., 2017) worldviews have also been proposed. The latter approach is reflected in the growth of Sustainable, Ethical and Entrepreneurial (SEE) enterprises and their shift towards 'the natural environment as the foundation on which society resides and the economy operates' (Markman et al., 2016: 674), which in turn builds on the notion of nesting: that is, if the economy is nested in society, which is nested in the environment, then this needs to be reflected in organizational priorities (2016: 674). This idea of nesting has resonance with both the 'wedding cake' model of the UN Sustainable Development Goals and the requirement for both society and the economy to operate within planetary boundaries (Partzsch, 2023). Similarly, Cornelissen et al.'s (2021) suggestion of 're-keying' as a leader sense-making device for reconciling social and commercial goals and shifting the discourse of organizational purpose in social enterprises speaks to the need for re-education as an intrinsic foundation for changes in practice and the development of a 'hybrid' – part commercial, part social – organizational identity. The reframing of figure and ground which this 're-keying' entails is a classic example of leaders as 'managers of meaning' (Smircich and Morgan, 1982).

The implications of the Covid-19 pandemic as a catalyst for change have found an application in this context as well as many others. Spyropoulos and Markowitz (2021: 1), for example, theorize that the pandemic

> has potentially activated and made more salient some key psychological mechanisms—including norms of fairness and reciprocity, feelings of gratitude, and consideration of personal legacies—that previous empirical work suggests can be harnessed to promote beneficent intergenerational decision-making aimed at solving the environmental challenges we and our descendants will face in the twenty-first century.

The key principle underlying their argument is the idea that coping with one existential threat may serve to focus our attention more fully on other existential threats that we have previously felt able to ignore. Tapping into another fundamental experience-based catalyst for change/learning, Schwass et al. (2021) advocate the power of the outdoors and, in particular, outdoor journeys. Drawing on interviews with participants on week-long Outward Bound Canada expeditions, they find a positive association between participants' exposure to natural environments and an increased sense of connection and stewardship towards nature. Participants reported a change in their values associated with nature, and experienced the journeys as a challenge to their current personal and employment situations. For some, the journeys inspired a willingness to change their employment or participate in voluntary initiatives to improve the state of the natural environment.

Focusing on the education of children rather than the re-education of adults, Taylor (2017) looks 'beyond' stewardship to consider 'common world' pedagogies for the Anthropocene. She draws attention to the fact that 'framed by humanist principles, most sustainability education promotes humans as the primary change agents and environmental stewards', and suggests that, although well-meaning, such 'stewardship pedagogies do not provide the paradigm shift that is needed to respond to the implications of the Anthropocene' (2017: 1448). Instead, Taylor draws on 'common world pedagogies' to suggest the need to move beyond humanist framings and embrace a more-than-human relational ontology, in order to present children with a means of learning 'with' non-human others rather than learning 'about' them and 'on their behalf'. This approach requires environmental educators to 'fundamentally rethink[] [their] place and agency in the world' and to 'move beyond humanist stewardship frameworks and their implicit human exceptionalist assumptions' (2017: 1449). This radical pedagogy goes further than the majority of attempts to break down the human–nature divide in acknowledging that the human species is 'just one of many that make and shape worlds together' (2017: 1449). Whilst, in doing so, it suggests the obsolescence of stewardship before it has properly taken hold, it nonetheless contributes to our understanding of the role of stewardship in meeting the challenges of the Anthropocene.

An alternative take on relational ontologies that is gaining momentum in the social sciences domain – and particularly in environment-related topic areas – is the recognition and adoption of Indigenous worldviews, and the suggestion that these stand as a counter-weight to Western understandings of the relationship between humans and nature. In the context of (re)education, Roe et al. (2017) consider the factors that support Indigenous involvement in multi-actor environmental stewardship, including the importance of recognizing and valuing the alternative forms of knowledge, expertise and perspectives Indigenous peoples represent. They also consider the challenges entailed in bringing together participants from Indigenous and non-Indigenous cultures in order to develop diverse multi-actor collaborations to achieve environmental protection and stewardship outcomes. Based on a case study of 39 regional partnerships across the Great Lakes basin of North America, Roe et al. find that respect for Indigenous knowledge, control of knowledge mobilization, intergenerational involvement, self-determination, continuous cross-cultural education and early involvement are all important in securing and maintaining Indigenous engagement. This paper thus highlights the challenges of grafting Indigenous thinking onto Western thinking, and the complexity of combining these disparate worldviews onto a shared source of stewardship wisdom.

This problem of securing Indigenous engagement is also addressed by Hansen and Antsanen (2018), who suggest that Indigenous knowledge has much to teach us about environmental stewardship. Based on interviews with elders of the Cree people, they see their worldviews and knowledge systems as offering both practical and theoretical contributions to current approaches to human activity and environmental issues, and suggest ways of 'importing' these into Western thinking. This approach reflects a mirror image of the problem noted by Bruton et al. (2022: 1059) – that the 'straight jacket of existing [Western] theory', when applied outside its originating context, can result in 'under-developed or inaccurate understanding of ... many regions of the world' – namely that a partial or Western interpretation of Indigenous wisdom can lead to faulty proposals for its application to Western problems and contexts. There is a parallel risk that the reductionism of Western epistemology

Table 3.1   Emergent themes – stewardship across research domains

WoS category	Stewardship of what	Core understanding
Arts and humanities	Global challenges	Relational ontology + governance
Human life sciences	Risks and benefits	Optimization
Non-human life sciences	Land and animals	Monitoring + conservation + optimization
Physical sciences	Resources	Resource management
Technology	Information/data	Data security
Social sciences	Anthropocene	Relational ontology + re-education + governance

will fail to grasp the more holistic foundations of Indigenous knowledge (Banerjee, 2022), leading to a similarly partial or faulty result. Indigenous worldviews are discussed in more detail in Chapter 5.

Finally, and linking forward to the tensions that will be discussed in Chapter 4, writing in this domain also explores how the ends of stewardship activity are perceived. Key themes here, reflected in the core terminology applied to characterize acts of stewardship, relate to whether the aim is the conservation or preservation of an existing situation or state of affairs (Bauer et al., 2018; Pitt et al., 2019), the restoration or regeneration of a previous heritage in some form (Beitl et al., 2019) or more open-ended perceptions of intergenerational trusteeship (Balakrishnan et al., 2017) and responsibility for future-facing pro-social decision-making (Syropoulos and Markowitz, 2021). The tensions between these perspectives can be seen as an echo of the 'management as complexity; leadership as change' trope (Kotter, 1990) common in the leadership and management literature, and raises interesting questions as to which (if either) end of this spectrum has most resonance with stewardship. The debate surrounding the purposes of stewardship finds echoes in the similar debates in relation to sustainability, the shift from 'doing less harm' to 'doing good' (Markman et al., 2016) – between becoming 'less unsustainable' versus becoming 'fully sustainable' (Shevchenko et al., 2016) – and the stakeholder awareness of grand challenges that is driving this shift.

A broad-brush summary of the emergent themes from each domain is set out in Table 3.1.

One of the stated aims of this chapter was to propose a nexus of stewardship meaning that might stand as a basis for future leadership practice. As the preceding discussion shows, this is no easy task – and perhaps not one that it is helpful to attempt. Rather than falling into the trap of reductionism common to many forms of leadership (and other) theorizing, it is perhaps more helpful to consider stewardship as a boundary object (Enqvist et al., 2018); that is, 'a conceptual tool that enables collaboration and dialogue between different actors whilst allowing for differences in use and perception' (2018: 17). Whilst Enqvist was writing specifically about sustainability research, and drawing only on the environmental science literature, much of what he suggests has resonance for leadership too, particularly his call for linking care, knowledge and agency. Similar to the current endeavour, he sought to make sense of the 'multiple meanings and framings of stewardship across [a] wide user base that reflect different disciplinary purposes, assumptions and expertise, as well as a long history of use in both academic and lay contexts' (2018: 16). The result was a model incorporating four distinct meanings of stewardship (ethic, motivation, action and outcome) and three dimensions (care, knowledge and agency) which is proposed as a 'centering device' for connecting practitioners, policy makers and researchers from multiple disciplines in pursuit of sustainability. The proposed model is certainly appealing, but, as we shall see in the next chapter, for leadership scholars and practitioners the picture is made more complex by a number of tensions which pull in different directions concerning what should be stewarded, how and for whom.

STEWARDSHIP AND LEADERSHIP

Before exploring these tensions, it is worth briefly considering where stewardship has appeared in the leadership literature already. Principal amongst these is Greenleaf's (1977) servant leadership. As noted in Chapter 1, whilst the aim of servant leadership was for the leader to place service before self-interest, the focus was not specifically on sustainability or global challenges. Rather it was a style of leadership that put people before tasks, and others before the self. This being the case, it is not surprising that stewardship was seen as an 'accompanying' – rather than a central or 'functional' – attribute of this kind of leadership. Servant leadership has subsequently found an echo in post-heroic models such as quiet leadership (Badaracco, 2002), shared or distributed leadership (Gronn, 2003) and Level 5 leadership (Collins, 2001), but none of these have a focus on stewardship in the context of grand challenges. Instead, they were seen as the antidote to the less-than-glorious outcomes of charismatic (Conger and Kanungo, 1987) and transformational (Bass and Avolio, 1994) leadership so lauded in earlier leadership writing.

More recently, Maak and Pless's (2006) responsible leadership comes much closer to the aim of the current review. Indeed, it was a definition from Maak and Pless that was used to introduce the idea of stewardship in the opening pages of Chapter 1. Their notion of holding in trust or custodianship – be it of environmental resources or social and moral values – and their focus on future generations as the recipients of our leadership decisions is surely stewardship by any other name. This raises the question of why we need stewardship as a form of leadership when we already have responsible leadership occupying a very similar space. The answer is certainly not to set stewardship up as a competitor to responsible leadership, but to explore the 'mechanics' of responsible leadership – and other forms of leadership with broadly similar aims – through what is hopefully a useful interdisciplinary lens. For this reason – that is, to place the emphasis on the practicalities of stewardship rather than the rhetoric of leadership and to hopefully avoid creating yet another incarnation of 'aspirational' leadership – I will be using the phrase 'leadership-as-stewardship' rather than the other way around, except where the context makes this clumsy or misleading.

CONCLUSION: LEADERSHIP AS STEWARDSHIP?

The aim of this chapter was to review extant literature on stewardship across a range of disciplines, to arrive at a nexus of understanding that might serve as a 'decluttered' marker for future leadership research. Instead, as Table 3.1 shows, what has emerged is a complex and nuanced collection of meanings and perspectives that is yet to coalesce into something workable for this purpose. The next step on this journey will surface a number of tensions that arise within the stewardship literature, to begin to consider what they might mean for 'leadership-as-stewardship', and to point to the value of relational ontologies to lead the way towards a stewardship-based agenda for leadership theory and practice.

4. Tensions and questions

INTRODUCTION

As already mentioned in the previous chapter, pulling the threads from the different research domains together suggests a complex understanding of stewardship that invites the positioning of the concept as a boundary object (Enqvist et al., 2018: 17). So, for example, the similarities in such notions as guardianship (McMillen et al., 2020), trusteeship (Balakrishnan et al., 2017), responsibility (García-Martín et al., 2018) and accountability (Bebbington and Rubin, 2022) that are common to all the research domains included within the review are intuitively obvious, but the differences of nuance contribute to the tensions that will be discussed in this chapter. For McMillen et al. (2020: 11) Indigenous kinship beliefs 'reinforce an understanding of reciprocal caring relationships between people and place' and engender 'relationships that place humans as guardians of nonhuman family members'. This worldview in turn drives 'perceptions of resource as family that are distinct from market driven perceptions of resource as commodity' (2020: 11). Following the teachings of Gandhi, Balakrishnan et al. (2017: 133) propose a 'trusteeship model' in which 'business managers and stakeholders integrate various rights and respon-sibilities to create both economic value and a just and prosperous society'. Not surprisingly, perhaps, given Gandhi's background, this is a much more legalistic perspective, and one which is less specific concerning the inclusion of non-human stakeholders. García-Martín et al. (2018) take a different view again, focusing on the ascription of personal responsibility for the adverse consequences human action might have on landscapes, and how this sense of responsibility is related to awareness, education, occupation, levels of income and socio-cultural context. What all three perspectives share is an undercurrent of the need for re-education as a driver for change, but both the underlying motivations and the proposed mechanisms for re-education are somewhat different.

Similarly, whilst these meanings can be seen to transfer across stewardship objects as wide-ranging as medical interventions (Cengiz et al., 2020; Pettit et al., 2019), land (Enqvist et al., 2018) and resource (Chandler, 2017) usage, data security (Bloemers and Montesanti, 2020) and the discoverability and curation of oral histories and library resources (Nunes, 2017), the underpinning research paradigms and perspectives within the different communities of practice can serve to give them significantly different connotations. In the case of medical interventions and antibiotic stewardship, the literature rests largely on positivist, quantitative, experimental research aimed at testing hypotheses relating to the efficacy of specific drugs, dosages or procedures in the context of potential side effects (most notably, the development of antibiotic resistance). So, for example, Cengiz et al. (2020) reported on the findings from a 'before and after' test of the outcomes from a change in antibiotic prophylaxis policy for preventing surgical site infections, drawing on secondary data from an American College of Surgeons-National Surgical Quality Improvement Program (ACS-NSQIP) data set. By contrast, Nunes (2017: 351) applied a critical theory perspective, within a social constructionist paradigm, to the shift from 'custody' of digital archives – 'connot[ing] physical guardianship, legal responsibility, and a one-time transfer of collections from originator to archive' – to 'stewardship', which 'connotes an ongoing collaborative relationship in which a repository manages but does not own a community's archives'. These quite different perspectives and paradigms can be understood as methodological 'boundaries' – sitting alongside the topic boundaries – that the notion of stewardship spans. At the same time, the effectiveness of stewardship as a boundary object can also be seen in the bricolage of imported stewardship notions found in the social sciences literature, and the resonance of these notions with existing debates in the field of management studies already discussed in Chapter 3.

As such, 'stewardship' is rich in nuance whilst still maintaining an 'inner jewel' (Hochschild, 1983: 34) of meaning that is grounded in a shared understanding of responsibility for something that we hold in trust for others. This said, the complexities and even contradictions inherent in the tensions which emerge from this literature require a degree of sensemaking (Huff, 2008) if they are to yield a defensible nexus for the proposal of a future research agenda for leadership scholarship. On this basis, we might reasonably retain Maak and Pless's (2006) language, noted in Chapter 1, as a working definition for stewardship at the same time as recognizing the need to substantiate this with additional 'scaffolding': to flesh out stewardship's potential operationalization and embodiment in light of the emergent tensions.

Specifically, these tensions relate to the focus, enactment and orientation of stewardship activity within and across the different research domains, and a recognition of the contextual complexity within which stewardship necessarily takes place. *Focus*, in this context, refers to what is being stewarded and for whom, and how far we should go in our definition of stakeholders to the process. *Enactment*, here, concerns the mechanisms underpinning stewardship activity and, in particular, whether stewardship occurs through governance frameworks or voluntary action. *Orientation* to change explores the degree of

Table 4.1   *Tensions and their parameters*

	Stewardship focus
Target – what	Good in and of itself (altruistic) Preservation of affordances (self-serving)
Stakeholders – for whom	Whole-Earth ecosystem (non-anthropomorphic) Future generations/society as a whole (anthropomorphic)
	Enactment mechanisms
Mechanisms	Top-down (governance) Bottom-up (voluntary action/agency)
Motivation	Governance – reward/benefit or avoidance/punishment (carrot or stick) Voluntary – immediate others or general benevolence (scope)
Responsibility	Government vs business vs activists/individuals (keystone actors)
	Intervention orientation
Degree of change	Preserving the status quo (static) Change/improving/enhancing (incremental) Change arising from scientific innovation (significant) New perspectives arising from change of mindset (radical)
Purpose of intervention	Restoring previous state (restoring) Preserving current state (preserving) Developing new solutions (developing)
	Contextual complexity
Understanding required	Grasp of whole ecosystem (holistic – non-anthropomorphic) Grasp of whole 'socio-system' (holistic – anthropomorphic) Grasp of system interdependencies (system complexity)

change required to meet the goals or purpose envisaged by specific stewardship interventions, and the balance between preserving, restoring and innovating that may be involved. Finally, there are a number of tensions that arise from the *contextual complexity* within which stewardship takes place. These include the limitations on our knowledge of whole ecosystems and/or socio-systems, the challenges of evaluating the impact of previous interventions, and the time-frames over which stewardship activities frequently play out. The parameters of these four tensions are summarized in Table 4.1.

These tensions are now discussed with reference to both their occurrence across the full range of research domains and their relevance for the social sciences, and in particular to management/leadership research and practice. The discussion draws on a number of 'mini-case studies' in which a selection of papers from the earlier review are analysed in relation to each of the tensions, to draw out the perspectives and assumptions which characterize them. This often relates to the underpinning worldview of the paper and its authors, rather than the specific findings which are conveyed. In total, 20 papers were analysed in this way, roughly in proportion to the overall number of papers in each domain of the original review. The exception is the Social Sciences domain – where more papers were included both because of their greater variety and because they represent the primary area of interest in connection with leadership. The papers selected for analysis are set out in Table 4.2.

STEWARDSHIP FOCUS: TARGETS AND STAKEHOLDERS

The first tension explores the *focus* of stewardship in terms of both its target (what is to be stewarded) and its stakeholders (for whom). As illustrated in Table 4.3, the target or object of stewardship (what) spans the preservation of a current situation or asset deemed valuable in and of itself (e.g. architectural heritage assets) versus the maintenance of the affordances associated with the current situation or asset (e.g. the continuance of food and water security), usually for human use. Thus, the underpinning issue of the 'what' tension is whether stewardship is predominantly altruistic or self-serving, at a macro, human level. These alternatives may be in direct competition where the 'rights' of that which is under stewardship are shared or contested by more than one perceived 'owner' (Knauß, 2018). This is often the case where Indigenous and colonial perspectives are in tension (Reo et al., 2017) or where proposals to return human-made habitats, such as land that has been brought into human cultivation, to their previous status (usually as native forest or wilderness) (Landres et al., 2020) are seen as threatening the livelihoods of local populations. An added tension arises where there is a mismatch between the countries called upon to take remedial action to secure future planetary health and those countries perceived to have benefited from past depredations (Blicharska et al., 2017), often referred to as the Global North and Global South respectively. Tensions may also arise in relation to the prevention of a future situation (e.g. the onset of antimicrobial resistance – Ang et al., 2021) through stewardship *against* a potential situation rather than *of* an existing one.

The preservation-of-affordances approach is prevalent in the human life sciences, physical sciences and technology, where the focus is on the continued effectiveness and availability of medicines and physical resources, and the security of data. Arts and humanities appear firmly grounded in big philosophical questions underpinned by a focus on aims that are good in themselves, albeit not without benefits to humans, whilst the social sciences span the two extremes. This domain is also more complex and nuanced in its application of theories and perspectives found elsewhere and the uses to which they are put: once again, this suggests the idea of bricolage as the social sciences draw from other domains to position human concerns in a wider, ecological context. A significant outlier here – and throughout the analysis that follows – is

Table 4.2   *Selected papers*

Domain	Authors	Date	Title
A&H	Knauß	2018	Conceptualizing human stewardship in the Anthropocene: The rights of nature in Ecuador, New Zealand and India
A&H	Nunes	2017	'Connecting to the ideologies that surround us': Oral history stewardship as an entry point to critical theory in the undergraduate classroom
HLS	March-Lopez et al.	2020	Impact of a multifaceted antimicrobial stewardship intervention in a primary health care area: A quasi-experimental study
HLS	Rezel-Potts et al.	2021	Antimicrobial stewardship in the UK during the COVID-19 pandemic: A population-based cohort study and interrupted time-series analysis
HLS	Rush et al.	2019	Communicating antimicrobial resistance and stewardship in the national press: Lessons from sepsis awareness campaigns
HLS	Van der Wees et al.	2017	Stewardship of primary care physicians to contain cost in health care: An international cross-sectional survey
HLS	Tiseo et al.	2021	Diagnostic stewardship based on patient profiles: Differential approaches in acute versus chronic infectious syndromes
HLS	McLeod et al.	2019	A whole-health–economy approach to antimicrobial stewardship: Analysis of current models and future direction
NHLS	Coley et al.	2021	Beliefs about human-nature relationships and implications for investment and stewardship surrounding land-water system conservation
NHLS	Ding and Schuett	2020	Predicting the commitment of volunteers' environmental stewardship: Does generativity play a role?
NHLS	Sangha	2020	Global importance of Indigenous and local communities' managed lands: Building a case for stewardship schemes
Phys S	Tsolakis et al.	2019	Sensor applications in agrifood systems: Current trends and opportunities for water stewardship
Phys S	O'Brien et al.	2021	The nature of our mistakes, from promise to practice: Water stewardship for sustainable hydropower in Sub-Saharan Africa

Domain	Authors	Date	Title
Tech	Bloemers and Montesanti	2020	The FAIR funding model: Providing a framework for research funders to drive the transition toward FAIR data management and stewardship practices
Tech	Van Donge et al.	2022	Data-driven government: Cross-case comparison of data stewardship in data ecosystems
Soc Sci	Bebbington and Rubin	2022	Accounting in the Anthropocene: A roadmap for stewardship
Soc Sci	Hansen and Antsanen	2018	What can traditional Indigenous knowledge teach us about changing our approach to human activity and environmental stewardship in order to reduce the severity of climate change?
Soc Sci	Taylor	2017	Beyond stewardship: Common world pedagogies for the Anthropocene
Soc Sci	Schillemans and Bjurstrøm	2020	Trust and verification: Balancing agency and stewardship theory in the governance of agencies
Soc Sci	Chan et al.	2018	Stewardship of quality of care in health systems: Core functions, common pitfalls, and potential solutions

Taylor's (2017) common worlds pedagogy approach, founded on 'learning "with" nonhuman others rather than "about" them and "on their behalf" [which] offers an alternative to stewardship' (2017: 1448). Thus, Taylor agues for the need to 'move beyond the limits of humanist stewardship framings' and base our pedagogies on 'a more-than-human relational ontology' (2017: 1448). This shift is said to be necessary to counter the persistence of education that 'privileg[es] human welfare and economic redistribution within sustainable development frameworks' (2017: 1541) and perpetuates belief in human exceptionalism. This radical position suggests that even our most successful attempts at environmental stewardship fall short of what is required because they are still grounded in an anthropocentric paternalism towards Earth ecosystems. Implicit in this perspective is the recognition of Earth resources as a boundary condition (Partzsch, 2023) and hence the overarching tension between affordances that extend human lifespans and population numbers and what the planet can ultimately sustain.

As noted above, the question of for whom stewardship is undertaken, and who pays the price, is another source of tension. For example, when stewardship takes the form of curation and preservation of heritage assets (such as cultural artefacts and oral histories), it is not always clear who are the beneficiaries or what are the perceived benefits to be reaped. Such preservation is simply seen as a good thing in and of itself: part of a place or region's history and hence of its regional or national identity, perhaps. Conversely, ensuring that a given resource is sustainably available to future generations (Darkson et al., 2020)

Table 4.3   *Stewardship focus – target*

Stewardship focus		
Domain	Authors	Target – what
A&H	Knauß	*Good in and of itself* – whole-Earth stewardship – focus on rivers, mountains, forests with cultural significance
A&H	Nunes	*Good in and of itself* – 'practical experience of digital archival stewardship [as a means of clarifying] theoretical understandings of the features of responsible community engagement' (p. 348)
HLS	March-Lopez et al.	*Preservation of affordances* – reduction/prevention of antimicrobial resistance in primary health care via evaluation of multifaceted antimicrobial stewardship interventions
HLS	Rezel-Potts et al.	*Preservation of affordances* – evaluating impact of Covid-19 prescribing on overall levels of UK National Health Service antibiotic prescribing
HLS	Rush et al.	*Preservation of affordances* – 'threat to human health from increasing ineffectiveness of antibiotics as a result of antimicrobial resistance … predicted ten million deaths from resistant infections annually by 2050' (p. 88)
HLS	Van der Wees et al.	*Preservation of affordances* – 'Physician stewardship towards cost control is potentially important in enhancing the financial sustainability of health care systems' (p. 717)
HLS	Tiseo et al.	*Preservation of affordances* – 'Multidrug resistant organisms represent a threat to healthcare systems and the containment of their spread represents a global priority' (p. 1373)
HLS	McLeod et al.	*Preservation of affordances* – 'One Health' approach connecting the health of humans, animals, and the environment as a means of tackling antimicrobial resistance [AMR]; 'propose that policymakers, clinical leaders, and healthcare managers assess and consolidate AMR activities across the whole health economy' (p. 2)
NHLS	Coley et al.	*Good in and of itself* – 'Sustainable and equitable solutions to the persistent and accelerating threats posed by climate change and habitat destruction require effective stakeholder engagement and public support' (p. 1293)
NHLS	Ding and Schuett	*Good in and of itself* – 'examined factors that contribute to the commitment of volunteers' environmental stewardship through motivations, satisfaction, and generativity' (p. 6802)
NHLS	Sangha	*Preservation of affordances* – 'importance of natural resources for supporting our economies and human well-being' is highlighted by 'many ecologists and ecological economists' (p. 7839)

Stewardship focus		
Phys S	Tsolakis et al.	*Preservation of affordances* – 'freshwater overexploitation in agriculture … emphasises the vital role of appropriate water-saving irrigation techniques to ensure natural resources sustainability in food supply networks' (p. 44)
Phys S	O'Brien et al.	*Preservation of affordances* – 'With up to 2/3 of Africa's feasible hydropower potential waiting to be tapped, the growing demand for power must be weighed against water scarcity and the need for water resources to be managed sustainably' (p. 1538)
Tech	Bloemers and Montesanti	*Preservation of affordances* – research funding organizations (RFOs) 'taking responsibility to increase the scientific and social impact of research output' through the promotion of 'FAIR (findability, accessibility, interoperability, and reusability) research data management and stewardship (RDM)' (p. 171)
Tech	Van Donge et al.	*Preservation of affordances* – 'government agencies increasingly depend on other organizations for high-quality data' such that 'data stewardship across organizations is becoming more critical … for the planning, implementation, execution, and enforcement of policies' (p. 101642)
Soc Sci	Bebbington and Rubin	*Good in and of itself* – roadmap for biodiversity stewardship by corporates through the mechanism of accounting regulations
Soc Sci	Hansen and Antsanen	*Preservation of affordances* – 'Harmful climate change has become a crucial issue [for humans]' (p. 1); 'Indigenous knowledge … provides us with a model for environmental stewardship [] to reduce the severity of climate change' (p. 1)
Soc Sci	Taylor	*Good in and of itself* – 'Anthropocene-attuned "common worlds" pedagogies move beyond the limits of humanist stewardship framings. Based upon a more-than-human relational ontology, common world pedagogies reposition … learning within inextricably entangled life-worlds, and seek to learn from what is already going on in these worlds' (p. 1448)
Soc Sci	Schillemans and Bjurstrøm	*Preservation of affordances* – combining agency and stewardship theories to 'provid[e] specific recipes for the governance of agencies' by developing a model that 'translate[s] both theories to ideal typical measures for governing agencies' (p. 654)
Soc Sci	Chan et al.	*Preservation of affordances* – health system stewardship is entrusted to governments 'with the role of global oversight of the functioning of the health system, to ensure that it contributes to the population's well-being and improved health outcomes' (p. 34)

has a clear focus on future beneficiaries across society as a whole. There are material benefits to be provided to those who come after us. This said, the notion of 'society as a whole' may be problematic when society itself is riven with inequalities and diverse identities and perspectives in relation to steward-ship issues. As suggested by Table 4.4, the 'what' and 'for whom' of stew-ardship focus are not unconnected. An overarching tension here is between anthropomorphic and non-anthropomorphic perspectives.

In the majority of cases, the focus of stewardship action is perceived as bene-fiting society as a whole (i.e. a broad-based anthropocentric perspective) with an implicit assumption of future generations as the eventual recipients. This aligns well with the instrumental preservation of affordances and the more altruistic good in and of itself perspectives discussed above. This anthropo-centric view of relevant stakeholders is not surprising in relation to the human life sciences and the social sciences, where it is prevalent, and also in the non-human life sciences and technology, which both operate as 'handmaidens' to the human agenda. Interestingly, it is in the arts and humanities, and in the social sciences, that we see the wider 'whole ecosystem' stakeholder view emerging, with Taylor (2017) once again going one step further than the rest of the field. Also emergent is the distinction between Western and Indigenous perspectives, and the consequent disconnect between those who receive/have received the benefits and whose who pay/have paid the price.

ENACTMENT MECHANISMS: GOVERNANCE OR VOLUNTARY ACTION

The second tension considers whether the *enactment* of stewardship needs to be underpinned by governance frameworks or rests on voluntary action driven by 'hearts and minds' agency. It also considers the motivations behind govern-ance frameworks (i.e. whether they take a carrot or stick approach to achieving regulation) and where the ultimate responsibility for action resides. In terms of actual mechanisms, enactment is divided into top-down governance and bottom-up agency/voluntary action, as summarized in Table 4.5.

Reliance on bottom-up voluntary action versus the imposition of top-down governance frameworks is mixed across most of the research domains, with only the physical sciences (voluntary) and technology (governance) showing a clear trend. In the case of the physical sciences, activism in favour of land, water and other resource usage has been a powerful force in recent decades, driving innovation rather than regulation. In the field of technology, the advent of ever-increasing access to information and data has sparked a growing wave of activity around data security, which tends to be based on regulation. This said, the key message here, across all the domains, is the interweaving and interdependence of the two approaches to achieve maximum effect. An inter-

Table 4.4   Stewardship focus – for whom

Stewardship focus		
Domain	Authors	Stakeholders – for whom
A&H	Knauß	*Whole-Earth ecosystem/future generations* – 'necessary to secure the ability of ecosystems to remain healthy and thrive' (p. 714)
A&H	Nunes	*Future generations/silenced or under-represented minorities* – 'oral histories [as] intersubjective ... creatively co-constructed by interviewer and narrator' as 'a useful entry point to critical theory' (p. 349) for students as 'next generation' society members
HLS	March-Lopez et al.	*Future generations/society as a whole* – 'Antimicrobial resistance is growing and is now recognized as a major global health threat (WHO, 2014). It is responsible for an estimated 700,000 deaths a year ... and is associated with annual expenditure and productivity losses amounting to €1.5 billion' (p. 399)
HLS	Rezel-Potts et al.	*Future generations/society as a whole* – 'Antibiotic prescribing in primary care accounts for 70% of medical antibiotic use' and is thus a 'significant driver of antimicrobial resistance' (p. 331)
HLS	Rush et al.	*Future generations/society as a whole* – setting treatment threshold for some illnesses 'in the context of evidence that, for health professionals, preventing harm in individual patients overrides longer-term societal benefits of stewardship' (p. 88)
HLS	Van der Wees et al.	*Future generations/society as a whole* – financial sustainability of health care systems
HLS	Tiseo et al.	*Future generations/society as a whole* – role of new diagnostics in clinical practice, in contexts of high prevalence of multidrug-resistant organisms (MDRO), where 'misuse of diagnostic tools may lead to increased costs and worse patient outcomes' (p. 1373)
HLS	McLeod et al.	*Future generations/society as a whole* – improving the sustainability of microbial stewardship through whole-Earth–economy approach
NHLS	Coley et al.	*Future generations/society as a whole* – encouraging affected individuals to 'prioritize the conservation of their local ecosystems within the larger context of global climate change' (p. 1); 'ensuring that decisions are equitable and consider the views of vulnerable and underserved populations' (p. 1294)
NHLS	Ding and Schuett	*Future generations/society as a whole* – examining generativity, a focus on the next generation, in the context of environmental stewardship

Stewardship focus		
NHLS	Sangha	*Future generations/society as a whole* – raising awareness of 'Indigenous peoples and local communities' (IPLC) efforts to preserve nature and/or of their abilities to astutely use nature's resources that contribute to delivering many environmental benefits for the wider regional and global public' (p. 7840)
Phys S	Tsolakis et al.	*Future generations/society as a whole* – 'Growing global food demand and security concerns dictate the need for state-of-the-art food production technologies to increase farming efficiency' (p. 44)
Phys S	O'Brien et al.	*Future generations/society as a whole* – bringing together 'government agencies, scientists, private sector financiers, developers and operators, civil society and development partners' (p. 1538) as key stakeholders to hydropower in sub-Saharan Africa
Tech	Bloemers and Montesanti	*Future generations/society as a whole* – through the more effective generation of knowledge and research impact arising from data re-use
Tech	Van Donge et al.	*Society as a whole* – via government agencies: 'Public agencies fulfil a wide array of public tasks, ranging from tax collection and social benefits allocation to the procurement of services' (p. 101642)
Soc Sci	Bebbington and Rubin	*Society as a whole* – changes in 'the context in which economic activity is played out, the role of organisations in responding to socio-ecological (cf. social and environmental) challenges and the underpinning contribution of accounting' (p. 584)
Soc Sci	Hansen and Antsanen	*Society as a whole (affordances) + whole-Earth ecosystem* (relational ontology from Indigenous perspective)
Soc Sci	Taylor	*Whole-Earth ecosystem* – 'cumulative body of scientific evidence of the Anthropocene … heralds uncertain ecological futures, profound challenges for the children who will inherit these uncertain futures, and a whole new level of responsibility for educators who are tasked with the job of preparing children to meet these profound challenges' (p. 1448)
Soc Sci	Schillemans and Bjurstrøm	*Society as a whole* – via semi-autonomous government agencies: stewardship and agency theories 'focus on the relationship between a delegator and a delegatee, which is the central object of analysis in the design of governance regimes' (p. 651)
Soc Sci	Chan et al.	*Society as a whole* – resilience and efficiency of health care provision, now and into the future

esting example here is Schillemans and Bjurstrøm's (2020) combination of agency theory and stewardship theory to craft a governance framework underpinned by trust as well as verification. Another is Bloemers and Montesanti's

Table 4.5   Enactment mechanisms

Enactment mechanisms		
Domain	Authors	Mechanisms
A&H	Knauß	*Top-down governance with legal status* – 'rights of nature' approach: that is, nature is given rights in the same way as people have rights and, as such humans have a responsibility to nature rather than being entitled to treat it as a resource. Giving nature the 'rights, duties and obligations of a living person, in order to preserve and conserve them' (p. 712)
A&H	Nunes	*Bottom-up voluntary action facilitated by increased awareness* – education through practical involvement in archiving activities which demonstrate the social construction of knowledge, meaning and identity and how some societal 'voices' can be suppressed or distorted
HLS	March-Lopez et al.	*Top-down governance via policy frameworks* – 2016 Centres for Disease Control and Prevention (CDC) publication on outpatient antibiotic stewardship describes 'four core elements for assessing and improving antibiotic prescribing in outpatient settings: 1) commitment, 2) action for policy and practice, 3) tracking and reporting, and 4) education and expertise' (p. 399)
HLS	Rezel-Potts et al.	*Top-down governance via evaluation and monitoring of government policy* – evaluating the impact of the Covid-19 pandemic on antimicrobial stewardship in primary care
HLS	Rush et al.	*Bottom-up voluntary action via education* – 'Media framing of health issues can influence public understandings by assigning different degrees of salience to specific aspects, opinions and risks reported … influenc[ing] decision-making about healthcare, for example in relation to vaccine uptake' (p. 88–89)
HLS	Van der Wees et al.	*Top-down governance (policy) and bottom-up voluntary action (education)* – 'Making information about costs available and easily accessible can stimulate cost awareness, but our data suggest that policy focusing on physician attitudes may be more important to stimulate cost consideration' (p. 721)
HLS	Tiseo et al.	*Bottom-up voluntary action by clinicians* – proposed algorithms to support physicians use of new diagnostics 'in well-defined diagnostic processes [that] may be implemented in all types of infectious disease' (p. 1380); top-down government via policy required to ensure implementation – 'should be included in a global diagnostic strategy' (p. 1380)
HLS	McLeod et al.	*Top-down governance of health care* – 'way people access healthcare has evolved: the availability of blended care and complex patient-care pathways … allows for patient-centred approaches as well as more rational use of services' (p. 2)

Enactment mechanisms		
NHLS	Coley et al.	*Bottom-up voluntary action via awareness and perceptions –* stakeholder engagement with environmental management is influenced by 'how a person considers their own relationship to nature, and ... the degree to which they consider themselves as part of a coupled human-natural system, as opposed to being apart from nature and the services it provides' (p. 1294)
NHLS	Ding and Schuett	*Bottom-up voluntary action –* environmental stewardship volunteers assist park and natural resource management agencies in 'restoring ecosystems, monitoring resources, citizen science, policy planning, and decision-making. By involving volunteers, agencies obtain the benefit of getting essential work completed and reducing personnel expenses' (pp. 6802–3)
NHLS	Sangha	*Top-down governance –* 'support mechanisms including respecting IPLCs' rights and access to land and appropriate financial instruments such as Payments for Ecosystem Services (PES)' (p. 6): 'the wider public is the main beneficiary, and therefore requires specific Indigenously designed PES mechanisms that go beyond geographical boundaries' (p. 7845)
Phys S	Tsolakis et al.	*Bottom-up voluntary action –* by food producers of monitoring systems designed to 'monitor the freshwater needs of crops and acquire data for guiding real-time precision farming and irrigation operations' (p. 45)
Phys S	O'Brien et al.	*Bottom-up voluntary action –* 'conference to: (a) promote the water stewardship approach to the hydropower industry, showcasing responsible hydropower development in the region, and (b) create interest, influence policies and renewable energy portfolio development, and (c) stimulate the involvement of hydropower developers and operators in water stewardship initiatives' (p. 1539)
Tech	Bloemers and Montesanti	*Top-down governance and bottom-up voluntary action –* 'RFOs also encourage research institutions to improve facilities and support for their researchers to create FAIR data, as they need to comply with the funder's requirements' (p. 173)
Tech	Van Donge et al.	*Top-down governance and bottom-up voluntary action* – 'three different configurations of inter-organizational data stewardship: 1) the government-led ecosystem, 2) the government-business-led ecosystem, and 3) the regulation-led ecosystem' (p. 101642)
Soc Sci	Bebbington and Rubin	*Top-down governance via accounting regulations –* 'governance systems ... shape the actions of both organisations and their economic stakeholders and introduce social, economic and ... environmental dimensions of responsibility' (p. 583)

Enactment mechanisms		
Soc Sci	Hansen and Antsanen	*Bottom-up voluntary action* – 'Indigenous knowledge is considered a major factor in challenging climate change even though some parts of Indigenous knowledge have been eroded or lost through colonization' (p. 1)
Soc Sci	Taylor	*Bottom-up voluntary action* – 'calls for a new kind of scholarship and practice that firstly resists modern humanist tendencies to enact the epistemological nature-culture divide that separates our species off from the rest of the world; and secondly to think and act as if we are the only ones that shape the world' (p. 1449)
Soc Sci	Schillemans and Bjurstrøm	*Top-down governance (trust and verification)* – combining agency and stewardship theory to ask: '[W]hat combination of steering measures in the governance regime of agencies is found to be most satisfactory by participants?' (p. 652)
Soc Sci	Chan et al.	*Top-down governance* – 'governments are expected to make informed decisions, follow ethical guidelines, work within a framework of societal norms and values, and be accountable and transparent to the public about results' (p. 34); 'six-point framework for stewardship (strategy formulation, intersectoral collaboration, governance and accountability, health system design, policy and regulation, and intelligence generation)' (p. 34)

(2020) exploration of the balance between making the creation of FAIR (findable, accessible, interoperable, and reusable) data a funding requirement for researchers at the same time as encouraging them to comply via the provision of improved facilities and support. As we shall see, the motivations (Table 4.6) and responsibilities (Table 4.7) which underpin these mechanisms are closely interwoven. In the case of enactment mechanisms, governance may be motivated by either reward (carrot) or compliance (stick), whilst voluntary action may seek to benefit specific others or be driven by general benevolence (scope). Similarly, responsibility for the implementation of governance frameworks largely resides with governments and their agencies, whilst voluntary action rests with a wider spread of individuals, activists and groups.

As can be seen from Table 4.6, motivations for stewardship can be complex and/or ambiguous. For example, corporate social responsibility (CSR) activities may be undertaken for reasons of genuine philanthropy, for the perceived spin-off benefits in terms of customer loyalty and brand enhancement (Wulfson, 2001), or even as a 'requirement' of doing business. This latter is becoming a frequent component of the tendering process for public contracts, for example in the building sector. However, the experiences of companies such as BP, with their less-than-successful adoption of the Helios logo in 2000 as an indicator of a supposed shift towards more sustainable energy produc-

Table 4.6   *Enactment mechanisms – motivation*

Enactment mechanisms		
Domain	Authors	Motivation
A&H	Knauß	*Carrot and/or stick* – values-based altruism or practical fear of an unliveable Earth: 'our common obligation to save the Earth' (p. 707); 'duty to prevent further damage to the Earth' (p. 706)
A&H	Nunes	*General benevolence* – via drive for equality based on personal values: 'Equality is thus both an ethical and a methodological value in oral history practice' (p. 348); 'advocate values of inclusion by insisting on the visibility of archival labour' (p. 350)
HLS	March-Lopez et al.	*Carrot* – clinicians implementing the policy to achieve benefits of reduced deaths and cost savings
HLS	Rezel-Potts et al.	*Carrot* – ensuring the achievement of reduced deaths and cost savings though effective antibiotic prescribing has not been hampered by Covid-19
HLS	Rush et al.	*General benevolence* – positive influence on health care decisions, such as increased uptake of voluntary vaccination programmes
HLS	Van der Wees et al.	*Carrot* – of cost savings; general benevolence – enhanced health care system sustainability
HLS	Tiseo et al.	*Carrot* – 'Developing diagnostic algorithms that combine old and new diagnostic tools may help clinicians in the prompt diagnosis of some challenging clinical syndromes and improve patient outcomes' (p. 1379)
HLS	McLeod et al.	*General benevolence* – of sustainable, efficient health care across all aspects of the system
NHLS	Coley et al.	*General benevolence* – whole-Earth sustainability
NHLS	Ding and Schuett	*Immediate others* – benefits to volunteers include 'helping the environment, socializing with people with similar values and improving areas that volunteer use for their own recreation' (p. 2); general benevolence through 'generativity' – volunteering as 'future-oriented, targeting the next generation … or preserving and improving the natural environment for posterity' (p. 6803)
NHLS	Sangha	*Carrot* – of support mechanisms for ecosystem services provision by IPLCs
Phys S	Tsolakis et al.	*General benevolence* – supporting overall food production and food security
Phys S	O'Brien et al.	*Immediate others* – to influence stakeholders in hydropower in Africa; general benevolence – policy around hydropower generation more broadly

Enactment mechanisms		
Tech	Bloemers and Montesanti	*Carrot and stick* – RFOs 'combine their funding requirements and funding policies with guidance and financial support for researchers to incorporate tools and standards that fit their research objectives and make their data FAIR' (p. 173)
Tech	Van Donge et al.	*Carrot and stick* – 'links responsibilities to data, which may include the responsibility for acquiring, storing, safeguarding and the use of data, as well as monitoring compliance with law and regulations' (p. 101643)
Soc Sci	Bebbington and Rubin	*Stick* – via mandatory accounting regulations: 'stewardship might be redefined as a new normative ideal for organisations in the Anthropocene' (p. 584)
Soc Sci	Hansen and Antsanen	*General benevolence* – reduction of climate change impact on the planet as a whole
Soc Sci	Taylor	*General benevolence* – including 'more than human' stakeholders: planet, not just people
Soc Sci	Schillemans and Bjurstrøm	*Carrot and stick* – 'Agency theory assumes self-centred actions and extrinsic motivation to be the primary sources of human behaviours. Stewardship theory … is based on psychological and sociological analyses of human behaviour and assumes that intrinsic motivation and collectivism go a long way to explain behaviours' (p. 653)
Soc Sci	Chan et al.	*Carrot and stick* – driving compliance with the government's agenda for quality improvement in health care

tion, are indicative of the troubled history of CSR and its tendency to be seen as 'greenwashing' (Kassinis and Panayiotou, 2018) rather than more 'genuinely' motivated shifts towards stewardship behaviours, driven by a values-based sense of duty or trusteeship. At an individual level, increasing public awareness of sustainability issues on a global scale and widespread acceptance of the notion of the Anthropocene (Taylor, 2017) has become a source of powerful motivation for many, both for themselves and for future generations (Vecsey and Venables, 1980). Enlightenment narratives of progress and growth – and human dominance over natural resource – are thus being superseded by more relational worldviews that incorporate notions of trusteeship (Balakrishnan et al., 2017).

Not surprisingly, responsibility tends to follow motivation. Historically, the incentive – or pressure – to undertake stewardship activities has been driven by government legislation or other forms of mandatory governance framework (Romero and Putz, 2018), often prompted by grass roots activists pressing for change. There are also 'softer', voluntary certification schemes (e.g. forestry conservation – Kill, 2016) that seek change through rewarding merit rather than punishing non-compliance. An argument increasingly exists for saying

Table 4.7   *Enactment mechanisms – responsibility*

Enactment mechanisms		
Domain	Authors	Responsibility
A&H	Knauß	*Government via legislation drawing on Indigenous cultural values and relational ontology –* 'rights of nature' as a 'useful tool to frame human stewardship in the Anthropocene, on the basis that giving rights to entities that previously were considered as mere objects is the most powerful normative tool of Western modernity' (p. 704).
A&H	Nunes	*Government via public-funded educational establishments* – but down to individual teachers to adopt a critical theory approach to archival practice
HLS	March-Lopez et al.	*Government via policy and public health sector* – health care professionals
HLS	Rezel-Potts et al.	*Government via policy and public health sector* – health care professionals
HLS	Rush et al.	*Media via their framing of health issues* – creating salience and shaping understanding
HLS	Van der Wees et al.	*Government via policy and public health sector* – health care professionals
HLS	Tiseo et al.	*Clinicians* – voluntary adoption of algorithms as a new diagnostic tool
HLS	McLeod et al.	*Government via health care policy and structure of provision* – creation of a whole health care/One Health framework
NHLS	Coley et al.	*Activists/individuals* – engaging in conversation/activities concerning climate change and habitat destruction
NHLS	Ding and Schuett	*Individuals/activists* – people who choose to volunteer in order to make a difference
NHLS	Sangha	*Governments and government/international agencies* – initiating policies that support the preservation of natural resources
Phys S	Tsolakis et al.	*Individual food producers* – 'management of freshwater resources from a holistic supply chain perspective' (p. 2)
Phys S	O'Brien et al.	*Individuals/activists* – key stakeholders arriving at a synthesis of perspectives and then trying to influence policy makers and others with the power to implement their conclusions
Tech	Bloemers and Montesanti	*Research funders, institutions and individual researchers* – 'Integrating FAIR RDM into good research practice requires a joint effort from researchers, their institutions and research communities, service providers and RFOs' (p. 173)

Enactment mechanisms		
Tech	Van Donge et al.	*Government agencies* but ... 'embracing a data ecosystems approach requires rethinking the distribution of those responsibilities. Both public and private organizations can fulfil data stewardship responsibilities, since both types of organizations might collect and process part of the data' (p. 45)
Soc Sci	Bebbington and Rubin	*Corporates* – as 'keystone actors' (p. 587); 'The role of organisations in biosphere governance/stewardship is predicated on the hypothesis that a relatively small number of large (most often transnational corporations) have a significant effect on the earth system and that, in combination, these companies could be mobilised to act in areas where formal inter-governmental governance is difficult to achieve' (p. 584)
Soc Sci	Hansen and Antsanen	*Educators, planners, government, individuals* – 'Indigenous knowledge needs to be incorporated into training programs related to disaster planning, land-use development, environmental preservation, and strategies for sustainable development. Indigenous knowledge holders are dedicated to raising awareness about climate change because without social change harmful climate effects will continue to develop to the detriment of all people throughout the world' (p. 11)
Soc Sci	Taylor	*Educators, planners, government, individuals, but also non-human actors* – 'Socio-ecological approaches ... have consistently promoted an eco-centric disposition that values the environment for its own sake, in lieu of the entrenched anthropocentric disposition that only values the environment in terms of its usefulness for humans' (p. 1451)
Soc Sci	Schillemans and Bjurstrøm	*Government agencies* – 'Stewardship theory views the delegatee as a trustee, more strongly focused on collective goals than on individual goals ... agency theory is essentially a theory of conflicting interests, whereas stewardship theory departs from aligned and overlapping interests' (p. 653)
Soc Sci	Chan et al.	*Government via health ministries' policy making* – resource for policy makers to 'identify options for driving the quality agenda and address anticipated implementation barriers' (p. 34)

that in the modern, commercially driven, consumerist world, big corporations are the only entities with the power to prompt real change. Bebbington and Rubin highlight the role of 'keystone actors' in this regard, defined as 'corporations whose size and connectivity in global production systems shape the fields in which they operate' (2022: 587–578). Increasingly, however, the emphasis is shifting towards education, and hence the responsibility of all to enact stewardship in whatever spheres they operate and/or have influence. This approach seeks to influence the purchasing decisions we make in the supermarket, through to the political parties we vote for and the issues over which we might choose to become activists. Once again, Taylor's (2017) is the stand-out perspective here, extending responsibility beyond educators, planners, governments and individuals to include non-human actors. Her call is for root and branch changes in education that seeks to replace 'the entrenched anthropocentric disposition that only values the environment in terms of its usefulness for humans' (2017: 1451) with 'socio-ecological approaches [that] have consistently promoted an eco-centric disposition that values the environment for its own sake' (2017: 1451).

INTERVENTION ORIENTATION

The third tension relates to whether the *orientation* of stewardship is to maintain the status quo or to initiate positive change. This can be broken down into the components of the degree of change and the purpose of the change intervention. The degree of change – summarized in Table 4.8 – spans a continuum from protecting/maintaining something in its current state, usually for its own sake (Lacatus, 2018); through incremental change to maintain the affordances of an asset or situation (Tsolakis et al., 2019); to more significant change to retain existing affordances at current levels or to ensure sustainability; to instigating radical innovation (Dominguez-Escrig et al., 2019) to improve/enhance affordances or their means of delivery in a way that does not cause further damage. The existence of competing interests and perspectives in making these decisions (Reo et al., 2017) frequently results in partial or negotiated outcomes and 'satisficing' (Simon, 1955). As is apparent, the 'degree of change' continuum overlaps with the 'stewardship of what' discussed above, to generate significant complexity, and even conflict, in relation to the corollary effects of any given change/maintain decision.

Whilst a number of the changes contemplated can be described as incremental, even these may require a degree of culture or practice change that may be challenging to achieve in practice. For example, the development of diagnostic algorithms by Tiseo et al. (2021) to improve diagnostic efficiency would seem like a useful tool that would be willingly adopted by clinicians, yet the existence of inertia, time pressures, and insecurities in relation to learning a new practice may still result in limited uptake. More significant change – such as that involving a change in role (e.g. from outright guardian to collaborative curator of archival material – Nunes, 2017) or of responsibilities (e.g. the formation of data ecosystems through shared data exchange processes – Van Donge et al., 2022) – can be expected to meet more resistance. And radical change, requiring a major restructuring of our health care provision (McLeod et al., 2019), a fundamental reshaping of how we account for corporate value (Bebbington and Rubin, 2022) or – most radical of all – an existential shift in our understanding of ourselves and/or our relationship with nature (Hansen

Table 4.8   Intervention orientation – degree of change

Intervention orientation		
Domain	Authors	Degree of change
A&H	Knauß	*Radical change* – fundamental shift in mindset re relationship between humans and nature. Catalyst for radical change in resource usage and decision-making criteria
A&H	Nunes	*Significant change* – 'whereas custody connotes physical guardianship, legal responsibility, and a one-time transfer of collections from originator to archive, stewardship connotes an ongoing collaborative relationship in which a repository manages but does not own a community's archives' (p. 351)
HLS	March-Lopez et al.	*Incremental change* – in relation to antimicrobial prescribing to reduce spread of antimicrobial resistance and reduce cost to primary health care providers of over-prescribing
HLS	Rezel-Potts et al.	*Preserving status quo (pre-covid state)* – 'serious consequences of unnecessary or inappropriate prescribing necessitate ongoing commitment to antimicrobial stewardship, even in the context of COVID-19' (p. 337)
HLS	Rush et al.	*Incremental change* – more balanced media reporting and/or reducing 'culture of defensive practice' (p. 93)
HLS	Van der Wees et al.	*Incremental change* – through policy changes to enhance education and awareness
HLS	Tiseo et al.	*Incremental change* – application of diagnostic algorithms 'improve the appropriate use of microbiological diagnostics to guide therapeutic decisions through appropriate and timely diagnostic testing' (p. 1373)
HLS	McLeod et al.	*Radical change* – restructuring of health care provision to 'enhanc[e] the delivery of AMS [antimicrobial stewardship] through an integrated approach' (p. 1); 'Fundamentally, AMS is lagging behind the advances made in health service delivery and patient behaviours by remaining sector-based' (p. 2)
NHLS	Coley et al.	*Incremental change* – increasing stakeholder engagement with conservation at a local level
NHLS	Ding and Schuett	*Incremental change* – in relation to attracting and retaining volunteers: 'increasing volunteers' long-term commitment to a nonprofit organization is a crucial responsibility for managers' (p. 6804) in natural resource management agencies
NHLS	Sangha	*Significant change* – environmental sustainability and human well-being through changing Western mindsets
Phys S	Tsolakis et al.	*Significant change* – 'digital technologies applied for monitoring and assessing freshwater utilisation in the food commodities sector' (p. 44)

Intervention orientation		
Phys S	O'Brien et al.	*Significant change* – 'four interrelated themes: (a) stakeholder engagement, (b) climate and water risks, and the resulting decision making under uncertainty, (c) strategic and system-scale planning and water allocation, and (d) resource protection and benefit sharing' (p. 1539)
Tech	Bloemers and Montesanti	*Radical change* – 'The current transition of "science" to "open science" requires a cultural change throughout all levels of academic organizations. The transition is also a technological change, requiring the implementation of new guidelines and practices, anchored in corresponding policies' (p. 173)
Tech	Van Donge et al.	*Significant change* – 'lack of formats and standards … legal regulations, security, privacy, outdated information infrastructures … makes data sharing more difficult. The shift towards data ecosystems requires dealing with the scattered execution of data exchange processes and the accompanying responsibilities' (p. 101643)
Soc Sci	Bebbington and Rubin	*Radical change* – from purely financial stewardship to corporates as biodiversity stewards
Soc Sci	Hansen and Antsanen	*Radical change* – adoption of a relational ontology in which humans are part of nature rather than above nature, with a consequent duty of stewardship
Soc Sci	Taylor	*Radical change* – 'At the very time in which the inseparability of cultural and natural worlds is finally, slowly and rudely dawning upon those of us well-schooled in dualistic western knowledge traditions, stewardship pedagogies seem particularly out-dated. Although well meaning, they do not lead us towards radically rethinking ourselves, our place and our agency in the world. Indeed, drawing directly upon a resolutely twentieth century humanist social change agenda, stewardship pedagogies inadvertently rehearse the entrenched sense of human exceptionalism. … Consciously or not, humanist stewardship pedagogies still operate from the premise that humans have exceptional capacities, not only to alter, damage or destroy, but also to manage, protect and save an exteriorized (non-social) environment' (p. 1453)
Soc Sci	Schillemans and Bjurstrøm	*Incremental change* – developing and embedding different ways of working and different relationships between agencies and the executive
Soc Sci	Chan et al.	*Incremental change* – in relation to quality and sustainability of health care systems

and Antsanen, 2018; Knauß, 2018), can be expected to meet challenges and barriers at every stage of the process. The combination of regulation, activism and education can all be expected to play a role here, with many dilemmas and false steps along the way. Once again, it is Taylor (2017) who sets out the depth and breadth of the challenges by articulating how firmly embedded existing worldviews – and hence views of ourselves – are in religion, science, education and in the whole fabric of Enlightenment thinking. From her perspective, even stewardship is part of the problem rather than part of the solution.

It is a measure of the scale and/or seriousness of the issues addressed within the stewardship literature that the purpose of the majority of stewardship initiatives (see Table 4.9) is the development of new solutions to previously intractable or presently embedded problems. In the domain of technology, these solutions focus around balancing the risks and rewards of the wealth of data to which we now have access (Van Donge et al., 2022) and to ensuring that research data is utilized more effectively for the wider good (Bloemers and Montesanti, 2020). In the physical sciences, the imperative is to support ways of utilizing the Earth's limited resources more efficiently (O'Brien et al., 2021; Tsolakis et al., 2019), with implications for sustainability. In the human life sciences, too, the ubiquitous problem of the efficient and effective utilization of medical advances – such as antibiotics (March-Lopez et al., 2020; Rezel-Potts et al., 2021) and diagnostic procedures (Tiseo et al., 2021) – place the emphasis on the contribution to be made through the development of new approaches.

It is in the social sciences, and arts and humanities, however, where the truly 'big picture' solutions are being proposed. The 'new' solutions here are actually very old, residing in a call for the recognition and adoption of Indigenous worldviews and their implications for the relationship between humans and nature. The call by Knauß (2018) to enshrine in law the 'rights of nature' stems from an Indigenous belief in the obligation to preserve 'Mother Earth' for the next generation. Sangha (2020) draws attention to the role already played by Indigenous peoples and local communities in sustaining biodiversity, and the need for Western societies to recognize and support the work they do for the good of all. And Hansen and Antsanen (2018) emphasize the importance of education programmes that raise awareness of the reality of how Indigenous knowledge supports sustainable development. The 'solution' in these cases is about rediscovering traditional and cultural knowledge we, in the West, have lost rather than about relying on technology and science to discover new ways of resolving the problems we have created for ourselves. Another aspect of the need for Western 'un-knowing' and 'un-doing' comes in the form of Nunes' (2017) work on decolonizing archival practice in order to restore the suppressed 'voices' of oral histories.

Table 4.9   Intervention orientation – purpose of intervention

Intervention orientation		
Domain	**Authors**	**Purpose of intervention**
A&H	Knauß	*Preserving current state and/or restoring previous state* – to facilitate future thriving; 'The past generations have handed over the "Mother Earth" to us in its pristine glory and we are morally bound to hand over the same Mother Earth to the next generation' (p. 713)
A&H	Nunes	*Restoring previously suppressed 'voices' through oral history* – thereby contributing to more critically informed understanding of the relevant communities
HLS	March-Lopez et al.	*Preserving current state and/or restoring previous state* – developing solutions to known/existing problems; potentially 'restoring' a time when we were less dependent on antibiotics as a first resort for the treatment of infections
HLS	Rezel-Potts et al.	*Preserving current state* – by evaluation/maintaining past efforts to control overall levels of antibiotic prescribing
HLS	Rush et al.	*Developing new solutions* – 'disjunction' of different health issues in media coverage 'compromises messages about the importance of balancing the need for sufficient access to antibiotics to protect individual health outcomes with safeguarding population health in the longer term' (p. 93)
HLS	Van der Wees et al.	*Developing new solutions* – 'Graduate and postgraduate education should focus on stimulating stewardship for responsible and efficient health care use. Stewardship should also be included in the evaluation of health care systems' (p. 721)
HLS	Tiseo et al.	*Developing new solutions* – algorithms for more effective decision making on use of diagnostic tests: 'practical diagnostic guide for the appropriate use of old and new diagnostic tools in some chronic and acute syndromes' (p. 1373)
HLS	McLeod et al.	*Developing new solutions* – 'Consolidating the sometimes disparate programs and initiatives within the health sector is necessary, and integrated models of care across primary, secondary, tertiary, and long-term care can help with coordinated implementation of AMS' (p. 2)
NHLS	Coley et al.	*Developing new solutions* – 'application of cognitive frameworks is needed to improve communication, integrate multiple sources of knowledge, and promote shared ownership of the prevailing issue and initiatives' (p. 2) to address the 'planning-implementation gap' in conservation

Intervention orientation		
NHLS	Ding and Schuett	*Preserving current state* – in relation to attracting and retaining volunteers: 'The past quarter-century's fiscal constraints have led natural resource management agencies ... to be increasingly dependent upon volunteer work as a critical resource' (p. 6802)
NHLS	Sangha	*Developing new (old/Indigenous) solutions* – by changing perceptions of traditional/Indigenous worldviews: 'worldwide recognition is required of the role of IPLCs for protecting biodiversity, water, and other natural resources that support life on Earth' (p. 7840)
Phys S	Tsolakis et al.	*Developing new solutions* – sensor-based freshwater monitoring framework 'aims at supporting the agrifood system's decision makers to identify the optimal sensor applications for improving sustainability and water efficiency in agricultural operations' (p. 44)
Phys S	O'Brien et al.	*Developing new solutions* – 'synthesise the key messages of experts who attended the conference; present the emerging body of good practice policies; suggest plans and actions for developing sustainable hydropower in Sub-Saharan Africa; and provide recommendations for future sustainable management of the sector in the future' (p. 1539)
Tech	Bloemers and Montesanti	*Developing new solutions* – 'elaborate on the role of RFOs in developing a FAIR funding model to support the FAIR RDM in the funding cycle, integrated with research community specific guidance, criteria and metadata, and enabling automatic assessments of progress and output from RDM' (p. 171)
Tech	Van Donge et al.	*Developing new solutions* – 'we know that poor data quality can lead to inefficiency and economic losses and incorrect decisions with a negative impact on the lives of citizens ... Maximizing the benefits and minimizing the risks of the ecosystem approach requires government agencies to be cautious when selecting a specific ecosystem configuration' (p. 101642)
Soc Sci	Bebbington and Rubin	*Developing new solutions* – 'focuses on the practice of accountants in the Anthropocene and developing a roadmap for stewardship' (p. 582)
Soc Sci	Hansen and Antsanen	*Developing new (old/Indigenous) solutions* – through re-education: 'Integrating Indigenous knowledge into schools will contribute to conscious awareness of the reality that Indigenous knowledge supports sustainable development, with the implication that the land is to be protected and preserved for future generations' (p. 11)

Intervention orientation		
Soc Sci	Taylor	*Developing new (post-humanist) solutions* – through re-education towards a 'common worlds' approach: 'to make a complete paradigm shift … to make a radical break with humanism's established disorders and to risk experimenting with new modes of collective thinking, or thinking with more-than-human others' (p. 1458); 'To fully engage with the profound implications of the Anthropocene, including the uncertainties of our ecological future, the complex ecological challenges we bequeath to children, and the new onus of responsibility borne by environmental educators, we need to move beyond humanist stewardship frameworks and their implicit human exceptionalist assumptions' (p. 1449)
Soc Sci	Schillemans and Bjurstrøm	*Developing new solutions* – more effective governance of semi-autonomous government agencies through a combination of trust and verification
Soc Sci	Chan et al.	*Developing new solutions* – 'The focus is on activities which directly influence health care providers to optimize the patient care delivered, in terms of effectiveness, safety, efficiency, timeliness, patient experience, and equity' (p. 35)

CONTEXTUAL COMPLEXITY

Finally, and to some extent underpinning all the tensions already discussed, is the degree of *complexity* surrounding stewardship decision-making parameters. The inherently interactive nature of ecosystems (Mathevet et al., 2018) and socio-systems, together with our incomplete understanding of the interdependencies within these complex systems, make it impossible to make a universally beneficial decision in any given case. Solving one problem is likely to create another (O'Brien et al., 2021), either recognized but considered of lesser importance or not recognized at all. These challenges are multiplied by the difficulties of accurately monitoring and evaluating the effects (good and bad, direct and indirect) of any given intervention, in order to inform the next decision that needs to be made. The chequered history of our understanding of climate change (Williams and Whiteman, 2021) speaks to the potentially dire consequences of (inevitably) making decisions in this inherently underspecified context. A key tension here is whether a supposedly holistic view of context is anthropomorphic only or embraces the non-anthropomorphic, with a significant ratcheting up of the system complexities to be considered in the case of the latter.

As Table 4.10 illustrates, to have any chance of making successful – let us not even suggest they can be 'right' – decisions, the level of understanding required can be expected to constitute whole ecosystems, socio-systems or socio-ecosystems. In a relatively focused context, this could mean the interdependencies between different aspects of medical care (March-Lopez et al., 2020; Tiseo et al., 2021), or the structuring of an entire health care (McLeod et al., 2019) or data-sharing system (Van Donge et al., 2022). At its broadest, we are talking about the whole of society and its relationship with the planetary ecosystem (Tsolakis et al., 2019). In between fall the nuanced relationships between the winners and losers of human history (Nunes, 2017) and how they might be addressed, and the checks and balances that encourage the sharing of research data in an often performative and instrumental research funding system (Bloemers and Montesanti, 2020).

What is true of the majority of the programmes, interventions and mind-shifts proposed in these case study papers is the long-term or ongoing nature of the struggle they represent and the requirement to bring to bear every available weapon (governance, activism/personal agency, education) to produce the underlying culture change for which they are calling. It is here that the sense of tension in how best to enact stewardship principles is at its most pronounced. For every noble cause or well-intentioned intervention, there is a counter-cause, an unintended effect or a compromise to be made. These tensions are exacerbated by the challenges of measuring and evaluating the impacts of any given decision or intervention over the vast area of stakeholders, time-periods, interconnecting consequences and differing priorities which complex socio-systems and ecosystems necessarily entail. For some systems – such as medical research and interventions – the use of trails and evaluations that directly inform future policy and interventions are integral to the system, yet even here some effects may take decades to filter through, during which period poor decisions are still being (unknowingly) made. Scale this up to the level of the whole-Earth ecosystem, and the task becomes incomprehensible and impossible: as Taylor's (2017) thesis against human exceptionalism suggests, it is arrogant of us to believe we can ever hope to get these decisions 'right'. And yet we have to do something. So how, as leaders, can we ensure we make the best decisions we can? What values-based navigational compass can we use to guide us through these tensions and dilemmas?

THE CHALLENGE FOR LEADERS: CHANGE *AND* COMPLEXITY

As already noted, the three tensions also interact with each other, and are potentially exacerbated by the complexity of the contexts in which they require to be addressed. The next chapter will consider the wisdom of relational worldviews as a potential guiding framework for making decisions in this bewildering arena for enacting stewardship, but first it may be helpful to more clearly articulate the challenge for leaders. There is a received wisdom that management is about complexity and leadership is about change (Kotter,

Table 4.10   *Contextual complexity – understanding required*

Contextual complexity		
Domain	Authors	Understanding required
A&H	Knauß	*Whole ecosystem* – understanding the role of 'resources' (e.g. rivers, forests, mountains) in Indigenous cultures and how they are connected with other elements of the Earth ecosystem
A&H	Nunes	*Whole socio-system* – emergent post-colonialism and the role of critical theory in understanding oral histories
HLS	March-Lopez et al.	*System interdependencies* – widely understood causal relationship between over-prescribing of antibiotics and the spread of antimicrobial resistance
HLS	Rezel-Potts et al.	*System interdependencies* – 'hypothesised that the [SARS-CoV-2 virus] pandemic might be associated with heightened antibiotic prescribing' (p. 332)
HLS	Rush et al.	*System interdependencies* – widely understood causal relationship between over-prescribing of antibiotics and the spread of antimicrobial resistance
HLS	Van der Wees et al.	*Whole socio-system* – 'The physician's primary duty, first and foremost, is to the individual patient … But the physician should also use health care resources responsibly and efficiently' (p. 721)
HLS	Tiseo et al.	*System interdependencies* – 'Diagnostic stewardship indicates the role of diagnostic tests in improving the use of antibiotics and promoting the appropriate use of microbiology diagnostic methods' (p. 1373)
HLS	McLeod et al.	*Whole socio-system* – 'One Health perspective on integration involves multiple sectors communicating and working together to design and implement programs, policies, legislation, and research to achieve better public health outcomes' (p. 2)
NHLS	Coley et al.	*Whole socio-ecosystem* – 'need to understand the conceptual frameworks with which humans make sense of the world around them in order to facilitate stakeholder engagement in finding effective solutions to environmental challenges arising from the complex interactions of land, water, and human society' (p. 12)
NHLS	Ding and Schuett	*Whole socio-system* – underpinning volunteers' decisions to participate in environmental stewardship activities and why they subsequently drop out
NHLS	Sangha	*Whole ecosystem* – 'the actions of wider mainstream society have made many IPLCs much more vulnerable to natural disasters such as climate change in the recent decades' (p. 7840)

Contextual complexity		
Phys S	Tsolakis et al.	*Whole socio-ecosystem* – 'considering the increasing global population and associated elevated nutritional needs, along with the intensifying anthropogenic activity in the international business landscape that raises societal and organisational competition over the scarce natural resources' (p. 44)
Phys S	O'Brien et al.	*Whole socio-ecosystem* – 'Hydropower has an immediate and direct dependence on both global and local ecosystem services, but also has the potential to cause significant environmental impacts with extensive consequences upstream and downstream of the development, at times leading to destructive social impacts at large spatial scales' (p. 1539)
Tech	Bloemers and Montesanti	*Whole research/funding cycle* – 'widely accepted that the FAIR principles, new practices for research data management and stewardship, and data management plans are essential elements in creating reusable data, and optimizing data sharing' (p. 172)
Tech	Van Donge et al.	*Whole data ecosystem* – 'In the past, each agency organized its own data exchange system according to its own needs. Today, data is distributed over many organizations, and government agencies need to adopt an ecosystem approach for data exchange' (p. 101642)
Soc Sci	Bebbington and Rubin	*Whole ecosystem* – 'the Anthropocene is a term used to describe the current state of the planet and highlights the increasingly dominant effects that human activities have on the nature and functioning of earth system processes (for example, in terms of climate change and biodiversity loss)' (p. 582)
Soc Sci	Hansen and Antsanen	*Whole ecosystem* – Indigenous worldviews 'compel people to respect human and non-human life, including the land, plants, and water … [and] teach that humans are not above nature' (p. 3)
Soc Sci	Taylor	*Whole socio-ecosystem* – 'Intersectionally-attuned scholars and educators who take a critical socio-ecological approach emphasise the interconnections and interdependencies of social, political, economic and ecological systems and concerns' (p. 1451)

Contextual complexity		
Soc Sci	Schillemans and Bjurstrøm	*Whole socio-system* – 'Modern governance is very much like herding: it is the art and craft of coordinating, steering, and controlling a large flock of individual agencies threatening to go it alone ... modern governments need to find ways to steer and coordinate these diverse agencies and to control and hold them effectively accountable' (p. 650)
Soc Sci	Chan et al.	*Whole socio-system* – 'There are typically many layers of organizational hierarchy between the Ministry of Health and the front line ... Intermediaries such as nongovernmental organizations, unions, professional associations, or community groups also shape how front-line care is delivered' (p. 35)

2001), but the understanding of stewardship developed above, when enacted as a form of leadership, suggests that leadership is about change *and* complexity. Even where stewardship is about preserving an existing state of affairs or set of affordances, it may still require changed mindsets and changed behaviours to achieve it. And the complexity of the relationships and underpinning knowledge systems within which such change is undertaken presents an immensely challenging decision matrix for determining what change to make. Pulling the threads of this chapter together as they relate to leadership, then, these challenges can be summarized under the following headings:

1. Political and practical realities – may constrain a leader's ability to make what they believe to be the 'right' decision. The former could take the form of intractable power relations between stakeholders themselves or between stakeholders and the leader. Practical realities are usually in relation to the cost of implementing an otherwise desirable decision or the necessity of demonstrating a suitable 'return on investment' in whatever form is deemed appropriate.
2. Making decisions without an understanding of the full complexity of the eco/socio-system – can be expected to lead to less-than-optimal decisions, however well-intentioned. Even in a relatively contained socio-system – such as a national health care system – the interdependencies between different functions, activities and actors are hard to estimate with sufficient accuracy to make well-grounded decisions: how much more so is this the case for a decision made within a full ecosystem.
3. Monitoring and evaluating the effects of decisions once made – in many cases, the time it takes for the consequences of a decision to filter through and for its full impact to be evaluated (or even recognized) exacerbates the challenges relating to the next decision down the line. Problems can arise through unexpected consequences – which therefore may not initially have been monitored – or through the absence of appropriate evaluation

measures or proxies, or through differing interpretations of the data once collected.

4. Satisfying the needs and respecting the rights of different stakeholders – the different interests and perspectives of different stakeholders regarding a decision can make it impossible to satisfy everyone. On a grand scale, we see this in the tensions between the Global North and Global South (Helliwell and Tomei, 2017) and between the beliefs and traditions of Indigenous peoples and those who settled their lands (Knauß, 2018). More parochially, the need for implicit (if not explicit) rationing of resources in health care sees decisions having to be made between different patient groups, different treatment types and the length of waiting lists for surgical interventions.

5. Trade-offs and compromises – encompassed within all of the previous challenges is that of making decisions that optimize the various trade-offs and compromises inherent in the various complexities they entail. In the absence of a single 'right' answer, the need for a solid values-based foundation for making any decision at all becomes imperative – without it, the tendency to comply with the voice that shouts loudest or to go with the 'least worst' choice in terms of personal or immediate consequences will inevitably rear its head.

6. Choosing the right intervention to achieve the desired goal – once the best possible goal, taking into account all the known circumstances, has been determined, there still remains the challenge of selecting the best possible intervention for achieving this goal. Inevitably, this decision may result in going round some of the previous loops – particularly in relation to practical costs and political agendas – again.

Clearly not every leader will be making world-changing decisions every day. But even if we are only 'leading by example' in our own everyday lives, the need for a guiding principle – for scaffolding to support the exhortation to be 'responsible' or 'sustainable' – is surely much needed if we are not to be paralysed into inaction.

CONCLUSION

This chapter has laid out a series of heavy challenges and tensions facing leaders in today's – and tomorrow's – world. It has 'laid it on thick' in suggesting the intractability of these challenges and tensions, and the onus on ill-equipped (by current leadership theories) leaders to meet them. It would be foolish to blithely suggest that stewardship is the solution to all of these problems – and it would, indeed, merely be setting up another form of 'aspirational' leadership, already critiqued in Chapter 1, to do so. All that can be offered are some touchpoints or scaffolding to support decision making in the face of complexity. The application of a relational ontology – drawing on both Indigenous and Western worldviews – is suggested as a hopeful point of departure, and one worthy of exploration. It is with a view to exploring these worldviews and their implications for leadership-as-stewardship that the next chapter turns to the generative potential of relational thinking (Walsh et al., 2021).

5. A return to relational ontologies: what's old is new again

INTRODUCTION

I want to begin this chapter with a reflexive caveat. I am not from an Indigenous people, nor have I had extensive contact with Indigenous communities. I am necessarily a product of the Western culture in which I have grown up – with all the 'baggage' of Enlightenment thinking and Empire that come with that heritage. I am – often unknowingly – caught in the language and tropes of that upbringing, and – try as I might to do otherwise – I inevitably see the world through this lens. In seeking to write about relational ontologies in this book – and particularly those of Indigenous cultures – I was very conscious of my lack of knowledge and understanding. I had only interest and a sense that I was groping after something of tremendous value. My Western – although I did not recognize this at the time – solution was to seek an Indigenous co-author. I approached four or five people with whom I had some connection, and received polite negatives from them all. It felt like a closed shop. It took the intervention of someone who had worked closely with Native American peoples, but was not herself Indigenous, to explain to me what was actually happening here and how deep the meaning of a relational ontology really runs. She explained that to invite a single person who I did not really know to write with me was to invoke all the individualism of Western ontology, along with the colonialist practice of viewing others as instrumentally useful to us and at our command. It showed not a willingness to learn, as I had intended, but just another intention to exploit.

In the context of a truly relational worldview – in which we are all part of the same human/nature collective – I could only expect to gain the understanding I was seeking through the building of long-term paths to engagement with Indigenous communities. And I could only do that from a position that acknowledged the false hegemonies of my colonialist past. There would need to be a prolonged period of trust building before I was entitled to make such a request as co-authorship. And even then, as the historical oppressor, I should probably wait to be invited. In offering – as I thought – a relationship of 1:1 co-authorship, I was assuming a position of individualistic equality, when

I actually (unthinkingly) represented a historical, cultural collective of oppression and disrespect. I had asked for the wrong thing in the wrong way – and received the answer I deserved!

In explaining this to me – or rather, laying out the context to enable me to realize it for myself – my informant talked about ideas of 'truth and reconciliation' and the work she had been doing in this area. She mentioned the depth of feeling with which she apologized to the Native Americans with whom she was working for their treatment at the hands of the settlers – indeed, from generations of Americans since. Thinking of my own (limited) knowledge of truth and reconciliation activities involving England and Ireland, I said – still not getting what it means to be relational! – that it felt meaningless to me to apologize for something I had not done; something that others had done in the past and for which I had no way of knowing whether they were actually sorry or not. It was then that the true meaning – the all-encompassing 'historicity' of a relational ontology – was brought home to me. Not only are we part of nature – rather than standing 'above' it – we are also inextricably part of our heritage and ancestry. In an Indigenous worldview, it *was* meaningful to make this apology, because it was inherently framed by an understanding of intergenerational connectedness.

I am ashamed to say that I was not very receptive to my colleague's prodding and prompting. We had met because she was interested in some other work I was doing and then suddenly I felt as if I was being carpeted for something I had not even done yet (i.e. writing with an Indigenous co-author). The realization of her wisdom took a little time to land – once my ruffled (individualist) feathers had settled. I would like to thank her now, as I should have done then, for her perception, wisdom and generosity. I was suitably chastened, and I believe the whole project of writing this book has benefited from that early lesson.

So, what does this mean for this chapter and the decision to write it alone? What are the implications of my Western heritage for my reading of relational ontology literature? On what basis am I able/entitled to interpret literature on Indigenous ontologies? I hope by starting with the reflexive caveat above to position the chapter as the inevitably flawed perspective it will necessarily be: I can only offer *my perspective* on relational ontologies and how they might support sense-making in relation to leadership-as-stewardship, and ask for the forbearance of readers from different worldviews and with different perspectives. As a further footnote to my somewhat abrupt (but still ongoing) learning journey in this regard, I would recommend that everyone read Tara McAllister's (2022) '50 reasons why there are no Māori in your science department'. The 50 reasons of the title offer an impassioned and visceral personal perspective on what it is like to be a young, Māori scientist being at once courted and disrespected by Western colleagues who want to gain access to Indigenous knowledge and claim diversity and inclusivity for their institution, whilst remaining deeply and unapologetically embedded in their colonialist values, practices and worldviews. Whilst McAllister claims – somewhat self-effacingly – that this is a 'personal, somewhat cheeky, reflection' (2022: 1) on what it means to be on the receiving end of the recent Western romance with Indigenous ideas, for me it came as a powerful and painful reminder of the old adage that 'the fish doesn't see the water it swims in': when we try to reach out to cultures we do not understand, we still view them from our perspective and never truly cross the divide between our world and theirs. In writing this chapter, and attempting to bridge this divide, I have drawn heavily on colleagues who have travelled this journey before me …

RELATIONAL ONTOLOGIES: SETTING THE SCENE

Relational thinking, from whatever worldview, calls for a re-evaluation of the relationship between humans and nature when compared with the traditional Enlightenment perspective of nature as a resource for humans to utilize from a position of exceptionality and superiority. In approaching the characteristics of relational ontologies, I draw on the work of Walsh et al. (2021), and in particular their connecting of 'ways of being (ontologics), thinking (epistemologies) and acting (ethics)' (2021: 5). Also pertinent is their incorporation of key features of both Western and Indigenous relational perspectives, in contrast to the explicitly post-colonial – and hence potentially more political – focus of the emerging body of work drawing exclusively on Indigenous worldviews (e.g. Henry and Wolfgramm, 2018).

Writing in the context of sustainability research, Walsh et al. (2021: 455) noted that a number of disciplines have started to 'reformulate [their] understanding of nature-cultures based on relational thinking', thus suggesting the timeliness of adopting a relational approach in other contexts. They characterize ways of being, thinking and acting as 'a single tri-partite constellation— an ethico-onto-epistemology—that does not presuppose subject-object and nature-culture binaries' (2021: 5). With Wildman (2006), they consider both Indigenous and Western traditions in examining relational discourses, on the rationale that historically most relational ontologies have developed outside the Western worldview (Todd, 2016). The inclusion of Indigenous perspectives is also justified – particularly in the context of their sustainability-driven focus – as a response to what they call the 'broad consensus that modern Western epistemologies arising from the Enlightenment and scientific revolution are largely responsible for creating profound divisions and patterns of exploitation between humans and nonhumans' and producing the 'philosophy of empiricism that shaped the development of science, technology, and industry throughout the modern period' (Walsh et al., 2021: 458). Wildman's (2006) focus is more specifically religious – comparing Buddhist and Christian faiths – noting that in both traditions 'the ruling understanding of relations suggests that we are intimately connected with aspects of the world we normally think have no claim upon us, and this in turn may evoke greater compassion and responsibility among human beings' (2006: 2).

From an ontological standpoint, Walsh et al. (2021) consider Western discourses such as Latour's (2017) argument that 'the Earth should be conceived as a complex assemblage of living and agential processes which should be given political standing' (2021: 458). From an Indigenous perspective, they highlight the kinship-based philosophies of the Indigenous peoples of North and South America, who 'perceive themselves and nature as part of the same family sharing origins and ancestral bonds' (2021: 458). Significant here is that these peoples 'never inherited the bifurcation of nature/culture characteristic of the Western modern worldview' but instead 'focus on the inter-related, inter-dependent, and inter-active aspects of nature-cultures' (2021: 458).

Epistemologically speaking, this bifurcated Western epistemology, inherited from Enlightenment thinking and the Scientific Revolution which followed, is 'largely responsible for creating profound divisions and patterns of exploitation between humans and nonhumans' (Walsh et al., 2021: 458). Walsh et al. seek to counter the prevalence of this bifurcation by arguing that '[d]espite modern people believing nature could be understood objectively, scientific knowledge is fundamentally shaped by social relations and practices' (2021: 458). For them, the key consequence of a biocentric or eco-centric position is the commitment to 'non-anthropocentrism, meaning that they do not position human interests at the centre of moral concern' (2021: 460). Put simply – and in relation to management – people are not the only, or even the most important, stakeholders to decision-making processes. Drawing all of these threads together, Walsh et al. (2021: 461) propose a definition of a relational paradigm that '(i) is grounded in a relational ontology, (ii) emphasizes the need for understanding human and non-human nature as mutually constitutive, and (iii) values more-than-human relations'.

From a communications perspective, Cooren (2018) sees the world as bifurcated in terms of materiality and sociality, such that 'two realities coexist separately, without much connection to each other: on one side, the so-called material world, i.e., the world of technologies, tools, furniture, architecture, and rocks; on the other side, the human/social world, i.e., the world of sensations, emotions, symbols, meanings, ideas, and ideologies' (2018: 278). For her, these features of materiality and sociality should be understood as essentially and inextricably entwined, such that post-humanistic attempts to treat them additively – for example, Orlikowski's (2007) sociomaterial assemblages or Barad's (2007) matter/meaning entanglements – tend to reproduce the very dualism they are attempting to refute. Rather, materiality and sociality need to be considered as two sides of the same coin: two ways by which anything is experienced and/or identified. From this perspective, 'insisting on the sociality of anything amounts to focusing on the relations that sustain its existence and identity, while insisting on its materiality consists of highlighting what this thing is made of, which also leads us to acknowledge its relationality' (Cooren, 2018: 279). Drawing on James (1909/1977), this leads to an understanding of humans as 'pluriverse … an assemblage of flesh, bones, nerves, organs, and skins, but also of sensations, emotions, attitudes, ideologies, thoughts, and beliefs that relate us to our environment' (2018: 283). More importantly, and similar to Walsh et al. (2021), this kind of post-humanist perspective requires us to decentre ourselves from our analysis, and to consider more seriously the 'becoming/evolution of these other beings throughout space and time' (Cooren, 2018: 279).

The long view inherent in this position is made explicit in Cooren's (2018: 282–283) view of human beings as societies: 'We are societies because our existence is the result of relations that connect us to our ancestors, genes, bodies, names, colleagues, ideologies, environment, etc., knowing that the pronoun "our" has, of course, to be understood relationally, that is, these characteristics that seem to be ours never are absolutely ours.' In this sense, we are inextricably embedded in both contemporary societies and the heritages that have shaped those societies down the years. From this perspective, it is clearly meaningful to engage in processes of truth and reconciliation – as discussed in the introduction – in which we take responsibility for and apologize for the failings of our forebears. We would not be who we are if they had not been who they were, and in accepting and living within the cultural milieu they bequeathed us, we must also see ourselves as needing to atone for the injustices and environmental damage that resulted. Hence, these fundamental and enduring relationships between humans and non-humans/nature, on an equal footing, inevitably have ethical implications. The 'polyphony' of our being – the tendency of humans to 'speak in the name of principles, values, situations, other people, organizations, or even ecosystems' (2018: 282) is an important stepping stone towards understanding and addressing the questions of both ethics and responsibility attaching to the decisions we make for ourselves and for others (both human and non-human). As Cooren concludes (2018: 285), 'it is in recognizing the multiple authors of our positions, decisions and actions that the question of our responsibilities can be meaningfully addressed'.

Wildman (2006) offers a more explicitly philosophical perspective on relationality, having first noted that relational ontology has become popular in recent years in a range of fields, from theology to information science, and from political theory to education. Despite this emergent interest, he sees the notion of a relational ontology as problematic because – whilst it is clearly premised on the notion that relations between entities are ontologically more fundamental than the entities themselves – there remains confusion and a lack of clarity concerning what constitutes a relation. Whilst acknowledging that for most of us, most of the time, a relation is a fairly simple and self-explanatory notion, he sets out a number of bases that make them philosophically trouble-some. Firstly, the 'sheer variety of relations' – 'logical, emotional, physical, mechanical, technological, cultural, moral, sexual, aesthetic, logical, and imaginary relations, to name a few' (2006: 1) – are said to make the category itself intractable and a unified philosophical account unachievable. Also problematic for philosophers is the fact that relations often encode or express personal, aesthetic or moral values, the fundamentals of which are unlikely to be simultaneously embraced by a single overarching theory.

Most importantly for Wildman (2006), the theological characters of some important relations are said to present special problems, in particular whether ordinary, physical relations should be understood as only analogies for meta-physical God/world relations. As a counterpoint to this essentially Christian perspective, he draws on 'non-theistic religious traditions such as Buddhism [that] speak centrally of relations, and … claim that it is liberating to realize that we have no substantive being of our own but are only ephemeral bundles of relations' (2006: 1). The exposition of Buddhist and Christian understand-ings of relational ontology which follows is instructive more for their similar-ities than their differences. In terms of this current chapter, the juxtaposition of the two, as follows, is key. Wildman (2006: 2) notes that 'in the context of Christian theology, if the God-world relation is the metaphysical basis for all relations, then in some beautiful sense the divine suffuses all of reality, making everything sacred and worthy of respect'. This aligns more with pre-Enlighten-ment beliefs than with post-Enlightenment, scientific Western practice. In the context of Buddhist thought, Wildman states that 'if the doctrine of pratītya-samutpāda (dependent co-origination) is correct, then every kind of relation is a cause of suffering and simultaneously an opportunity for enlight-enment, which dramatically changes the way we engage the world' (2006: 2).

From both perspectives, Wildman draws the importance of a

> ruling understanding of relations [that] suggests that we are intimately connected with aspects of the world we normally think have no claim upon us, and [that] this in turn may evoke greater compassion and responsibility among human beings, thereby helping to overcome bigotry, oppression, injustice, cruelty to animals, and ecological neglect. (2006: 2)

Whilst much of Wildman's philosophical argument is beyond the scope of this discussion, his conclusions are pertinent. As he notes, it is not necessary to understand the philosophical underpinnings of relationality to be influenced by the life-changing impact of recognizing a profound connection to nature and to those around us (2006). As he concludes, 'to be true to oneself is to acknowledge this value-laden interconnectedness among entities, and the responsibilities we incur because of it' (2006: 12).

EXAMPLES OF A WESTERN PERSPECTIVE ON RELATIONALITY

In much Western academic writing, the notion of a relational ontology has a somewhat technical meaning, as, for example, in relation to Actor–Network Theory (ANT) (Latour, 2007). In this context, relational ontology represents the 'philosophical position that what distinguishes subject from subject, subject from object, or object from object is mutual relation rather than substance' (Schaab, 2013: 1974). ANT thus assumes a 'flat' ontology in which any phenomenon is the result of associations between humans and non-humans in which either can have agency as an actor (Latour, 2007). Whilst this usage certainly has connotations of a shift away from anthropocentrism, it is not the sense in which we are concerned with relationality in connection with ideas of stewardship and the worldviews from which this duty might be seen to arise. Rather, we are concerned with how Western thinking has attempted to capture relational ontologies as a values-driven worldview, and to do so without having a relational historical/cultural heritage to draw upon. As already noted in previous chapters, it is a consequence of Enlightenment thinking that Western worldviews privilege humans over nature and see the relations between the two as being essentially hierarchical and instrumental. As a basis for developing an inclusive, relational ontology this is clearly going to require a significant shift in both values and practice. As the examples below demonstrate, whilst well-intentioned, the required shift is seldom completely successful and the development of a holistic, non-anthropocentric perspective is never completely realized.

The first example critically explores the 'relational turn' in sustainability science (West et al., 2020). As such, it problematizes the adoption of the 'coupled social-ecological and human-environment systems perspectives' (2020: 304) said to be at the heart of sustainability science. In particular, West et al. (2020) see the assumption that social and ecological entities belong to different classes that interact, rather than being the same type of thing, as resulting in a paradox such that 'coupled systems perspectives insist on the inextricability of humans and nature in theory, while requiring researchers to extricate them in practice – thus inadvertently reproducing the separation they seek to repair' (2020: 304). This problematization speaks to the challenge noted above of truly casting off our exceptionalist, instrumentalist view of the human–nature relationship and adopting a thorough-going non-anthropocentric position of the value and rights of nature (Knauß, 2018). In exploring the relational turn – and a consequent emphasis on continually unfolding processes and relations rather than distinct entities – as a proposed paradigm shift for sustainability science, the authors draw on their own research interests to suggest how it can be operationalized. The result is the identification of three broad 'transformative opportunities' (West et al., 2020: 319) relating to (1) more holistic, dynamic analysis of human/nature connectedness; (2) more situated and diverse knowledges to support decision making; and (3) new approaches and interventions that nurture relationships in place and practice. This is clearly a big step in terms of recognizing the 'stakeholders' of sustainability science, and yet these are still positioned in terms of their ability to 'better reflect the complexity of *human* experiences' (2020: 319, emphasis added).

A second example that helps to characterize Western perspectives on relationality is Gupta et al.'s (2023b) Earth system justice framework. This paper takes a pragmatic approach to suggesting how 'the global community could share limited ecospace' (2023: 1) at the same time as remaining within Earth system boundaries. Their justice model aims to ensure minimum (human) needs are met within safe and just resource boundaries at the same time as maintaining Earth system stability over time. The model itself sets out the '3 I's' of ecospace justice within Earth system boundaries, drawing on the needs and rights of both anthropocentric and non-anthropocentric stakeholders. In defining the ecospace in this way, they offer a number of useful categories. So, for example, non-anthropocentric justice is said to be owed to 'other beings that can "feel" (sentientism); justice for all living beings (biocentrism); and justice which includes all biotic communities and ecosystems (ecocentrism)' (2023: 10). At the same time anthropocentric justice is divided into 'justice between generations (intergenerational), within generations (intragenerational), between fellow citizens (nationalist), between states (international), and between individuals irrespective of domicile (global)' (2023: 10). These various potential stakeholders are condensed into (I1) interspecies justice and Earth system stability, (I2) intergenerational justice and (I3) intragenerational justice. As 'ends' these seem to constitute a reasonable justice-based lens for resource allocation and decision making, albeit with an implicit (if not explicit) instrumentalist view of planetary sustainability. The problem arises in relation to the mechanisms – or lack of them – through which some of the more transformational elements of the resultant justice will be delivered – and who gives ground (sometimes literally) in order to make space for the needs of others. Most problematic of these means' proposals is that of 'economic limitarianism' (Robeyns, 2019), which requires that 'no-one should hold surplus money, defined as money that one has in addition to what is needed for a fully flourishing life' (Gupta et al., 2023b: 13), but rather that it should be redistributed to meet the needs of others. Gupta et al. (2023b) propose extending this concept to refer to key natural resources – such as water, food, energy and living infrastructure – as well as money, but make no suggestions as to how this redistribution would be assessed, implemented or policed, beyond recognizing that market mechanisms would need to change and economic transformations would be required. It is here that the anthropocentric underpinnings of their thesis begin to bite: referring to the interlocking crises (climate change, deforestation/land degradation and biodiversity loss) identified by the United Nations Environment Programme *Making Peace with Nature* synthesis report (UNEP, 2021), they frame their significance in terms of the extent to which they will 'reduce human wellbeing now and into the future' (Gupta et al., 2023b: 3). Thus, it is still human needs that are at the forefront and – perhaps more importantly – human resistance that can be expected to scupper any initiative of this type in the absence of a deep-seated heritage of human–nature (and even human–human?) relationality.

The final example I want to explore is Kenter and O'Connor's (2022) Life Framework of Values model, in which they attempt to connect the different ways we can experience and think of nature with the ways in which nature itself can be said to matter. In particular, their addition of 'living *as* nature' to O'Neill et al.'s (2008) three frames of living *from*, living *with* and living *in* nature is intended to capture a holistic 'oneness' between humans and nature that is more reflective of a relational ontology. At the same time, they seek to instil more nuance in the tripartite values framework – consisting of instrumental, intrinsic and relational – that had previously been presented as a one-on-one match with the three framings of nature. They make the case that the mapping is not that straightforward – for example, living *from* nature could be understood as relational as well as instrumental – and that none of the three frames fully capture the relational ontology suggested by relationality as a value. Whilst the proposed framework is clearly anthropocentric in its positioning, it is – so to speak – honestly so: that is, it is not trying to fudge the issue of human usage of nature and the instrumental aspect of the human–nature relation, but is setting out a reasoned argument for how the previous exceptionalism accorded to humans can be countered through the application of the four frames. Specifically, the suggestion is that 'the four distinct frames, *presented on an equal footing*, intuitively support an approach where values and interests associated with frames are *regarded with similar consideration*' (Kenter and O'Connor, 2022: 2538, emphasis added) as a counterweight to the previous privileging of the living-*from*-nature frame. They thus suggest the power of social learning, and the identification of shared frames together with their underlying ontological worldviews, in shifting research, policy and priorities towards a realization of oneness with nature. In many respects, this paper attempts the least of the three discussed – or is, perhaps, the least grandiose in its stance – and thereby achieves the most.

AN APPRECIATION OF INDIGENOUS WORLDVIEWS

> In South Africa, with its challenges of drought, poverty, epidemics, and pandemics, an ontology of immanence can be harnessed by invoking words derived from aphorisms found in African languages such as the Shona word Ukama (relatedness of everything in the cosmos) and the isiXhosa word, Ubuntu (because we are, I am) [...]. Both these words express the oneness of everything in the cosmos and the imperative to care for the "living" and "non-living" (the more-than-human world). This imperative to care is within us as part of our being in the world, but becomes eroded or obfuscated by our cultures, schooling and limitations of society. (Le Grange, 2017: 104, cited in Filho and Tillmanns, 2020)

Whilst the African narrative of relational ontology has been less prominent in the academic literature than other first nation heritage writing, the quote above beautifully captures the notion of oneness as deriving from Indigenous peoples, with their worldviews of profound connections between humans and nature. This stands as a counterpoint to both the human–nature dualism which has tended to be prominent within Western cultures since the Enlightenment, and the recently constructed 'ungrounded' – by which I mean lacking this heritage-based grounding – relational ontologies now appearing in the literature. In what follows, I attempt to respectfully engage (Muller et al., 2019) with Indigenous worldviews and scholarship to give a flavour of the heritages from which these relational ontologies derive, and to explore some perspectives on how these worldviews differ from the Western perspectives discussed above. In doing so, I fully acknowledge the troubled colonial history which has inevitably politicized relations between Indigenous and non-Indigenous peoples, and of which I – through the heritage of my country – am guilty.

Firstly, it is important to note that Indigenous worldviews are not all the same: they do, however, have common themes. In the context of seeking to decolonize environment management, Muller et al. (2019) identify these as an ethos of care, reciprocal responsibilities and interconnectedness/sacredness as a basis for stewardship. For Indigenous peoples, an *ethos of care* refers to a way of being in the world which informs their entire way of life and their relations with both human and non-human sharers of the Earth. As such, it is 'embedded in kinship and genealogical connections to everything in the world such that each person has "a spiritual bond in a relationship of reciprocity" with all other species' (Muller et al., 2019: 407; citing Whyte et al., 2016: 29). The recognition of non-human agency, and the impossibility of separating human and non-human recipients of care, is an important underpinning here, whilst the importance of kinship is exemplified by the notion, attributed to the Iroquois (Iroquois Constitution, n.d.), of acting for the seventh generation forward. It likewise has resonance with the Māori notion of Kaitiakitanga – meaning guardianship, stewardship or trusteeship (Harmsworth, 2008).

This ethos of care is closely related to the second theme, that of *reciprocal responsibilities*. As Ziker et al. (2016) note, this refers to a mindset of reciprocity rather than to direct, potentially instrumental, exchanges between individuals. As such, it resides in an ongoing responsibility to enact reciprocity in one's dealings with others, both human and non-human, and to extend the notion of exchange across generations into the future. This concept has been found under different names across a number of Indigenous peoples: for example, the Māori refer to it as 'hau' (Salmond, 2014); in Australia, it can be either 'wirnan' in the Kimberleys (Doohan, 2008) or 'wetj' in Bawaka (Suchet-Pearson et al., 2013). In the Arctic, the Ust'-Avam principles of kinship, reciprocity and generosity are summarized in the phrase 'I give it, if I have it' (Ziker et al., 2016: 48).

Finally, the *interconnectedness* of humans, non-humans and places – and the sacredness of the relations between them – emerge as a fundamental underpinning of many Indigenous worldviews. It is the sacredness of these relationships, and their corollary of ethical and respectful interacting, which is at the heart of the duty of stewardship as a central feature of Indigenous worldviews. In the context of environment management, Muller et al. (2019) see this sense of the sacred as a key driver in the depth and intimacy of Indigenous understandings of nature that are precluded by Western, scientific objectivity. They draw on Kealiikanakaoleohaililani and Giardina (2016) to argue that it is this sense of the sacred that enables 'informed stewardship and passionate guardianship to occur' (2016: 65), and that 'it is this embracing of resources from within a network of sacred relationships that distinguishes Indigenous from Western approaches to sustainability' (2016: 59).

Muller et al. (2019) go on to problematize the Western discourses of 'conservation' and 'development' for their downgrading of Indigenous knowledge systems. Glazebrook (2021) likewise sees this devaluing of Indigenous knowledge systems as problematic, and sees the Enlightenment-based focus on objectivity in contemporary philosophy of science as continuing to preclude recognition of knowledge systems which do not fit this template. This being the case, the 'inserting' (Muller et al., 2019: 405) of Indigenous knowledge systems into Western environment management frameworks 'can be felt as violent political acts enabled by the exercise of power to control financial, institutional and political resources'. (From this perspective – and returning to my opening caveat – it is clear how my request to co-author with Indigenous colleagues was, quite reasonably, interpreted as another example of the 'bolt-on' insertion of Indigenous knowledge systems with the potential to perpetuate existing colonial positions.) The problem here is that these Western power structures fail to acknowledge Indigenous peoples as sovereign partners, and thus perpetuate the 19th-century Western exceptionalism that was the basis for the colonialism from which Indigenous peoples have suffered.

From this perspective, even the term 'environmental management' is seen as problematic, since it depends upon a separation of people from place which Indigenous, relational perspectives do not perceive (Muller et al., 2019). There is an irony, therefore, in the fact that a notable attempt to honour Māori knowledge systems in the furthering of landcare research has been undertaken by a research organization owned by the Crown Research Institute (Reynolds and Gordon, 2021), which arguably still represents an echo of the historical colonial oppressor.

One specific form of 'insertion' of Indigenous knowledge systems is the concept of 'ecosystem services', which emerged from the United Nations Millenium Ecosystem Assessment, identifying a number of benefits derived by people from Indigenous ecosystems. In particular, cultural benefits are the 'nonmaterial benefits people obtain … through spiritual enrichment, cognitive development, reflection, recreation, and aesthetic experiences' (United Nations, 2003: 58), and often derive from the care and stewardship enacted by Indigenous peoples of land and resources which are then experienced as beneficial by non-Indigenous incomers. As a related issue, the long history of cultural misrepresentation and appropriation or 'theft' (Ward, 2011) serves as an ongoing form of colonization from which those doing the appropriation derive a false sense of shared heritage and personal enrichment. In the context of teaching American Indigenous history and culture, Ward (2011: 104) suggests that 'the single greatest remedy [to these problems] involves open communication and unbiased recognition of indigenous authority' in relation to their own culture and heritage. Whilst this is clearly an important point of departure for progress, if we do no more than this then the dangers of entrenched 'standpoint epistemologies' (Toole, 2021) and the retention of past positions and injuries seem all too likely. So how can we move forward, and what signs are there that this is already happening in the years since Ward was writing?

As highlighted by Muller et al. (2019), Indigenous science methodologies are now beginning to be recognized and their different epistemology valued. In particular, such methodologies are reliant on long-term, situated observations and a deep place-based knowledge of the phenomena under study (Johnson et al., 2016). As such, the power of Indigenous science is said to be in its 'ability to make connections and perceive patterns across vast cycles of space and time' (Worldwide Indigenous Science Network, 2018, n.p.). Wildcat (2013) coins the term 'Indigenuity' to capture this rich knowledge and understanding, whilst Muller et al. (2019) highlight the unique insights that can be gained through bringing this ancient knowledge system together with modern scientific approaches. To achieve the latter, it is important to safeguard the rights of Indigenous peoples to manage their own territories through their traditional governance structures and decision-making processes, at the same time as acknowledging the need for multi-epistemic literacy and ontological pluralism. Thus, a willingness to learn from Indigenous science methodologies requires Western scientists to recognize that Indigenous understanding of the world, based on generations of situated experience, is not to be dismissed via such demeaning phrases as 'primitive' or 'old wives' tales' but must be accepted as offering reliable, functional understanding of nature that has served the Indigenous inhabitants of the land for generations (Glazebrook, 2021). Glazebrook (2021) gives a telling example of where the Chicano community of Colorado refused to cut down forests on the basis that the god of the mountain would be angry and punish the community. Western loggers, thinking they knew better, harvested the trees only to find that the absence of shade from the trees' canopy resulted in early snow melt and flooding, followed by insufficient water for the crop growing season. When the crops failed, the logging company were baffled: their knowledge system was unable to comprehend the knowledge system of the Chicano. As Glazebrook (2021: 732) notes, 'the ideology of universal truth applied across cultures to preclude practical wisdom of knowing how to feed the community is dangerous'. It is also disrespectful.

Underpinning these examples of working respectfully with Indigenous peoples to share their knowledge rather than appropriate it is the importance of building trusting relationships over time. The work of the Bawaka Collective offers an inspiring example of what this relationship-building might look like. The Bawaka Collective is an Indigenous and non-Indigenous, human-more-than-human research collective in the Yolŋu homeland of Bawaka in North East Arnhem Land, Australia. The Collective includes elders of the Indigenous Datiwuy people, who are also family members and are caretakers for Bawaka Country, and non-Indigenous human geographers from the Universities of Newcastle and Macquarie, who have been adopted into the family as kin. The Collective also includes the Bawaka Country itself as a member, with the whole Collective having worked together since 2006, to share their respective knowledge and skills on an equal footing as the basis for intercultural learning and respect. The strapline of the Collective is simply 'learning both ways'.[1]

CONCLUSION: RELATIONAL THINKING AS A SENSE-MAKING LENS

The idea of relational thinking as an approach to advancing leadership understanding is not new. A number of more or less successful attempts have been made to combine appreciation of difference with attempts at convergence. Examples include Nicholson et al.'s (2019) call for 'ambicultural governance' as a mechanism for harmonizing Indigenous and Western business practices and worldviews, and Ruwhiu and Elkin's (2016) paper on the similarities between the tenets of Māori leadership and servant leadership. The former builds on the idea of the balanced scorecard (Kaplan and Norton, 1996) to develop a business strategy model that is designed to act as a 'decision making tool that facilitates both tangible and intangible benefits for organizational success and collective well-being' (Nicholson et al., 2019: 31). It draws on a case study of creative governance structures that bring together a relational Māori approach to stewardship – Kaitiakitanga – with Western ideas of commercial practice to derive a 'balanced landscape', or He Whenua Rangatira, a decision making tool underpinned by an 'informed and dynamic of both/and [Indigenous/Western practice and knowledge] to facilitate holistic, sustainable [business] decision-making' (2019: 31). Ruwhiu and Elkin (2016) see convergence between the individual and collective moralities of Māori and servant leadership, both of which draw their significance from a relational perspective, albeit within potentially different domains. Servant leadership rests on the importance of service to others (Greenleaf, 2002; Van Dierendonck, 2011) and includes stewardship as one of its attributes, whilst, as we have seen, the Māori worldview incorporates broader relationships with and service to non-human as well as human kin. Located primarily in a work-based context, servant leadership consists in a primary objective of meeting the needs of others through a desire to serve through acts of leading. It aims to achieve communal goals and has a 'strong ethic of contributing to the betterment of society' (Ruwhiu and Elkin, 2016: 311). Māori leadership is more spiritually grounded in terms of genealogies, inherited and endowed authority, life force and reciprocity, and is 'informed by collective and intergenerational wisdom' (2016: 313). Areas of convergence between the two approaches are summarized in a table which maps the servant leader values of integrity, empathy, foresight, stewardship and community against the Māori leader values of Manakitanga (respect for others), Whanaungatanga (familial relations), Wairuatanga (respect for the spirit of the cosmos) and Kaitiakitanga (guardianship of the environment). Whilst acknowledging that the proposed intersecting touchpoints between the two forms of leadership require further research, the authors nonetheless see this as a productive avenue of exploration for developing cross-cultural leadership perspectives.

This latter paper reflects the burgeoning literature drawing on Māori perspectives as informing Western leadership – where it appears to be more prominent than most other Indigenous worldviews. So, for example, Spiller et al. (2020) propose an integrated ecosystem approach to (Western) collective leadership by expanding it to encompass the 'extraordinary set of relationships ... including those across generations and across living and non-living entities' (2020: 517) understood within the Māori worldview. Henry and Wolfgramm (2018) reframe relational leadership from a Māori perspective by exploring it as a dynamic interaction between ontology (way of being) and praxis (ways of doing), whilst Spiller and Stockdale (2012) draw on conceptualizations of 'nourishing' life-energies to offer a series of touchstones as to how managers and leaders can bring 'new life and dignity into dispirited modern enterprise' (2012: 1). Katene (2010) utilizes principles of Māori leadership as benchmarks for evaluating how 'good' Western forms of leadership might be considered, and Forster et al. (2016) present case studies of Māori women's leadership as an invitation to others to 'join in the dynamic process of storytelling so that the plurality of Indigenous women's leadership perspectives, experiences and performances are recognized and celebrated' (2016: 324). Interestingly, what appears to be unique about the Ruwhiu and Elkin (2016) paper is its recognition of servant leadership as one of the few (if not the only) Western leadership theories that directly incorporates notions of stewardship.

Whilst these green shoots of intercultural understanding and onto-epistemological pluralism are yet to become a mainstream feature of Western leadership literature, they do point the way towards a fruitful direction for future research and a foundational grounding for a stewardship-focused research agenda in the domain of leadership scholarship. As will be laid out in Chapter 7, a mindset of openness to other forms of knowledge and 'oneness' (Le Grange, 2017: 104, cited in Filho and Tillmanns, 2020) with the ecosystem of which we are a part have the potential to serve as an anchor for decision making under leadership-as-stewardship. These ideas stand as touchpoints for the final two chapters – which drive the ideas presented so far into the practical realm of corporate biodiversity stewardship and propose a future research agenda respectively.

NOTE

1.   https://bawakacollective.com/about-us/.

6. Corporate biosphere stewardship

With Jan Bebbington, Director of the Pentland Centre for Sustainability in Business, Lancaster University Management School

THE PLANET: THE ULTIMATE CONTEXT FOR LEADERSHIP

Earth systems science is an area of study that seeks to understand how global ecological systems operate in concert and what drives trends in global environmental change (Steffen et al., 2020). Whilst change is a constant and a natural feature of the Earth system, enhanced/accelerated climate change, biodiversity loss and disruption of chemical cycles (such as nitrogen, phosphorus and novel materials cycles) are a matter of concern with the field developing (at least in part) by the need to understand and predict drivers of global climate change. The idea that we are living in the onset of the Anthropocene has also emerged from this field of study (Steffen et al., 2011). The Anthropocene is a description of our current time that identifies that human actions drive global-level Earth system changes (Davies, 2016; Lewis and Maslin, 2015; Malhi, 2017). Framing this change as the Anthropocene, as distinct from the Holoscene, indicates the epochal nature of the time we are living in and what is at stake as a result: there is a well-founded fear that our collective actions are eroding the 'habitable space' for humans and other living creatures (Folke et al., 2021). For organizational scholars, the Anthropocene invites us to better understand the connection between corporations[1] and planetary-level impacts, bringing into focus how and in what way corporate behaviour might mitigate or drive negative effects and what might be done to address these effects. Management literature on corporate-environmental (cf. ecological)[2] impacts has existed for many years, often framed with 'grand challenge' narratives (Brammer et al., 2019; Ferraro et al., 2015; George et al., 2016; Seelos, 2023). What is evident, however, is that these concerns have yet to penetrate the mainstream of management scholarship, but may yet do so as transnational policy and national regulations asks more of corporations.

Table 6.1   The conceptual underpinning for corporate biosphere stewardship

Reflexive capabilities	Informing the elements necessary for stewardship
• *Connecting corporations* to the biosphere which is underpinned by a belief in the biophysical reality of connections and data that geo-spatially locates corporate activities, as well as their supply chains • *Values orientation* that sees the necessity of becoming biosphere stewards • Development of '*markets for responsibility*' that have an impact on corporate behaviour (e.g. through 'ethical' consumers, 'responsible' investors and 'green clubs' of likeminded business partners)	1. *Alignment* of corporate and social goals, in contrast to accepting tradeoffs or the inevitability of externalities 2. *Frameworks* that help corporations to understand what goals are being pursued, such as the Sustainable Development Goals 3. Changes in the regulatory framework to make stewardship behaviour key to the '*social licence*' to operate 4. An *aligned finance* sector (including banks and owners) who will support stewardship actions 5. Radical *transparency* regarding where stewardship actions are being focused as well as the outcomes of actions taken (and not taken) 6. *Scientific knowledge* to inform action that is presented in a way that corporations can access and use (for example, the Science Based Targets initiative)

There is also literature that considers the implications of living in the Anthropocene for business organizations (see Bebbington and Rubin, 2022; Bebbington et al., 2020; Gasparin et al., 2020; Hoffman and Jennings, 2015; Tarim, 2022; Wright et al., 2018), albeit that an Anthropocene framing is not widely adopted or understood. Moreover, it has proven difficult for scholars to span the conceptual gap from Anthropocene thinking and its application to an individual business entity. To help in this translational task, Bebbington et al. (2024) have developed propositions for what needs to happen for corporations to be biosphere stewards in the Anthropocene, and Table 6.1 summarizes the organizational capabilities and elements that underpin such an outcome.

A different way that Earth system science thinking has 'spilled over' to business and management studies is through the planetary boundaries framework (Antonini and Larrinaga, 2017; Edwards et al., 2021; Whiteman et al., 2013). In this framework (see Rockström et al., 2009; Rockström et al., 2023; Steffen et al., 2015) a series of critical elements of the Earth system have been identified (climate change, biosphere integrity, novel entities, stratospheric ozone, atmospheric aerosol, land system change, ocean acidification, freshwater use, biochemical cycles) along with the 'safe operating space' they collectively foster. Over time the science behind the planetary boundaries' framework has been further refined by data on each of the boundaries with the most recent assessment noting that six of the nine planetary boundaries are being exceeded

(Richardson et al., 2023). If the planetary boundaries are consistently exceeded the concern is that a new operating space might emerge that is less conducive to human flourishing. In addition, the physical science behind this work has been integrated with questions of equity and the social minimums that would be required to make a 'safe and just' (Gupta et al., 2023a) operating space. Moreover, the translation of these global boundaries for cities and businesses is starting to emerge (Bai et al., 2024) and this work might form the basis for integrating planetary boundary concerns into questions of stewardship.

Whilst this material might seem a long way from the concerns of business and management scholars, we believe that this is not the case. Rather, the question of how corporations might contribute to tipping points in a negative sense as well as the potential for business leadership to navigate us into a safe and just operating space is highly salient. This chapter contributes insight to this area by focusing on the notion of 'corporate biosphere stewardship' and an exploration of what kind of leadership would be necessary to achieve such an outcome.

CORPORATE BIOSPHERE STEWARDSHIP

Folke et al. (2019) first coined the phrase 'corporate biosphere stewardship' and to understand what they meant by this, we need to unpack the meaning of 'biosphere' and 'stewardship'. The biosphere is the living part of the physical world that surrounds us and is the source of all materials that we use to feed ourselves as well as providing fuel and fibre to sustain our lives (Brondizio et al., 2019; Millennium Ecosystem Assessment, 2005). At the same time, the biosphere is often the receiving environment for negative impacts of our lives (*externalities* in the language of economics). The idea of stewarding the biosphere comes from these concerns with the hope that corporations, by virtue of their key role in mobilizing resources and possessing economic power (Österblom, 2022a), may be able to do so in a way that does not undermine the productivity and resilience of the biosphere (see Nyström et al., 2019) but stewards it instead.

In this context, stewardship is a normative ideal that has considerable traction in natural science and has, at various times, found resonance in business and management studies. Given that a broader conception of stewardship is laid out in the preceding chapters, this chapter will draw on the synthesis of the idea undertaken by Enqvist et al. (2018) to frame our leadership discussion (see also Bennet et al., 2018; Blasiak et al., 2021; and Mathevet et al., 2018, who address similar issues). As already mentioned in Chapter 3, Enqvist et al. (2018) propose stewardship as a boundary object that has the ability to create a 'conversation space' amongst practitioners, policymakers and researchers to frame responses to sustainability challenges. They identify four dimensions of stewarding activity that focus on: (1) understanding the ethical position behind the stewarding activity, (2) whose preferences inform stewardship, (3) what activities are identified as expressions of stewarding and (4) what outcomes could be designated as stewardship. They then distil three dimensions of stewardship: care, knowledge and agency. *Care* relates to the values that underpin stewardship activity, which include beliefs about what responsibilities an individual (or collective, in the case of a firm) has for stewardship. *Knowledge* refers to the information drawn from practice to develop understanding of what stewardship activities might be required and where these activities need to be conducted. *Agency* models the capabilities of individuals, companies or collectives to undertake action and produce stewardship effects. These elements articulate with our characterization of corporate biosphere stewardship in Table 6.1 and feed forward to the discussion of what conceptions of leadership might allow these values to come to the fore. In addition, if we anticipate that it is possible to mobilize corporate action we need to identify which companies might become stewards and how they could realize agency as stewards. To answer these questions, it is important to note that stewardship is not achievable within existing regulatory structures and organizational norms. For example, although many aspects of biosphere interaction (such as acquiring resource access or discharging wastes to the biosphere) are governed by regulatory requirements, the collective impacts of corporate activities are still undermining the Earth system. Likewise, it is unrealistic to expect corporations to act outside of the economic rules that they operate within. This is a conundrum that sits at the heart of business and management sustainability-focused research: we want corporations to act according to sustainability criteria in an economic system that is unsustainable. This implies that leadership for corporate biosphere stewardship will have to be working in, and simultaneously against, the existing economic system. At the same time, however, the regulatory and corporate governance requirements do not have to be a straightjacket and innovative companies have always found ways to expand the art of the possible.

Folke et al. (2019) identified which companies to target based on an analysis of the largest corporations in sectors that have significant environmental impacts (namely agriculture and forestry, seafood, agrochemicals, fossil fuels and mining). The focus on large transnational companies is premised on the belief that these entities have the reach and resources to understand their impacts and to change how they operate. Moreover, it is likely that these companies are also able to shape regulatory regimes in which they operate. A striking feature of the corporate cohort Folke et al. (2019) identify is that just under 200 companies account for relatively large proportions of industry turnover. As a result, their work suggests that stewarding behaviours might not require every company to drive outcomes from a combination of care, knowledge and agency. Rather, a smaller group might be able to exert a normative change in their respective industries. This proposition has found realization in the idea of 'keystone actors' (see Hileman et al., 2020; Österblom et al., 2015; and Virdin et al., 2021) and the development (for one of the industry segments examined by Folke et al., 2019) of a keystone dialogue process (see Österblom, 2023; Österblom et al., 2017; and Österblom et al., 2022b, who document and evaluate the Seafood Business for Ocean Stewardship, or SeaBOS, cohort). Here the hypothesis is that a group of companies (driven by CEO engagement and leadership) may engender changes in actions and impacts along steward-ship dimensions. The propagation of stewardship norms is predicated on these keystone actors having multiple physical connections across the whole indus-try (in terms of who they buy from, sell to and operate alongside in particular locations) that result in novel norms, practices and outcomes. In this way, lead-ership from a cohort of CEOs may leverage critical transitions (see Scheffer et al., 2012). Whilst there is evidence of a movement towards stewardship from this cohort, the process is still in play and begs the question what kind of leadership would support these keystone actors (and other corporations) to become biosphere stewards.

LEADERSHIP FOR CORPORATE BIOSPHERE STEWARDSHIP

This section addresses the question of what kind of leadership/approaches to leadership would be necessary to support corporate stewardship action: what principles might be needed to support the alignment of corporate and social goals, and what 'scaffolding' can be offered to support practising leaders in bridging the gap between conceptual thinking concerning stewardship in the Anthropocene and its practical application to individual business entities. In particular, it considers approaches to strategic leadership: that is, leadership *of* the organization rather than leadership *in* the organization. Here we acknowl-edge the insight of Ghoshal (2005), concerning the absence of a sense of moral responsibility in most leadership theories and education, and begin by identifying theories of leadership that do not offer much hope in attempting to understand how, and under what circumstances, strategic leadership will support corporate biosphere stewardship. For example, 'classic' theories of strategic leadership (such as Hitt and Ireland, 2002) take a narrow perspective, seeing leadership as a process of managing human and social resources to create competitive advantage in a process called effectuation. This frame takes a resource-based[3] view of the firm, thereby leaving little room for management discretion. In this view, leaders would also have a low propensity to wish to consider aspects beyond narrow financial interests. From this perspective, the kind of values-based acceptance of a duty of stewardship mentioned earlier in the chapter would not be seen as part of the remit of strategic leaders. Firmly grounded in Enlightenment-based notions of progress and profit, the relational underpinnings of biosphere stewardship and the potential for a 'market for responsibility' are similarly absent.

Still based on the assumption that the goal of the firm is to maximize value for its owners, positive agency theory (Jenson and Meckling, 1976) sought to address the issues arising from the separation of ownership and control in organizations. In this context, agency theory stands as a way of explaining managerial behaviour, where managers are agents of the firm's owners performing services for them under contract through the delegation of decision-making authority. The problem arises when the interests of owners and managers diverge: agency theory then posits that 'if both parties to the relationship are utility maximisers, there is reason to believe that the agent will not always act in the best interests of the principal' (1976: 308) and that extrinsic motivation in the form of monitoring and incentives will be required to minimize the aberrant activities by the agent. The economic underpinnings of this theory see the gap between the interests of managers and owners characterized purely in terms of personal benefits to the manager (which make the performance of the firm sub-optimal) rather than, for example, being values-driven and/or pertaining to the interests of wider stakeholders. This is clearly very different from Enqvist et al.'s (2018) use of the term 'agency', in which agency stands as the capabilities of individuals or collectives to undertake positive action to produce stewardship effects. Indeed, for Jenson and Meckling (1976: 211) it would be misleading to treat the firm as an individual and hence suggest it has social responsibility, since it is only 'a legal fiction which serves as a focus for a complex process in which the conflicting objectives of individuals are brought into equilibrium within a framework of contractual relations'.

The difficulty with these early attempts at codifying strategic leadership is that the internal focus on firm resources combined with the goal of competitive advantage reduce firm aspirations and purpose to nothing more than the future viability of the firm itself (Hitt and Ireland, 2002), whilst references to 'stakeholders' – where they occur – do not look wider than the board of directors and institutional investors. Under this rubric, the sole purpose of strategic leadership is to ensure that resources are organized and utilized effectively to create competitive advantage and hence economic value. This implies that a very different conception of strategic leadership is required to support corporate biosphere stewardship.

Problematically, however, a purely economic perspective on strategic leadership still persists in more recent literature, and broader conceptions of organizational purpose are yet to be reflected in this research domain. So, for example, in a critical review of agency theory published in 2017, Zogning is still defining the aims of the theory in terms of explaining organizational behaviours based on the assumption that actors who work in organizations have a 'utility maximization logic' (Eisenhardt, 1989) and seek to get what is in their best interest even if it is not in the best interest of the organization. At the same time, agency theory implicitly assumes the interests of the principal are always morally acceptable. In terms of broader perspectives on firm purpose and manager motivation, Zogning (2017: 5) notes that 'actions of the manager, like all social actions, [are] rooted in the social structures in progress and [are] not entirely determined by economic incentives and information asymmetries' but sees the other factors at play here in terms of status, community and need for self-fulfilment. He goes on to note that various theories and approaches have emerged balancing the risks and rewards associated with agents pursuing their own interest rather than the principal's, but none of them bring in the interests of wider stakeholders and all are driven by economics rather than broader values. New governance structures reducing the power of executive management, and with a focus on increased transparency as well as business outcomes, are said to have arisen as a result of mass/institutional share ownership rather than moral imperatives, arguably supporting Boal and Hooijberg's (2001) view that agency theory (Jenson and Meckling, 1976) is a theory of corporate governance rather than a theory of leadership.

Similarly, Cullen et al.'s (2006) attempt to bridge the gap between 'pure' stewardship theory and 'pure' agency theory via the positing of 'stakeholder theory' – as a reframing of the purpose of the firm towards value creation for wider stakeholders rather than merely maximization of shareholder value – falls short of what is required, and of what the name implies. According to Freeman (1984) stakeholder theory identifies and acknowledges the emergence of stakeholder groups – beyond shareholders – requiring organizational consideration, and identifies a stakeholder as 'any group or individual who can affect or is affected by the achievement of the organization's objectives' (1984: 46). Donaldson and Preston (1995) identify stakeholders as governments, investors, political groups, customers, communities, employees, trade associations and suppliers. On this definition, stakeholders are largely related to the traditional, commercial goals of the firm – although communities and political groups could potentially be interpreted as representing interests beyond this remit – and the concept is a pragmatic rather than moral one. Thus, it potentially fails to answer the need for the environment or ecological resilience, say, to be considered as a stakeholder in the operations of business organizations.

The proposed tripartite justification for stakeholder theory (Donaldson and Preston, 1995) also falls short of the mark. Whilst including a normative justification as one of the three pillars on which stakeholder theory stands (the other two are as a descriptive reflection of reality and as an instrumental linkage between managerial action and corporate performance), the adoption of a moral/ethical position based on the legitimate interest and intrinsic right to consideration this entails remains constrained to a very limited understanding of who – or what – might constitute a stakeholder. The further division of stakeholder theory into deontological (right in and of itself) versus consequentialist/teleological (right based on the consequences it generates) streams of thought does nothing to rectify this limited view. The stakeholder approach does, however, mark an emergent challenge to the sovereignty of shareholders, with the normative justification in particular suggesting that a shareholder perspective is morally untenable (Donaldson and Preston, 1995) and that it should not be assumed that shareholder rights stand above those of other stakeholders. On this reading, agents should be understood as representatives of other stakeholders, not just shareholders, and the main aim of stakeholder theory is 'to question the purpose of the firm and who management are responsible to, rather than the control of the manager and interest alignment' (Cullen et al., 2006: 40). As a counterpoint to this view, however, it has been suggested (Sundaram and Inkpen, 2004) that identifying all relevant stakeholders is an unrealistic task for managers. Whilst this seems like a reasonable observation, the suggestion that maximizing shareholder value will necessarily be good for all stakeholders, through creating the 'greatest value for the greatest number of stakeholders' (Cullen et al., 2006: 25), seems dangerously wide of the mark.

There have, however, been some formulations of strategic leadership, and/ or attempts to broaden our understanding of the strategic leader's remit, that offer a more promising point of departure for the thesis of this chapter. One example is O'Shannassy's (2021: 235) framing of a special issue of the *Journal of Management and Organization* with the observation that 'the effective work of strategic leaders plays a key role in enhancing the well-being of society and delivering sustainable triple bottom line economic, environmental and social outcomes'. He expanded on what is a significant shift in the positioning of the role of strategic leaders by juxtaposing 'economic sustainability [which] considers the ongoing financial viability and solvency of the firm, environmental sustainability [which is] the firm's commitment to environmental quality, [and] social sustainability [which is] the health and well-being of organization stakeholders and the community' (2021: 235) as a rationale for why we should understand strategic leadership of organizations as being 'important to business, society and the planet'. This language, representing a fundamental change in our understanding of both the purpose of the firm and the remit of those who lead it, is likewise reflected in the mapping of the evolution of the strategic leadership literature over time (Tao et al., 2021). Early scholarship saw strategic leadership as a special competence drawn from the individual characteristics of leaders which allow them to set the purpose and direction of the organization (Hosmer, 1982). This then shifted to a unique series of processes that determine the degree to which organizations are effective in making fundamentally sound connections between people, technology, work processes and business opportunities (Sosik et al., 2005). More recently, the focus has shifted to leadership style, often linked to transformational leadership (Azbari et al., 2015; Vera and Crosan, 2004). These latter perspectives are said to incorporate the notion that the aim of strategic leadership is to 'add economic, social, and intellectual capital for shareholders, society, and employees' (Tao et al., 2021: 440). Whilst these perspectives accord with several normative elements identified in Table 6.1, they do not explicitly frame the goals of leadership in terms of ecological ideals that are being sought, nor the challenge posed by the Anthropocene.

Another aspect of the broadening of the strategic leaders' remit that has emerged in the literature is corporate social responsibility or CSR (Wang et al., 2023), defined as the 'organizational actions and policies that take into account stakeholders' expectations and the triple bottom line of economic, social, and environmental performance' (Aguinis and Glavas, 2012: 933). As noted in earlier chapters, however, this has not been a happy tale, with more examples of 'greenwashing' (Kassinis and Panayiotou, 2018) coming to the fore than what might be seen as 'genuine' acts of social responsibility. This is, perhaps, not surprising given the frequently instrumental reasons – including boosting stakeholder support; image and reputation; political influence; strategic leaders' careers and status; pressures from stakeholders, governments and other business leaders – for which executives and boards have been shown to pursue CSR policies and actions. Even here, however, there is hope in the mere inclusion of social responsibility on the agenda of otherwise commercial organizations: but the problem remains of the frequently limited scope of CSR initiatives compared with the need for fully fledged stewardship perspectives, and the frequent lack of leadership for these initiatives at the apex of the organization.

Not all attempts to 'extend the boundaries of strategic leadership research' (Vera et al., 2022) have really achieved their aim. For example, a special issue of *The Leadership Quarterly* edited by Vera et al. (2022) produced a collection of fairly 'traditional' strategic leadership papers, and an editorial that is still largely grounded in economic perspectives of competitor advantage and shareholder value. Themes include executive attributes, managerial discretion and executive compensation/agency theory. To the extent that the word 'stakeholder' is used, it still has a very narrow capitalist/economic focus. Only in the setting of a future research agenda for the field do Vera et al. (2022) recognize the role of strategic leaders in setting the vision and purpose of the organization in the context of 'major environmental and climate challenges faced by modern societies' (2022: 8). Similarly, the potential for a shift away from the logic of profit-maximization (Mayer, 2019) and the embedding of a wider societal purpose (Malnight et al., 2019) in organizational governance structures and success indicators, whilst mooted, is all for the future.

More fruitful for the present chapter, Boal and Hooijberg's (2001) review of strategic leadership research positioned the construct as pertaining to absorptive capacity (the ability to learn), adaptive capacity (the ability to change) and managerial wisdom (discernment and Kairos time – the capacity to make the right decision at the critical moment; Bartunek and Necochea, 2000), and linked this to the importance of strategic leaders perceiving changes in the organizational environment and understanding the social actors and relationships within which they are called upon to operate (2001). They draw attention to the notion of strategic inflection points (2001: 520), caused by changes in fundamental industry dynamics, technologies and strategies, which strategic leaders need to anticipate and to which they need to respond, suggesting a cognizance of wider systems within which business is undertaken. We posit in the opening of this chapter that changing ecological conditions (such as the safe planetary boundary) might be a salient fundamental change in the business environment.

In building scaffolding for leadership-as-stewardship, we can consider absorptive capacity, adaptive capacity and management wisdom (Boal and Hooijberg, 2001) as foundational skills for strategic leadership, in need of principles and purpose to inform their application. The first principle to bring to bear here is the notion of stewardship itself, captured by our initial definition of stewardship as relating to the holding in trust of social, moral and environmental values and resources, and the responsibility for protecting and enriching them for future generations (Maak and Pless, 2006). In the context of strategic leadership, we will see below that the implementation of stewardship rests on the acceptance of a radical shift in our understanding of organizational purpose and the abandonment of economic value creation as the only goal of corporate entities. The broadening of the organizational remit to include other forms of value creation – such as social and environmental – is coming, but it will need to be anchored at the heart of the organization – through a reframing of the goal and remit of strategic leadership – if it is to meet our collective needs, and address the call for a new style of strategic leadership set out in this chapter.

In parallel with the principle of stewardship is the question of how widely we cast the net of stakeholders who have an interest in the stewardship process. If we adopt the relational perspectives discussed in Chapter 5, then we are able to extend the list of stakeholders to corporate activity to include the biosphere. This move rests on a number of tenets drawn from relational thinking. Firstly, it draws on the call made by Walsh et al. (2021), amongst others, for a re-evaluation of the post-Enlightenment understanding of the relationship between humans and nature, and moderation of the perspective of exceptionality and superiority that sees nature as a resource for humans to utilize at will.

Indeed, it has been argued in Bebbington et al. (2020) that the Anthropocene prompts us to realize that this is a physical reality, not only a conceptual move. Walsh et al. (2021) draw on Latour's (2017) argument that 'the Earth should be conceived as a complex assemblage of living and agential processes which should be given political standing' (2020: 7), again echoing Earth system science descriptions of the physical reality we inhabit. This argument is echoed in Knauß's (2018) work on giving nature the 'rights, duties and obligations of a living person, in order to preserve and conserve them' (2018: 712) and his suggestion that this approach is a 'necessary step towards securing the ability of ecosystems to remain healthy and thrive' (2018: 714). What these attempts to extend the reach of stakeholder concern have in common is the recognition that 'we are intimately connected with aspects of the world we normally think have no claim upon us' and that this should 'evoke greater compassion and responsibility among human beings' in relation to a range of challenges including 'ecological neglect' (Wildman, 2006: 2). This ecosystem-based interpretation of what constitutes a stakeholder stands as a second principle of strategic leadership for the biosphere.

This brings us to the question of the purpose for which these skills and principles should be activated. In seeking a new understanding of strategic leadership that supports corporate biosphere stewardship, it is proposed that we place leadership for organizational ambidexterity at the apex of the framework built so far. Organizational ambidexterity has been defined as the capacity of an organization to be 'aligned and efficient in their management of today's business demands while simultaneously adaptive to changes in the environment' (Raisch and Birkinshaw, 2008, cited in Havermans et al., 2015: 180). In business terms, this has been framed as the need to simultaneously exploit current knowledge and opportunities and explore future innovations within a subsystem (Havermans et al., 2015: 179) and has been recognized as an under-researched aspect of leadership research. The fundamental importance of organizational ambidexterity is seen as stemming from the need to implement both incremental and revolutionary change (Tushman and O'Reilly, 1996) in order to remain successful over long periods of time. Whilst Tushman and O'Reilly (1996) considered this need in terms of organizational sustainability, subsequent authors have recognized that the importance of leadership ambidexterity escalates in times of crisis, and draw attention to climate change and the sustainability crisis as examples of where this need is greatest (Singh et al., 2023). Similarly, Havermans et al. (2015) note the need for requisite complexity: that is, that the 'complexity of external stimuli has to be matched by the complexity of internal responses by an organization' (Boisot and McKelvey, 2010, cited in Havermans et al., 2015: 180). For them, as for Tushman and O'Reilly (1996), the 'real test of leadership, then, is to be able to compete successfully by both increasing the alignment or fit among strategy,

structure, culture, and processes, while simultaneously preparing for the inevitable revolutions required by discontinuous environmental change' (1996: 11).
For us, and in the context of corporate biosphere stewardship, ambidexterity
rests on the balance between planetary boundaries and human flourishing,
and the relational ontologies which radically reframe our understanding of
our standing within this relationship. Similarly, Gupta et al.'s (2023) Earth
system justice framework offers parallels with the notion of ambidexterity
interpreted at a more macro level by suggesting how 'the global community
could share limited ecospace' (2023: 1) at the same time as remaining within
Earth system boundaries, balancing present minimum (human) needs with
the maintenance of Earth system stability over time. Thus, it is also here that
a degree of alignment between the demand for corporate biosphere stewardship identified in the opening of the chapter and leadership conceptions really
start to emerge. Ambidexterity also underpins the keystone actor approach and
is, to some extent, starting to be evident in the SeaBOS initiative (Österblom
et al., 2022b).

The 'pyramid' of skills, principles and purpose suggested by this synthesis
of strategic leadership capacities, guided by stewardship and relationality, and
directed by the pressing need to find balance between present needs and future
potential, is summarized in Figure 6.1. Collectively these components, operating at different levels, are proposed as offering substantive scaffolding to the
practising leader in enacting both corporate biosphere stewardship and responsible leadership for the Anthropocine more broadly. As with all models, this
is inevitably a simplification, and cannot hope to capture all the complexities
of the systems within which leadership takes place. The focus of this chapter,
for example, has been broadly on ecosystems with less obvious emphasis on
socio-systems, but an argument can be made for these same skills, principles
and purpose serving both realms of activity equally effectively.

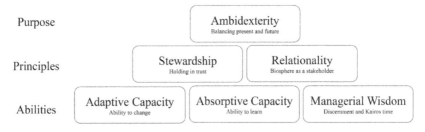

Figure 6.1   Strategic leadership for corporate biosphere stewardship

CONCLUDING OBSERVATIONS

In highlighting the SeaBOS project as an example of real-world corporate biosphere stewardship, and proposing the leadership ambidexterity model as a supporting framework for stewardship as a form of strategic leadership, this chapter has offered a hopeful glimpse of where progress is already being made in meeting the challenges of the Anthropocene, and how leadership-as-stewardship can contribute to that vital endeavour. It has started to answer the question of what kind of business leadership might be required to navigate us into a safe and just operating space, within present planetary boundaries but with a fundamental focus on a sustainable future. It suggests some of the points of leverage within the corporate world, and challenges entrenched Enlightenment ideas of progress as necessarily equating to economic growth. In so doing, it brings us back to a broader idea of the 'betterment of the human condition' (Robertson, 2015) with which Enlightenment thinking was originally associated: one which balances meeting the needs of humankind with maintaining the productivity and resilience of the biosphere from which the ability to meet future needs necessarily stems. The notion of ambidexterity is key here, as are notions of stewardship and relationality. This is only a point of departure, however, and there remains much to be done. In the concluding chapter, we will revisit the journey we have travelled so far, and explore the future research agenda suggested by the idea of stewardship as a successor to leadership and as a repository for so many of our hopes and aspirations. The final chapter likewise considers the 'so what?' of leadership-as-stewardship for both practitioners and management educators. If the SeaBOS project has shown us what *can* be done, then it is suggested that it is the remit of management education to embed this learning in the standard curriculum for future leaders.

NOTES

1. Here we are going to focus on corporations, rather than organizations more widely. The reason for doing this is that corporations, many of whom are large economic entities, often have a disproportionately negative environmental effect as well as global reach (Österblom et al., 2022a). That being said, organizations in the public sector should not be ignored in leadership and stewardship conversations because they are often guardians of environmental functioning in particular places (see Bebbington et al., 2023, who play out this point in more detail in relation to the Sustainable Development Goals).
2. The distinction between environmental and ecological relates to the relative focus placed on biological elements of the Earth system. Broadly speaking,

an environmental focus would examine the interactions between physical, chemical and biological aspects of a system whereas an ecological focus examined interactions between organisms and their environment. Taking an ecological focus to organizational impacts, therefore, would be more likely to examine corporate interactions with the living world, alongside physical interactions. Thus far, the management literature has focused on environmental more strongly than ecology.

3.   Given this theory developed without connection to natural science knowledge, resources such as a stable climate or a regenerative biosphere are not what is meant by 'resources'.

7.   Conclusion: *quo vadis*, stewardship?

INTRODUCTION: THE JOURNEY SO FAR

The origins of this journey into stewardship began with concerns about the research discipline (and the practice) of leadership, so this concluding chapter could just as easily be called '*Quo vadis*, leadership?' Indeed, whilst one of the more radical goals of the book might be said to be replacing leadership with stewardship in the management lexicon, a more reasonable direction of travel is that of bringing the two together to arrive at something more workable for practitioners and scholars alike. By 'more workable' I am not suggesting that stewardship is somehow easier than leadership, or that it addresses all the challenges currently inherent in the leadership construct. Rather, the aim is to suggest some productive ways in which we can continue to advance our understanding of both in a way that is fit for purpose for the 21st century. Before attempting this, it is perhaps worth recapping on the journey thus far.

The journey started with the post-Enlightenment baggage being carried by the leadership construct, and with the shift towards advocacy rather than enquiry in leadership research. The former has tended to saddle leadership inextricably with notions of profit and progress, and tied the remit of leaders to the interests of shareholders. Even in the public sector, the advent of 'new public management' (Lane, 2002) and calls for 'transformational leadership' (Fischer, 2016) have seen a shift in focus that brings previously private-sector concerns to bear in the running of public services. The latter is part of a shift towards the promulgation of a range of 'aspirational' forms of leadership – responsible (Pless and Maak, 2011), sustainable (Avery and Bergsteiner, 2010), authentic (Iszatt-White and Kempster, 2019) – that place additional, often unrealistic, burdens on practising leaders at the same time as seeing leadership scholars invade the territory of moral philosophy, often with limited empirical support for their well-meaning calls for purpose. The idea of stewardship as an alternative focus for academic attention that also offers better grounded 'scaffolding' for the practice of leadership was – perhaps, serendipitously – no more than a term that seemed to capture the 21st-century zeitgeist, but the critical exploration of the preceding chapters suggests that this proposed new focus might have 'legs'.

In reviewing the sizeable literature on stewardship, across a range of research domains, a number of useful tropes emerged. These started – and also finished – with Maak and Pless's (2006: 108) work in the field of responsible leadership, which defined a steward as someone who understands themselves 'as a custodian of social, moral and environmental values and resources', trusted with their protection and enrichment, and guided by the question 'What am I passing on to [] future generation[s]?' The emergent tropes included ideas of optimization, resource management, data security, governance, (re) education and relational ontologies. At the same time, differences emerged in relation to what is to be held in trust, for whom and to what end. Homing in on the management literature, and the social sciences more generally, the review highlighted the ways in which writers in this domain have drawn on other disciplines in crafting their understanding of stewardship, resulting in a bricolage of meanings that offer an interesting and nuanced source of inspiration for the discipline of leadership. Underpinning this bricolage is a leaning towards perspectives that acknowledge the idea of the Anthropocene – 'the proposed geological epoch in which human activities outstrip glaciers in changing the face of the Earth' (Tsing, 2016) – as a key underpinning of most management and social activities now and in the future. In response to this 'grand challenge' framing of the management remit, the two-pronged strategies of governance and re-education are much in evidence, as is the search for a 'better way' via an emergent interest in Indigenous peoples and relational ontologies that counteract the Enlightenment-based separation of humans and nature, and the exceptionalist assumption that natural resources are there for our sole use and benefit.

Further analysis of the stewardship literature revealed a number of tensions that highlight the difficulty of unquestioningly accepting stewardship as a 'good thing', and of rushing to offer it as a new 'miracle cure' for the world's ills. The tensions considered related to such issues as what is to be 'stewarded' and for whom, what mechanisms are required to enact stewardship and whose responsibility is it to enact them, what degree of change orientation might stewardship actually entail and how should stewards address the contextual complexities within which they are inevitably required to operate. Specifically, these tensions relate to the stewardship *focus*, *enactment* mechanisms and intervention *orientation* of stewardship activity, and the *contextual complexity* within which stewardship necessarily takes place.

The idea of *focus* covers what is being stewarded and for whom, and how far we should go in our definition of stakeholders to the process. The tensions here arise from whether we choose to steward something for altruistic reasons – as a good in and of itself – or for the more self-serving motive of retaining the affordances it provides to us as users. Related to this is the question of whether we view the stakeholders as including whole Earth ecosystems (i.e.

a non-anthropomorphic perspective) or as consisting of society as a whole, including future generations (i.e. an anthropomorphic perspective). As we saw with all the tensions, there are no right answers here, only the need for some kind of guiding framework to support leaders – and the rest of us – in making the best decisions, with all the trade-offs this will necessarily entail, in any given situation.

The challenge of *enactment* concerns the mechanisms underpinning stewardship activity and, in particular, whether stewardship occurs through governance frameworks or voluntary action. The three elements of tension – mechanisms, motivation and responsibility – which contribute to the tensions surrounding *enactment* relate to whether stewardship is enacted via top-down governance or bottom-up voluntary action; whether governance measures take a reward or punishment/carrot or stick approach; whether the scope of voluntary action encompasses general benevolence or only immediate others; and whether the keystone actors responsible for driving and undertaking stewardship are governments, businesses or individuals/activists. Inevitably, there are tensions between these tensions, and trade-offs within the *enactment* process as well as across the other three tensions.

Tensions also arise in determining the *orientation* of interventions undertaken, particularly with regard to the degree of change required to meet the goals or purpose envisaged by specific stewardship interventions, and the balance between preserving, restoring and innovating that may be involved. The degree of change can range from preserving the status quo, through incremental change to improve or enhance an existing situation, to significant change arising from scientific innovation, to radically new perspectives arising from a wholesale change of mindset or shift in understanding. Even the underlying purpose of the intervention can be a source of tension or uncertainty, spanning the desire to restore a previous state, preserve a current state or develop new solutions. Not surprisingly, there are significant overlaps here with what is to be stewarded and for whom.

Finally, even the context in which stewardship occurs can be problematic, with tensions arising from the *complexities* of the ecosystems and/or socio-systems within which leaders are required to operate. These include the limitations on our knowledge of whole ecosystems and/or socio-systems, the challenges of evaluating the impact of previous interventions and the timeframes over which stewardship activities frequently play out. As with the scoping out of stakeholders, the problem to be addressed may require a grasp of whole ecosystems and a non-anthropomorphic stance, or the (more limited?) grasp of a whole 'socio-system' and a purely anthropomorphic perspective. In either case, the challenges of achieving a holistic understanding of the system interdependencies within vastly complex contexts is something that has tripped up many well-intentioned stewardship interventions (think of the unanticipated effects of reintroducing animal species to environments in which their historical predator is no longer there to keep population growth in check) in the past and will no doubt do so again in the future.

Considering the sum total of the case study papers through which these tensions were illustrated, it becomes clear that leaders face an ongoing struggle to navigate the daily challenges of enacting leadership-as-stewardship and need to bring to bear every available weapon (governance, activism/personal agency, education) to produce the underlying culture change for which they are calling. As already noted in Chapter 4, for every noble cause or well-intentioned intervention, there is a counter-cause, an unintended effect or a compromise to be made: there is never a 'right' answer and leaders need (and deserve) to be better supported in arriving at the best possible answers than they are currently. For some systems – such as medical research and interventions – the use of trails and evaluations that directly inform future policy and interventions may allow an element of 'trial and error' to support progressive improvement. Even here, however, some effects may take decades to filter through, during which period poor decisions are still (unknowingly) being made. Scale this complexity up to the level of whole socio-systems or ecosystems and the task becomes almost incomprehensible and all but impossible. Yet we have act, we have to decide – even if we decide to do nothing, this will still have ongoing effects on the system. So how, as leaders, can we ensure we make the best decisions we can? What values-based navigational compass can we use to guide us through these tensions and dilemmas?

DESTINATION ACHIEVED?

In drawing the journey so far to a conclusion, we have considered three possible touchpoints to guide leadership-as-stewardship actions: (1) change and complexity, (2) a return to relational ontologies and (3) ambidexterity in balancing present and future concerns. The first of these touchstones derives from recognizing the interdependencies and interweaving of the four tensions discussed above, and a reframing of the old maxim that management is about complexity and leadership is about change (Kotter, 2001), suggesting rather that stewardship, when enacted as a form of leadership, requires a focus on both change *and* complexity. Even where stewardship is about preserving an existing state of affairs or set of affordances, it may still require changed mindsets and changed behaviours to achieve it. And determining what changes to make requires cognisance of the complexity of the relationships and underpinning knowledge systems within which such change is undertaken. This is perhaps no surprise to practising leaders, but is nonetheless something that current 'aspirational' leadership theories do not necessarily equipe leaders to do.

Another important touchstone stems from the recent groundswell of appreciation for Indigenous worldviews – such as the Māori notion of Kaitiakitanga or guardianship and the Iroquois notion of acting for the seventh generation forward – with their profound connections between humans and nature, as a counterpoint to the human–nature dualism within modern society. More broadly, and in both Western and Indigenous contexts, an exploration of relational ontologies and their implications for stewardship offers a profound opportunity to recalibrate the relationship between humans and nature. This stands as a counterpoint to both the human–nature dualism and the assumption of human exceptionalism which have tended to be prominent within Western cultures since the Enlightenment. Whilst there are clearly differences between the culturally grounded relational ontologies of Indigenous peoples and the 'ungrounded' – that is, lacking a heritage-based grounding – relational ontologies now appearing in Western literature, they nonetheless offer a valuable point of departure for a stewardship-focused research agenda in the domain of leadership scholarship.

It is worth noting that this book has been developed at a time when the importance of 'decolonizing management theory' (Banerjee, 2022) has drawn attention to the Western bias in management theorizing (Muzio, 2022) and the performative effects of Western theory in perpetuating neo-colonial and imperialist dynamics in non-Western contexts that have been pressured into conforming to theories that do not align with their ontological and epistemological beliefs. The resultant devaluing of Indigenous histories, practices and knowledges (Muzio, 2022), often as a result of continuing to view them from a Western perspective (Bruton et al., 2022), which was a feature of the colonial past is only now being recognized as a significant loss to the world. At the opposite end of the spectrum, the increasing interest in Indigenous worldviews has the 'danger of essentializing context by an uncritical privileging of the local' (Banerjee, 2022: 1084) that does a disservice to both Indigenous and Western orientations. The politicization of attempts to build synergies between these different worldviews, and the challenges of truly opening ourselves up to in-depth understanding of the worldviews of others (see my opening caveat to Chapter 5) should not deter academics and practitioners alike from attempting this journey.

The need for decolonization applies equally to leadership scholarship, which has also been shaped by the hegemony of Western, market-economy thinking (Banerjee, 2022), to arrive at a more 'connected' perspective of the different leadership challenges arising from the application of supposedly 'universal' (Bruton et al., 2022: 1058) theories to Western and Eastern contexts (Filatotchev et al., 2020). Examples explored in Chapter 5 included Nicholson et al.'s (2019) call for 'ambicultural governance' as a mechanism for harmonizing Indigenous and Western business practices and worldviews, and Ruwhiu and Elkin's (2016) paper on the similarities between the tenets of Māori leadership and servant leadership.

The third touchpoint, that of ambidexterity, emerged from Chapter 6's exploration of what it would entail if corporations were to become active stewards of the biosphere, the role of keystone actors in enacting biosphere stewardship and the pivotal role of leadership that would support corporate biosphere stewardship requirements. Working from the premise of the whole Earth ecosystem as the ultimate context for leadership, and an acceptance of the epochal nature of the Anthropocene as a period in which our collective actions are eroding the 'habitable space' for humans and other living creatures (Folke et al., 2021), it is likewise timely to acknowledge that the role of business – and in particular large corporations – is going to be foundational to preserving what habitable space we have into the future. As keystone actors, large corporations are able to mobilize resources and exercise economic power (Österblom, 2022a) in ways that steward rather than undermine the productivity and resilience of the biosphere (Nyström et al., 2019). Through the exercise of strategic leadership – that is, leadership *of* the organization rather than leadership *in* the organization – they have the ability to support environmental responsibility, promote social well-being and exercise self-governance towards an 'ambidextrous' balancing of present needs and future potential. It is a measure of the weight of influence wielded by the business world – and in particular by business investors – that the Environmental, Social and Governance (ESG) Standards for responsible investment have gained currency around the world. Promulgated initially by Larry Fink, head of the world's largest asset manager, Black Rock, the ESG framework has emerged as a catch-all term for a range of ethically responsible business practices, from decarbonization to discrimination in the workplace. According to investment bank Morgan Stanley,[1] sustainable/ESG funds rose to more than $3.1 billion in the first half of 2023, accounting for almost 8 per cent of total global assets under management.

Bringing these touchpoints together also brought us back to the underpinnings of strategic leadership, and specifically Boal and Hooijberg's (2001) review of strategic leadership research in which they positioned it as consisting of absorptive capacity (the ability to learn), adaptive capacity (the ability to change) and managerial wisdom (discernment and Kairos time). If we consider these to be the foundational skills and abilities of a strategic leader, then we can layer stewardship (as holding in trust) and relationality (to the biosphere as a stakeholder) on top as the principles by which the application of these skills and abilities should be guided. On top again is the notion of ambidexterity (the balancing of present and future) as the purpose these principles are directed towards achieving. As a purpose, organizational ambidexterity is about being 'aligned and efficient in their management of today's business demands while simultaneously adaptive to changes in the environment' (Raisch and

Birkinshaw, 2008, cited in Havermans et al., 2015: 180). To be sustainable both as businesses and in ecological terms, organizations need to simultaneously exploit current knowledge and opportunities and explore future innovations within, in order to implement both incremental and revolutionary change (Tushman and O'Reilly, 1996). As already stated in Chapter 6, in the context of strategic leadership, the implementation of ambidexterity rests on the acceptance of a radical shift in our understanding of organizational purpose and the abandonment of economic value creation as the only goal of corporate entities. The broadening of the organizational remit to include other forms of value creation – such as social and environmental – will need to be anchored at the apex of the organization.

LEADERSHIP-AS-STEWARDSHIP

At its outset, this book proposed stewardship as a new 'signifier' (Kelly, 2014) for leadership scholarship. The benefits of this shift were seen as being the introduction of a construct with less capitalist, aspirational and Enlightenment baggage than its predecessors, and with the potential to prevent the 'technosphere racing ahead without much concern for its own longevity' (Gasparin et al., 2020: 396). Conversely the pitfall was the potential to merely create another form of aspirational leadership with which to burden practising leaders. Whilst the jury may still be out on the success of the stewardship proposal, it is hoped that the preceding pages have done enough to establish it as one that is at least worthy of future research. To this end, the following research agenda sets out just some of the questions which arise from a desire to pursue the leadership-as-stewardship project.

In conceptualizing leadership-as-stewardship, the ontological and epistemological precepts can be seen as relatively clear cut, if challenging to enact. Ontologically, relational thinking demands that leaders consider the widest possible range of stakeholders in their decision making, and adopt a non-anthropocentric stance in doing so. A clear example of this stance from the stewardship literature was found in Knauß's (2018) 'rights of nature' approach to environmental stewardship, in which non-human stakeholders are placed on a par with human stakeholders in determining issues of usage and obligation. Knauß (2018: 703) proposes this approach as a means of 'transcend[ing] European Modernity', thus countering Enlightenment-driven progress and growth discourses already found in responsible and sustainable (Avery and Bergsteiner, 2011a, 2011b) leadership, but further anchored by heritage-embedded stewardship discourse. It has already been noted that care must be taken here to avoid the pitfalls of importing 'local' Indigenous theories wholesale into a supposedly 'universal' Western context (Bruton et al., 2022), rather than recognizing that Western ontologies represent an equally local and 'indigenous' context in their own right, but further research into the similarities and differences of relational ontologies is clearly needed if we are to blend them in any form of harmonious practice. And contrary to Bruton et al.'s (2022: 1057) premise, the insufficiency of 'placing bandages on existing theories' may be just as marked in moving East to West as West to East: another topic area open to research attention.

Perhaps equally challenging will be the change in epistemological commitments required to inform decision making that is resonant with a relational ontology. Embracing a stewardship-led, non-anthropocentric worldview will require the acceptance of a broader range of 'truths' and forms of 'evidence' within decision-making processes (Reo et al., 2017). This might include giving relevance to notions of place (McMillen et al., 2020) and feelings of environmental connectivity (Schwass et al., 2021), and will certainly require a greater affinity with Indigenous worldviews (Spiller, 2021). Running directly counter to the tenets of Enlightenment thinking, placing as it does science and rationality – with their inherent reliance on evidence – above faith, this is a big ask. The importance of sensitively squaring the circle between these very different bases of knowledge and action is already finding credence in the 'legitimizing' of Indigenous worldviews within academic literature, pushing against the 'epistemic blindness' (Bancrjee, 2022: 1079) which has historically resulted in a framing of 'Eastern' (Filatotchev et al., 2020) epistemologies as a deficit model such that the issue has been one of application rather than foundational understanding. The 'rights of nature' (Knauß, 2018) approach and place-based (García-Martín et al., 2018) writing are good examples of the emergent counter-trend to this hegemonic stance, but further research which explores the synergies between different worldviews and offers thoughtful frameworks for reconciling different forms of research evidence is much needed if we are to achieve the benefits which this direction of travel potentially offers.

Research that *synthesizes* Indigenous and Western understandings of relationality will be at a premium here. At the same time, however, such research needs to speak to the complexities of 'importing' – or exporting – theories from other contexts (Filatotchev et al., 2020) and the importance of developing a much deeper understanding of those contexts as a preliminary to this type of regrounding of management theory development. Another key aspect of this agenda relates to understanding the nature and implications of the human/ nature bifurcation (Walsh et al., 2021), its faith-based and non-faith-based origins (Wildman, 2006), and the role of Enlightenment thinking (Banerjee and Arjaliès, 2021) in the forms and prevalence this bifurcation has acquired in modern thinking. A historical approach to understanding how this has informed management scholarship would be particularly revealing, whilst a focus on the practical and theoretical implications of post-Enlightenment, relational thinking for existing management theory has the potential to shed fresh light on our attempts to address 'grand challenges' by extricating us from the 'straight jacket of theory' (Bruton et al., 2022: 1059) as it currently exists.

Relatedly, more needs to be understood concerning the consequences of dismantling commitments to Enlightenment-based epistemologies (Walsh et al., 2021) and the knowledge/evidence structures that are inherent in them. If we reduce our allegiance to the fiction of leader rationality (Miska et al., 2014) and at the same time consider the consequences of openness to pre-Enlightenment worldviews, with their acceptance of more spiritual, emotional and ancestral (Reo et al., 2017) sources of wisdom, what would this mean for decision-making processes, evaluative processes, and the role of values in organizational, governmental and societal contexts? The historical privileging of Western epistemologies and the 'epistemic blindness' (Banerjee, 2022) arising from colonial/Western ways of knowing and being are deep-seated in both business and academia, thus requiring a substantive 're-keying' (Cornelissen et al., 2021) of our understanding of rigour and robustness in both decision making and research.

A third aspect of a relationally driven research agenda would be the revisiting of existing writing on ethical leadership (Ciulla, 2004) as seen through a relational lens. How would both deontological and teleological drivers of action be influenced by the inclusion of non-anthropocentric considerations in management decisions? Alongside the philosophical underpinnings of these issues, empirical exploration is needed into the interaction of the three tensions of stewardship discussed above as experienced by practising leaders and managers. How do they, in practice, navigate these tensions, and what are both their espoused theories and their theories-in-use (Argyris, 1976) for achieving a sense of ethicality in their actions and decisions? Relatedly, there is significant work to be done in exploring the overlaps and tensions between the proposed framework and existing 'aspirational' forms of leadership (Iszatt-White et al., 2021), and evaluating their relative merits both as scaffolding for future leadership scholarship and as frameworks for practitioner guidance. Leadership-as-stewardship could be seen as just another aspirational form of leadership – and in some ways it is – but it seeks to anchor the ethical and practical enactment of modern leadership in a clearer understanding of the ontological and epistemological commitments from which our current challenges have arisen. Both theoretical and empirical studies to authenticate – or even reject – the benefits of a relational, stewardship-based perspective can only add value.

Finally, there is a need for research which builds on the proposed leadership ambidexterity model, and the recrafting and regrounding of strategic leadership which underpins it. Key questions here might revolve around the validity of repurposing the idea of organizational ambidexterity (Havermans et al., 2015; Raisch and Birkinshaw, 2008) to encompass a much broader frame of reference in terms of both current and future dimensions. Does the anchoring of this balanced agenda to ideas of stewardship and relationality hold good when empirically tested, and how might these connections between purpose and principle be further elaborated to offer more robust scaffolding for practising leaders? Similarly, how might Boal and Hooijberg's (2001) conception of the skills required by strategic leaders be revisited to test their applicability to leadership in the Anthropocene, and their appropriateness as the foundational component of leadership ambidexterity? Emerging from the exploration of keystone actors and large corporations, it will also be important to investigate the usefulness of the proposed framework for other corporate and non-corporate settings, and for leaders at other organizational levels. Indeed, how might the touchpoints offered by leadership ambidexterity inform other areas of activity and decision making that we all encounter in our daily lives?

STEWARDSHIP IN LEADERSHIP

Whilst further research is undoubtedly necessary in validating and elaborating the ideas put forward in the preceding chapters, and particularly those emerging from Chapter 6, this will be a wasted effort if they never progress beyond being well-founded academic theories. Bringing ideas of stewardship into everyday leadership – and into the accepted remit of practising leaders – will be a vital step in delivering on the agenda set out at the start of this book. That is, if we are to counter the unintended consequences of Enlightenment notions of progress (Banerjee and Arjaliès, 2021), reduce the unhelpful 'baggage' (Alvesson and Sandberg, 2020) carried by leaders attempting to enact aspirational (Avery and Bergsteiner, 2010; Ciulla, 2004; Pless and Maak, 2011; Walumbwa et al., 2008) forms of leadership and provide a more workable model of leadership to guide us into the future, then ideas of leadership-as-stewardship must make the transition from theory to practice. One important route is through the medium of management education.

   The question of what management education is for (Lavine et al., 2022) has risen to prominence along with many of the issues raised in this book. More specifically, some authors have asked why the world's grand challenges and the means to tackle them are not part of the core curriculum (Kempster and Jackson, 2023: 119), and have suggested making 'purpose' the 'superordinate agenda' (2023: 133) for leadership practice and research as a response. The shift from seeing business schools as a place for the gaining of instrumental knowledge connected with business/economic goals to seeing them as somewhere where deeper meaning 'that raises a sense of conscience about the human condition, society and its many challenges' (Holt, 2020; cited in Lavine et al., 2022: 4) is developed is gaining pace, albeit with a long way still to go. In many management education curricula, the notion of responsibility remains superficial or even absent, with understandings of responsible management practice being developed via the 'hidden curriculum of socialised learning in the background of formal education contexts' (Hibbert and Wright, 2023: 418), if at all. Where responsible management is part of the curriculum, it frequently goes only part way towards the kind of planetary stewardship suggested by relational ontologies and the notion of ambidexterity. Lavine et al. (2022), for example, suggest the enhancement of our response to societal challenges by the interweaving of positive organizational scholarship (POS) and critical management studies (CMS) in management education pedagogy: that is, an essentially anthropocentric perspective.

Elsewhere, a more thorough-going review of the purpose of management education has led to a vision of universities as civic institutions, through a process of 'back-casting' (Muff, 2013: 489) from the desired end result of what kind of world we want for the future to what kind of management education we need to get there. For Muff (2013), management education must provide a service to society that goes beyond supplying the demands of the current economic system, and positions business as a key player in trans- forming the current economic system into something that is fit for purpose in driving a better, more sustainable future. In delivering on this aim, manage- ment education is required to fulfil three fundamental roles: (1) refocusing education to develop globally responsible leaders, (2) transforming research into an applied field with a clear purpose of enabling business organizations to serve the common good and (3) engaging in the transformation of business and the economy by engaging in the ongoing public debate (Muff, 2013: 490). The notion of a 'collaboratory approach', in which business schools operate as a 'container' or 'holding platform' for the purpose of bringing these three roles together in order to transcend academic boundaries and generate practical learning and action clearly goes well beyond just transforming the content of the curriculum. It is a new way of thinking about management education that admits of no half measures. It is a measure of the challenges inherent in this approach that over a decade after Muff's vision for management education appeared, we are still a long way from enacting it in practice.

Inevitably, different institutions have taken different approaches and some are further along the road than others. It is suggested that there are three stages or orders of change to the process of curriculum transformation, namely, 'bolt-on', 'built-in' and 'platform' or embedded (Muff, 2013: 497). The 'bolting on' of new modules dealing with issues of responsibility and sustainability is reasonably well established in management education – and higher education more broadly – with formats including 'straight' academic teaching, the use of positive case studies, and student participation in sus- tainability-based business simulations. The inevitable drawback with this approach – whilst it may act as a 'quick fix' for institutions who need to be seen to be doing something in the sustainability space – is the potential for disconnects and tensions between these new modules and the more traditional teaching of topics such as economics, accounting and finance, and marketing which still persist within the same programmes. Another disconnect often exists between what the institution is teaching its management students and how it is managing its own operations, since the bolt-on approach requires very little in the way of fundamental change at an organizational level.

The 'built-in' approach goes further towards integrating sustainability and responsible leadership into the curriculum, via such initiatives as the creation of an overarching programme narrative around responsibility; the inclusion of more transformative, issue-based teaching and learning approaches (Muff, 2013); and assessment formats that promote critical reflection and personal change. Change at the programme level – and the 'built-in' approach more generally – requires greater institutional change and the support of a culture that is willing to examine its own purpose and contribution to the issues at hand. There are fewer disconnects here, but the tensions between developing into a truly civic institution and continuing to operate as part of the existing neo-liberal ideology in which business schools have historically been steeped remain substantial. There is a danger that, on the one hand, institutions are perceived as engaging in 'greenwashing' (Kassinis and Panayiotou, 2018) by jumping on the bandwagon of the sustainability trope for commercial reasons (because they expect it to put 'bums on seats' in the classroom), whilst on the other hand, they are seen as doing too little to address the need for radical change within the 'standard' management education curriculum.

Notwithstanding both the challenges and the potential for misperceptions, there is some evidence of frameworks appearing that shift the focus of management education programme design towards making positive social impact core to business leadership (Kempster and Jackson, 2023: 116). Kempster and Jackson's (2023) 'Good Dividend' framework – based on the need for businesses to create positive returns on a spread of six capitals (social, reputational, finance, natural, human, operational) rather than just financial returns – is one response to this challenge, based on a significant reframing of the purpose of business in meeting the challenges of the Anthropocene. Similar to the idea of 'keystone actors' (Österblom et al., 2022b) discussed in Chapter 6, they argue that the best way forward is to work *with* capitalism, rather than working against it, on the basis that the wealth, power, resources and influence to make a difference to global issues reside largely with corporations. This approach is not unique, with other manifestations appearing under the rubric of 'moral capitalism' (Young, 2003) – said to be capitalism that is underpinned by a plural set of capitals shaped by a societal 'invisible guiding hand' (Smith, 1776) to realize enlightened self-interest, 'stakeholder capitalism' (Freeman et al., 2007) and 'conscious capitalism' (Mackey and Sisodia, 2014). Kempster and Jackson (2023) call their version 'regenerative capitalism', and see management educations as a mechanism for generating the 'moral outrage' (2023: 125) required to create the sense of urgency needed to harness business as a mechanism for addressing grand challenges. Not surprisingly, they acknowledge that whilst purpose-driven value creation is undoubtedly desirable – or even necessary – it is 'much more difficult to make manifest, let alone sustain' (2023: 117) than the underpinning imperative suggests.

'Third-order change' (Muff, 2013: 497) requires the creation of a 'platform' on which a wide range of stakeholders to significant global issues can come together to seek practical solutions as well as theoretical understanding. Through what Muff (2013) refers to as 'collaboratories', this approach shifts the emphasis from the programmed learning of subject content to the creation of a learning environment in which self-directed stakeholders – including students, academics, policy holders, communities, and so on – come together to work on issues of mutual concern. At this level, notions of sustainability and responsibility are fully embedded in the programme design and reflect the wider ethos of the institution as a civic university. Third-order change requires a 'wholesale rethinking of current forms of social and economic organizing' (Wright et el., 2018; cited in Gasparin et al., 2020), and an acceptance of the notion that 'business as usual' is no longer possible, and hence that 'business (and management) education as usual' is no longer fit for purpose. As Gasparin et al. (2020: 386) note:

> business and management education continues to teach and promote human-centred economic models that are profoundly insensitive to the complex interdependencies between human action and the irreversible environmental changes that constitute the currently, and rapidly unfolding, reality of climate change.

Drawing on the notion of humans as parasites on Earth systems – and in particular of our 'mastery' of nature through the development of increasing levels of technology – they call for a complete re-think of the purpose of management education and suggest that 'the project for future business and management education can then be simply stated: How do we gain mastery over our own mastery' (Gasparin et al., 391). What they mean by this is that humans no longer have mastery over the technosphere they have created and that we need to 'turn[] that mastery back on itself, to slow the pace of [planetary] violence and damage caused by our own parasitism' at the same time as 'shifting toward a renewed mutualism or "reciprocal living together"' with other spheres (2020: 391) within the overall socio-ecosystem. Similar to the stance of Indigenous worldviews (Glazebrook, 2021; Nicholson et al., 2019; Spiller, 2021) and relational ontologies (Cooren, 2018; Kenter and O'Connor, 2022; Wildman, 2006) discussed in Chapter 5, Gasparin et al. (2020) draw on the work of Serres

(2011: 72) to suggest that 'we should no longer be the masters and possessors of nature. The new contract becomes a rental agreement.'

In terms of management education, this translates into a radical 'dehominization' of the curriculum, in which curricula are 'reworked to include cross-cultural dimensions, to be sensitive to historical changes, and to rise to the challenge of decolonialization' (Gasparin et al., 2020: 400) in order to move away from the current anthropocentric forms of reasoning that are taught as informing business decisions. We need to teach management students to 'Think[] like Biogea' (2020: 391), which means:

> understanding strategy from the perspective of a tree, marketing from the belly of the snake, finance amid the excess of frogspawn, innovation among coral. Management education needs to be "de-hominized" if we are to understand how we can live with rather than against Biogea. (Brown, 2016: 157)

In attempting to make the giant leap towards 'dehominization', a key obstacle is our 'limited human-centric conceptions of agency' (Gasparin et al., 2020: 401) and the constrained 'parasite' logic within which we manage our businesses and educate our next generation of leaders. The solution, they suggest, is a shift from the logic of the probable and rational to the realm of 'pataphysics', where anything is possible. Put simply, if you throw out all 'the rationalities and modes of reasoning that dominate the ways problems are framed and social and economic models of organizing are conceived' (Gasparin et al., 2020: 397), then you have the potential to let in some truly imaginative and creative possibilities.

One interesting output from Gasparin et al.'s (2020: 387) adoption of 'anything is possible' pataphysics and relationally derived reasoning derives from their agreement with Serres (1995, 2018) that we no longer have the power to reverse the 'Great Acceleration' in human progress and technology. The best we can do is to act to slow it down or to turn it back in itself by engaging with the planetary interdependencies through which it was constituted (e.g. the relationship of mutual dependency between the current state of the lithosphere and the extractive aspects of the technosphere). The resultant notion of 'slow design' – 'an approach predicated on slowing the metabolism of people, resources and flows, [which] could provide a design paradigm that would engender positive behavioural change' (Strauss and Fuad-Luke, 2008: 1) – is suggested as being a 'strong example of an emerging mutualistic business model that attempts to push beyond anthropocentric forms of organizing' (Gasparin et al., 2020: 388) in which 'production cycles are tied to the natural cycles of the raw materials' (Gasparin et al., 2020: 395).

Clearly leadership-as-stewardship could be incorporated into management education at any of the three levels proposed by Muff (2013). Arguably, modules with titles such as 'Responsible leadership and ethics', 'Leading responsibly' or 'Strategic purpose and responsible leadership' – all existing module titles from master's programmes within my own institution – have some resonance with notions of leadership-as-stewardship, albeit very much as first-order 'bolt-ons' to the more traditional curriculum. There is, however, a strong case for saying that a meaningful shift towards leadership-as-stewardship needs to be at the third-order 'platform' level of change, within which the relationality of Indigenous and other similar worldviews and the ambidexterity of purpose between present and future horizons form part of the foundational principles of programme design and institutional culture. Business schools – perhaps better known as management schools, as in the case of my own institution – need to begin with their own internal transformation into custodians of the future, and be brave enough to reflect this stance in all that they do. At the same time as taking a lead in tackling global challenges, they need to be open to the kind of engagement with other stakeholders – including, as seen in Chapter 6, the biosphere – suggested by the idea of problem-solving collaboratories in which learning is almost a by-product of actual, practical doing. For me, this brings us back to the ambidextrous leadership framework already discussed as a basis for the skills, principles and purpose that might offer scaffolding to the kind of interdisciplinary, real-world, solution-focused learning vehicles which the idea of a collaboratory suggests. Ironically, the more structures (global-challenge-related research funding calls and sustainability-related accreditations and rankings are notable examples to which we all seem to have mindlessly bought in) we put in place to promote research and teaching that address global challenges – and for which ideas of stewardship might be foundational – the further we seem to be from the kind of radical transformation of our curricula that might actually enable us to meet these agendas.

STEWARDSHIP OF LEADERSHIP

This book started with the idea of totally replacing leadership with stewardship: an admittedly bold and perhaps unrealistic goal given the tenacity of the leadership construct in our thinking and imagination over many years (Meindl et al., 1985). Subsequent chapters have suggested a more moderate aim – and a consequent reshaping of the argument – to consider how we can live with leadership, and make it fit for 21st-century purpose, rather than abandoning it completely. Slightly tongue-in-cheek, we might ask how we can 'reduce, reuse and recycle' existing elements of leadership scholarship to refocus and reground the construct around stewardship. How might we 'upcycle' it to give it a new lease of life and a renewed purpose?

Much has already been said about the potential for reducing the Enlightenment and capitalist 'baggage' carried by the leadership construct, as well as the aspirational burden recently advocated forms of leadership place on practising leaders. Collectively, this baggage constrains the remit of leadership to out-dated ideals of progress and profit within a predominantly capitalist economic model, at the same time as creating unrealistic expectations of what leaders and leadership can achieve that are not always supported by the practical guidance through which these aspirations can be realistically enacted. We are already, thankfully, moving away from the heroic (Carlyle, 1846) forms of leadership in which charismatic (Conger and Kanungo, 1987) or transformational (Bass and Avolio, 1990) leaders have all the answers and steer the world towards the goals of profit and progress to which we have long adhered. Instead, we are recognizing the need for more distributed (Bolden, 2011) and relational (Uhl-Bien, 2006) approaches to leadership that are underpinned by a shared sense of responsibility and the need to harness the skills and abilities of those who might previously have been relegated to the role of 'follower' (Kelley, 2008). Ideas of stewardship, relationality and ambidexterity can hopefully offer an anchor for the 'simplification' of leadership as a construct: an umbrella under which the best of recent scholarship can be collected, but which allows for the jettisoning of the redundant, the outdated and the burdensome.

Arguably, leadership scholarship takes the art of reusing and recycling to excess, with even the early essentialist (Kirkpatrick and Locke, 1991) and behavioural (Hersey and Blanchard, 1982) approaches yet to be removed from the canon. Nonetheless, there are some theories that might usefully be revisited – servant leadership (Van Dierendonck, 2011), as one of the few that explicitly refers to stewardship, is an obvious example – with the aim of bringing rele-vant aspects of past theories together under the stewardship banner. Perhaps more productive than simply massaging elements of past theorizing into a new stewardship-based format is the idea of retaining recent attempts to set a vison for the purpose of leadership (Kempster and Jackson, 2023) – such as respon-sible leadership (Pless and Maak, 2011) and sustainable leadership (Avery and Bergsteiner, 2010) – but with the addition of more practically grounded 'scaffolding' to support leaders in navigating the tensions and trade-offs inher-ent in enacting these aspirations in the real world. In effect, not recycling but upcycling! Supporting this practical grounding of aspirational imperatives for leadership will require a return to inquiry (i.e. empirical research on how to do leadership-as-stewardship better) rather than additional attempts at often quite philosophical advocacy.

Whilst refocusing leadership scholarship is a necessary condition of devel-oping leadership that is fit for purpose in the 21st century, we are merely moving the deckchairs on the deck of the *Titanic* unless this brings us closer to getting leadership as a discipline a seat at the table of grand challenges research. If we look at the research funding calls emerging in the social sciences, there are numerous agendas – the productivity agenda, the innovation agenda, the employability agenda, not to mention the net zero agenda and all those calls relating to specific aspects of environmental sustainability – encompassing a wide range of academic disciplines, but there does not appear to be a 'leadership agenda'. Like the Abominable Snowman (Bennis and Nanus, 1985), leadership's footprints are everywhere, but leadership itself is nowhere to be seen! One of the key aims of the leadership-as-stewardship trope, therefore, must be to use this revised profile for the leadership discipline as a vehicle for ensuring its voice is heard in the myriad of work that needs to be done – across all six of the research domains where stewardship was already in evidence – to turn the themes and ideas discussed in this book into a viable reality. We already know that any solutions to the global challenges we face will necessarily be interdisciplinary: hopefully leadership-as-stewardship can emerge as the glue that binds different disciplines together and a vehicle for transferring theoretical solutions and understanding, not practice.

CONCLUSION – FACING UP TO THE FUTURE

Notwithstanding the toning down of the original thesis that leadership as a signifier for our organizational aspirations should be abandoned, this book has set some ambitious goals for what leadership-as-stewardship as a potential successor might offer. It has laid out some thoughts on how stewardship might be embedded in leadership scholarship and management education, with the suggestion that these are likely to be the most fruitful routes towards embedding it in day-to-day leadership practice and the accepted remit of practising leaders. The imperative to take this huge leap towards a more relational – in the broadest sense – and ambidextrous approach to navigating today's challenges in a way that ensures tomorrow's possibilities is, I believe, clear, and others have set this out more clearly and powerfully than I. It is undoubtedly a daunting task, but one which we shirk at our peril. It would be pretentious to suggest the current work as more than a very small step on this momentous journey, or to fall back on the platitude that 'the longest journey begins with a single step', but I hope nonetheless that the idea of leadership-as-stewardship has some resonance for both scholars and practitioners of leadership, and offers some form of compass for the navigation of the many challenges we will all face along the way.

NOTE

1.   https:// www .morganstanley .com/ ideas/ sustainable -funds -performance -2023.

References

Acharya, K. R., Brankston, G., Soucy, J. P. R., Cohen, A., Hulth, A., Löfmark, S., Davidovitch, N., Ellen, M., Fisman, D. N., Moran-Gilad, J., Steinman, A., MacFadden, D. R., & Greer, A. L. (2021). Evaluation of an OPEN Stewardship generated feedback intervention to improve antibiotic prescribing among primary care veterinarians in Ontario, Canada and Israel: Protocol for evaluating usability and an interrupted time-series analysis. *BMJ Open, 11*(1), e039760.

Aguinis, H., & Glavas, A. (2012). What we know and don't know about corporate social responsibility: A review and research agenda. *Journal of Management, 38*(4), 932–968.

Akpan, M. R., Isemin, N. U., Udoh, A. E., & Ashiru-Oredope, D. (2020). Implementation of antimicrobial stewardship programmes in African countries: A systematic literature review. *Journal of Global Antimicrobial Resistance, 22,* 317–324.

Algera, P. M., & Lips-Wiesma, M (2012). Radical authentic leadership: Co-creating the conditions under which all members of the organization can be authentic. *The Leadership Quarterly, 23*(1), 118–131.

Alvesson, M., & Sandberg, J. (2020). The problematizing review: A counterpoint to Elsbach and Van Knippenberg's argument for integrative reviews. *Journal of Management Studies, 57*(6), 1290–1304.

Anderson, D. J., Watson, S., Moehring, R. W., Komarow, L., Finnemeyer, M., Arias, R. M., Huvane, J., Bova Hill, C., Deckard, N., Sexton, D., J., & Antibacterial Resistance Leadership Group (2019). Feasibility of core antimicrobial stewardship interventions in community hospitals. *JAMA Network Open, 2*(8), e199369.

Ang, C. Y., Dhaliwal, J. S., Muharram, S. H., Akkawi, M. E., Hussain, Z., Rahman, H., Kok, Y. Y., Dhaliwal, S. K. S., & Ming, L. C. (2021). Educational resource for antimicrobial resistance and stewardship for dentistry programmes: A research protocol. *BMJ Open, 11*(7), e048609.

Antonini, C., & Larrinaga, C. (2017). Planetary boundaries and sustainability indicators: A survey of corporate reporting boundaries. *Sustainable Development, 25*(2), 123–137.

Argyris, C. (1976). Theories of action that inhibit individual learning. *American Psychologist, 31*(9), 638.

Ashiru-Oredope, D., Doble, A., Thornley, T., Saei, A., Gold, N., Sallis, A., C. A. M. McNulty, Lecky, D., Umoh, E., & Klinger, C. (2020). Improving management of respiratory tract infections in community pharmacies and promoting antimicrobial stewardship: A cluster randomised control trial with a self-report behavioural questionnaire and process evaluation. *Pharmacy, 8*(1), 44.

Atif, M., Asghar, S., Mushtaq, I., & Malik, I. (2020). Community pharmacists as antibiotic stewards: A qualitative study exploring the current status of Antibiotic Stewardship Program in Bahawalpur, Pakistan. *Journal of Infection and Public Health, 13*(1), 118–124.

Avent, M. L., Cosgrove, S. E., Price-Haywood, E. G., & Van Driel, M. L. (2020). Antimicrobial stewardship in the primary care setting: From dream to reality? *BMC Family Practice, 21*, 1–9.

Avery, G. C., & Bergsteiner, H. (2010). *Honeybees & locusts: The business case for sustainable leadership.* Allen & Unwin.

Avery, G. C., & Bergsteiner, H. (2011a). How BMW successfully practices sustainable leadership principles. *Strategy & Leadership, 39*(6), 11–18.

Avery, G. C., & Bergsteiner, H. (2011b). Sustainable leadership practices for enhancing business resilience and performance. *Strategy & Leadership, 39*(3), 5–15.

Avolio, B. J., & Gardner, W. L. (2005). Authentic leadership development: Getting to the root of positive forms of leadership. *The Leadership Quarterly, 16*(3), 315–338.

Avolio, B. J., Gardner, W. L., Walumbwa, F. O., Luthans, F., & May, D. R. (2004). Unlocking the mask: A look at the process by which authentic leaders impact follower attitudes and behaviours. *The Leadership Quarterly, 15*(6), 801–823.

Avolio, B. J., Waldman, D., & Yammarino, F. (1991). Leading in the 1990s: The four I's of transformational leadership. *Journal of European Industrial Training, 15*, 9–16.

Azbari, M. E., Akbari, M., & Chaijani, M. H. (2015). The effect of strategic leadership and empowerment on job satisfaction of the employees of Guilan University. *International Journal of Organizational Leadership, 4*(4), 453–464.

Badaracco, J. (2002). *Leading quietly.* Harvard Business School Press.

Bai, X., Hasan, S., Seaby Andersten, L., Bjørn, A., Kilkiş, Ş., Ospina, D., Liu, J., Cornell, S. E., Sabag Muñoz, O., Bremond, A. de, Crona, B., DeClerck, F., Gupta, J., Hoff, H., Nakicenovic, N., Obura, D., Whiteman, G., Broadgate, W., Lade, S. J., … Zimm, C. (2024). Translating Earth system boundaries for cities and businesses. *Nature Sustainability, 7*, 108–119. https://doi.org/10.1038/s41893-023-01255-w

Baird, G. S. (2019). The Choosing Wisely initiative and laboratory test stewardship. *Diagnosis, 6*(1), 15–23.

Baker, K. M., & Reill, P. H. (Eds.). (2001). *What's left of the Enlightenment: A postmodern question.* Stanford University Press.

Balakrishnan, J., Malhotra, A., & Falkenberg, L. (2017). Multi-level corporate responsibility: A comparison of Gandhi's trusteeship with stakeholder and stewardship frameworks. *Journal of Business Ethics, 141*, 133–150.

Banerjee, S. B. (2022). Decolonizing management theory: A critical perspective. *Journal of Management Studies, 59*(4), 1074–1087.

Banerjee, S. B., & Arjaliès, D.-L. (2021). Celebrating the end of Enlightenment: Organization theory in the age of the Anthropocene and Gaia (and why neither is a solution to our ecological crisis). *Organization Theory, 2*, 1–24.

Barad, K. (2007). *Meeting the universe halfway: Quantum physics and the entanglement of matter and meaning.* Duke University Press.

Barsoumian, A. E., Roth, A. L., Solberg, S. L., Hanhurst, A. S., Funari, T. S., Crouch, H. et al. (2020). Antimicrobial stewardship challenges in the deployed setting. *Military Medicine, 185*(5–6), e818–e824.

Barthes, R. (1993). *Mythologies.* Vintage.

Bartlett, R. C. (2001). On the politics of faith and reason: The project of Enlightenment in Pierre Bayle and Montesquieu. *The Journal of Politics, 63*(1), 1–28.

Bartunek, J. M., & Necochea, R. A. (2000). Old insights and new times: Kairos, Inca cosmology, and their contributions to contemporary management inquiry. *Journal of Management Inquiry, 9*(2), 103–113.

Bass, B. M., & Avolio, B. J. (1990). Developing transformational leadership: 1992 and beyond. *Journal of European Industrial Training, 14*(5), 21–27.

Bass, B. M., & Avolio, B. J. (Eds.) (1994). *Improving organizational effectiveness through transformational leadership.* SAGE.

Bauer, N., Vasile, M. and Mondini, M. (2018). Attitudes towards nature, wilderness and protected areas: A way to sustainable stewardship in the South-Western Carpathians. *Journal of Environmental Planning and Management, 61*(5–6), 857–877.

Bebbington, J., Laine, M., Larrinaga, C., & Michelon, G. (2023). Environmental accounting in the European Accounting Review: A reflection. *European Accounting Review, 32*(5),1107–1128.

Bebbington, J., Larrinaga, C., & Michelon, G. (2024). A socio-ecological approach to corporate governance. In M. Magnan & G. Michelon (Eds.), *Handbook on corporate governance and corporate social responsibility* (pp. 360–371). Edward Elgar Publishing.

Bebbington, J., Österblom, H., Crona, B., Jouffray, J.-B., Larrinaga, C., Russell, S., & Scholtens, B. (2020). Accounting and accountability in the Anthropocene. *Accounting, Auditing & Accountability Journal, 33*(1), 152–177.

Bebbington, J., & Rubin, A. (2022). Accounting in the Anthropocene: A roadmap for stewardship. *Accounting and Business Research, 52*(5), 582–596.

Beccaria, C. (1764/2009). *Of crimes and punishments.* CreateSpace Independent Publishing Platform.

Beitl, C. M., Rahimzadeh-Bajgiran, P., Bravo, M., Ortega-Pacheco, D., & Bird, K. (2019). New valuation for defying degradation: Visualizing mangrove forest dynamics and local stewardship with remote sensing in coastal Ecuador. *Geoforum, 98*, 123–132.

Bennett, N. J., Whitty, T. S., Finkbeiner, E., Pittman, J., Bassett, H., Gelcich, S., & Allison, E. (2018). Environmental stewardship: A conceptual review and analytical framework. *Environmental Management, 61*(4), 597–614.

Bennis, W., & Nanus, B. (1985). *Leaders: The strategies for taking charge.* Harper & Row.

Bishop, J. L., Schulz, T. R., Kong, D. C. M., & Buising, K. L. (2019). Qualitative study of the factors impacting antimicrobial stewardship programme delivery in regional and remote hospitals. *Journal of Hospital Infection, 101*(4), 440–446.

Blake, R. R., & Mouton, J. S. (1981). Management by grid principles or situationalism: Which? *Group and Organizational Studies, 6*(4), 439–463.

Blasiak, R., Dauriach, A., Jouffray, J.-B., Folke, C., Österblom, H., Bebbington, J., Bengtsson, F., Causevic, A., Geerts, B., Grønbrekk, W., Henriksson, P. J. G., Käll, S., Leadbitter, D., McBain, D., Ortuño Crespo, G., Packer, H., Sakaguchi, I., Schultz, L., Selig, E. R., … Crona, B. (2021). Evolving perspectives of stewardship in the seafood industry. *Frontiers in Marine Science, 8.* https://doi.org/10.3389/fmars.2021.671837

Blicharska, M., Smithers, R. J., Kuchler, M., Agrawal, G. K., Gutiérrez, J. M., Hassanali, A., Huq, S., Koller, S. H., Marjit, S., Mshinda, H. M., Masjuki, H. H., Solomons, N. W., Van Staden, J., & Mikusiński, G. (2017). Steps to overcome the North–South divide in research relevant to climate change policy and practice. *Nature Climate Change, 7*(1), 21–27.

Bloemers, M., & Montesanti, A. (2020). The FAIR funding model: Providing a framework for research funders to drive the transition toward FAIR data management and stewardship practices. *Data Intelligence, 2*(1–2), 171–180.

Boal, K. B., & Hooijberg, R. (2001). Strategic leadership research: Moving on. *The Leadership Quarterly, 11*(4), 515–549.

Bolden, R. (2011). Distributed leadership in organizations: A review of theory and research. *International Journal of Management Reviews, 13*(3), 251–269.

Brammer, S., Branicki, L., Linnenluecke, M., & Smith, T. (2019). Grand challenges in management research: Attributes, achievements, and advancement. *Australian Journal of Management, 44*(4), 517–533.

Brand, D. (2017). Grand designs down under: Utopias and urban projects in mid-nineteenth century New Zealand. *Journal of Urban Design, 22*(3), 308–325.

Brink, A. J., Messina, A. P., Feldman, C., Richards, G. A., Becker, P. J., Goff, D. A., Bauer, K. A., Nathwani, D., & Van den Bergh, D. (2016). Antimicrobial stewardship across 47 South African hospitals: An implementation study. *The Lancet Infectious Diseases, 16*(9), 1017–1025.

Brinkerhoff, D. W., Cross, H. E., Sharma, S., & Williamson, T. (2019). Stewardship and health systems strengthening: An overview. *Public Administration and Development, 39*(1), 4–10.

Brondizio, E., Settele, J., Díaz, S., & Ngo, H. (Eds.). (2019). IPBES *global assessment report on biodiversity and ecosystem services of the Intergovernmental Science-Policy Platform on Biodiversity and Ecosystem Services.* IPBES Secretariat.

Brown, M. E., & Trevino, L. K. (2006). Ethical leadership: A review and future directions. *The Leadership Quarterly, 17*, 595–616.

Brown, S. D. (2016). They have escaped the weight of darkness: The problem space of Michel Serres. In C. Steyaert, T. Beyes, & M. Parker (Eds.), *The Routledge companion to reinventing management education* (pp. 144–160). Routledge.

Bruton, G. D., Zahra, S. A., Van de Ven, A. H., & Hitt, M. A. (2022). Indigenous theory uses, abuses, and future. *Journal of Management Studies, 59*(4), 1057–1073.

Buehrle, D. J., Phulpoto, R. H., Wagener, M. M., Clancy, C. J., & Decker, B. K. (2020). Decreased overall and inappropriate antibiotic prescribing in a Veterans Affairs Hospital Emergency Department following a peer comparison-based stewardship intervention. *Antimicrobial Agents and Chemotherapy, 65*(1), e01660-20.

Burns, J. M. (1978). *Leadership.* Harper & Row.

Burrell, G., & Morgan, G. (1979). *Sociological paradigms and organizational analysis.* Heinemann Educational.

Cameron, K. (2011). Responsible leadership as virtuous leadership. *Journal of Business Ethics, 98*, 25–35.

Carlyle, T. (1846). *On heroes, hero-worship and the heroic in history.* Wiley and Putnam.

Cengiz, T. B., Jarrar, A., Power, C., Joyce, D., Anzlovar, N., & Morris-Stiff, G. (2020). Antimicrobial stewardship reduces surgical site infection rate, as well as number and severity of pancreatic fistulae after pancreatoduodenectomy. *Surgical Infections, 21*(3), 212–217.

Chan, B. T., Veillard, J. H., Cowling, K., Klazinga, N. S., Brown, A. D., & Leatherman, S. (2019). Stewardship of quality of care in health systems: Core functions, common pitfalls, and potential solutions. *Public Administration and Development, 39*(1), 34–46.

Chandler, J. (2017). Stewardship of offshore petroleum: Where is the value? *Marine Policy, 81*, 64–70.

Chaparro, J. D., Beus, J. M., Dziorny, A. C., Hagedorn, P. A., Hernandez, S., Kandaswamy, S., Kirkendall, E. S., McCoy, A. B., Muthu, N., & Orenstein, E. W. (2022). Clinical decision support stewardship: best practices and techniques to monitor and improve interruptive alerts. *Applied Clinical Informatics*, *13*(3), 560–568.

Chatwood, S., Paulette, F., Baker, G. R., Eriksen, A. M., Hansen, K. L., Eriksen, H., Hiratsuka, V., Lavoie, J., Lou, W., Mauro, I., Orbinski, J., Pambrun, N., Retallack, H., & Brown, A. (2017). Indigenous values and health systems stewardship in circumpolar countries. *International Journal of Environmental Research and Public Health*, *14*(12), 1462.

Chisholm, H. (1911). East India Company. In H. Chishom (Ed.), *Encyclopaedia Britannica*, Vol. 8 (11th ed., pp. 834–835). Cambridge University Press.

Ciulla, J. B. (1996). Ethics, chaos, and the demand for good leaders. In P. Temes (Ed.), *Teaching leadership: Essays in theory and practice* (pp. 181–201). Peter Lang.

Ciulla, J. B. (2004). Ethics and leadership effectiveness. In J. Antoniakis, A. T. Cianciolo, & R. J. Sternberg (Eds.), *The nature of leadership* (pp. 302–327). SAGE.

Coley, J. D., Betz, N., Helmuth, B., Ellenbogen, K., Scyphers, S. B., & Adams, D. (2021). Beliefs about human-nature relationships and implications for investment and stewardship surrounding land-water system conservation. *Land*, *10*(12), 1293.

Collins, J. (2001). Level 5 leadership: The triumph of humility and fierce resolve. *Harvard Business Review*, *83*(7), 136.

Conger, J., & Kanungo, R. (1987). Toward a behavioural theory of charismatic leadership in organizational settings. *Academy of Management Review*, *12*, 637–647.

Conger, J. A. (1990). The dark side of leadership. *Organizational Dynamics*, *19*(2), 44–55.

Cooren, F. (2018). Materializing communication: Making the case for a relational ontology. *Journal of Communication*, *68*(2), 278–288.

Cornelissen, J. P., Akemu, O., Jonkman, J. G., & Werner, M. D. (2021). Building character: The formation of a hybrid organizational identity in a social enterprise. *Journal of Management Studies*, *58*(5), 1294–1330.

Costas, J., & Taheri, A. (2012). "The return of the primal father" in postmodernity? A Lacanian analysis of authentic leadership. *Organization Studies*, *33*(9), 1195–1216.

Cronin, M. A., & George, E. (2023). The why and how of the integrative review. *Organizational Research Methods*, *26*(1), 168–192.

Crutzen, P. J. (2016). Geology of mankind. In P. J. Crutzen & H. G. Baruch (Eds.), *Paul J. Crutzen: A pioneer on atmospheric chemistry and climate change in the Anthropocene* (pp. 211–215). Springer

Cullen, M., Kirwan, C., & Brennan, N. (2006). Comparative analysis of corporate governance theory: The agency-stewardship continuum. In *20th Annual Conference of the Irish Accounting & Finance Association, Institute of Technology, Tralee* (pp. 1–53).

Cumbraos-Sánchez, M. J., Hermoso, R., Iñiguez, D., Paño-Pardo, J. R., Bandres, M. Á. A., & Martinez, M. P. L. (2019). Qualitative and quantitative evaluation of the use of Twitter as a tool of antimicrobial stewardship. *International Journal of Medical Informatics*, *131*, e103955.

Daft, R. L. (2003). *Organization theory and design* (8th International Student ed.). Thomson Learning.

Darkson, C., Campbell, M. L., & Rockloff, S. (2020). Fostering marine environmental stewardship. *Conservation & Society*, *18*(4), 405–411.

Davies, J. (2016). *The birth of the Anthropocene*. University of California Press.

Davis, J. H., Schoorman, F. D., & Donaldson, L. (1997). Toward a theory of stewardship. *The Academy of Management Review*, *22*(1), 20–47.

Denyer, D., & Tranfield, D. (2011). Producing a systematic review. In D. A. Buchanan & A. Bryman (Eds.), *The SAGE handbook of organizational research methods* (pp. 671–689). SAGE.

Dhawan, N. (2014). *Decolonizing enlightenment: Transnational justice, human rights and democracy in a postcolonial world*. Verlag Barbara Budrich.

Dijkers, M. P. (2019). A beginner's guide to data stewardship and data sharing. *Spinal Cord, 57*(3), 169–182.

Ding, C., & Schuett, M. A. (2020). Predicting the commitment of volunteers' environmental stewardship: Does generativity play a role? *Sustainability, 12*(17), 6802.

Dmytriyev, S. D., Freeman, R. E., & Hörisch, J. (2021). The relationship between stakeholder theory and corporate social responsibility: Differences, similarities, and implications for social issues in management. *Journal of Management Studies, 58*(6), 1441–1470.

Domínguez-Escrig, E., Mallén-Broch, F. F., Lapiedra-Alcamí, R., & Chiva-Gómez, R. (2019). The influence of leaders' stewardship behaviour on innovation success: The mediating effect of radical innovation. *Journal of Business Ethics, 159*, 849–862.

Donaldson, T., & Preston, L. E. (1995). The stakeholder theory of the corporation: Concepts, evidence, and implications. *Academy of Management Review, 20*(1), 65–91.

Doohan, K. (2008). *Making things come good: Relations between Aborigines and miners at Argyle*. Backroom Press.

Du Toit, L., & Woermann, M. (2012). *When economy becomes ecology: Implications for understanding leadership*. [Paper presentation]. Reflections on Responsible Leadership: 2nd International Conference in Responsible Leadership, Pretoria, 18–21 November 2012.

Duara, P. (2021). The Ernest Gellner nationalism lecture: Nationalism and the crisis of global modernity. *Nations and Nationalism, 27*, 610–622.

Edwards, M., Alcaraz, J., & Cornell, S. (2021). Management education and Earth systems science: Transformation as if planetary boundaries mattered. *Business & Society, 60*(1), 26–56.

Eisenhardt, K. M. (1989). Building theories from case study research. *Academy of management review, 14*(4), 532–550.

Elsbach, K. D., & Van Knippenberg, D. (2020). Creating high-impact literature reviews: An argument for "integrative reviews". *Journal of Management Studies, 57*(6), 1277–90.

Enqvist, J. P., West, S., Masterson, V. A., Haider, L. J., Svedin, U., & Tengö, M. (2018). Stewardship as a boundary object for sustainability research: Linking care, knowledge and agency. *Landscape and Urban Planning, 179*, 17–37.

Ergene, S., Banerjee, S. B., & Hoffman, A. (2020). (Un)Sustainability and organization studies: Towards a radical engagement. *Organization Studies, 42*(8). https://doi.org/10.1177/0170840620937892

Fan, D., Breslin, D., Callahan, J., & Iszatt-White, M. (2022). Advancing literature review methodology through rigour, generativity, scope and transparency. *International Journal of Management Reviews, 24*, 171–180.

Ferguson, A. (1767). *An essay on the history of civil society*. Transaction Publishers.

Ferraro, F., Etzion, D., & Gehman, J. (2015). Tackling grand challenges pragmatically: Robust action revisited. *Organizational Science, 36*, 363–390.

Filatotchev, I., Wei, L. Q., Sarala, R. M., Dick, P., & Prescott, J. E. (2020). Connecting eastern and western perspectives on management: Translation of practices across organizations, institution and geographies. *Journal of Management Studies, 57*(1), 1–24.

Filho, A. S., & Tillmanns, T. (2020). "Radical" and beyond: An encounter between relational ontology and sustainability education. *Constructivist Foundations, 16*(1), 026–029.

Fischer, S. A. (2016). Transformational leadership in nursing: a concept analysis. *Journal of Advanced Nursing, 72*(11), 2644–2653.

Foley, K. A., MacGeorge, E. L., Brinker, D. L., Li, Y., & Zhou, Y. (2020). Health providers' advising on symptom management for upper respiratory tract infections: Does elaboration of reasoning influence outcomes relevant to antibiotic stewardship? *Journal of Language and Social Psychology, 39*(3), 349–374.

Folke, C., Österblom, H., Jouffray, J.-B. Lambin, E. F., Adger, W. N., Scheffer, M., Crona, B. I., Nyström, M., Levin, S. A., Carpenter, S. R., Anderies, J. M., Chapin, S., Crépin, A.-S., Dauriach, A., Galaz V., Gordon, L. J., Kautsky, N., Walker, B. H., Watson, J. R., ... Zeeuw, A. de. (2019). Transnational corporations and the challenge of biosphere stewardship. *Nature Ecology & Evolution, 3*, 1396–1403.

Folke, C., Polasky, S., Rockström, J., Galaz, V., Westley, F., Lamont, M., Scheffer, M., Österblom, H., Carpenter, S. R., Chapin, F. S., III, Seto, K. C., Weber, E. U., Crona, B. I., Daily, G. C., Dasgupta, P., Gaffney, O., Gordon, L. J., Hoff, H., Levin, S. A., ... Walker, B. (2021). Our future in the Anthropocene biosphere. *Ambio, 50*, 834–869.

Ford, J., & Harding, N. (2011). The impossibility of the "true self" of authentic leadership. *Leadership, 7*(4), 463–479.

Forster, M. E., Palmer, F., & Barnett, S. (2016). Karanga mai ra: Stories of Māori women as leaders. *Leadership, 12*(3), 324–345.

Freeman, R. E. (1984). *Strategic management: A stakeholder approach.* Pittman Publishing.

Freeman, R. E., & Auster, E. R. (2011). Values, authenticity, and responsible leadership. *Journal of Business Ethics, 98*, 15–23.

Freeman, R. E., Martin, K., & Parmar, B. (2007). Stakeholder capitalism. *Journal of Business Ethics, 74*, 303–314.

García-Martín, M., Plieninger, T., & Bieling, C. (2018). Dimensions of landscape stewardship across Europe: Landscape values, place attachment, awareness, and personal responsibility. *Sustainability, 10*(1), 263.

Gardner, W. L., & Schermerhorn, J. R., Jr. (2004). Performance gains through positive organizational behaviour and authentic leadership. *Organizational Dynamics, 33*(3), 270–281.

Garrard, G. (2006). *Counter-Enlightenments: From the eighteenth century to the present.* Routledge.

Gasparin, M., Brown, S., Green, W., Hugill, A., Lilley, S., Quinn, M., Schinckus, C., Williams, M., & Zalasiewicz, J. (2020). The business school in the Anthropocene: Parasite logic and pataphysical reasoning for a working earth. *Academy of Management Learning & Education, 19*(3), 385–405.

Gasparyan, D. (2016). What is Anti-Enlightenment? *Aurora, 28*(44), 607–632.

Gebretekle, G. B., Mariam, D. H., Taye, W. A., Fentie, A. M., Degu, W. A., Alemayehu, T., Beyene, T., Libman, M., Gedif Fenta, T., Yansouni, C. P., & Semret, M. (2020). Half of prescribed antibiotics are not needed: A pharmacist-led antimicrobial stewardship intervention and clinical outcomes in a referral hospital in Ethiopia. *Frontiers in Public Health, 8.* https://doi.org/10.3389/fpubh.2020.00109

George, G., Howard-Grenville, J., Joshi, A., & Tihanyi, L. (2016). Understanding and tackling societal grand challenges through management research. *Academy of Management Journal, 59*(6), 1880–1895.

Gerber, J. S., Jackson, M. A., Tamma, P. D., & Zaoutis, T. E. (2021). Policy statement: Antibiotic stewardship in paediatrics. *Journal of the Pediatric Infectious Diseases Society, 10*(5), 641–649.

Ghoshal, S. (2005). Bad management theories are destroying good management practices. *Academy of Management Learning & Education, 4*, 75–91.

Gibbon, E. (1776–1789/1994). *The history of the decline and fall of the Roman Empire.* Allen Lane.

Gibson, C., & Warren, A. (2018). Unintentional path dependence: Australian guitar manufacturing, bunya pine and legacies of forestry decisions and resource stewardship. *Australian Geographer, 49*(1), 61–80.

Glazebrook, T. (2021). What is worth knowing? Science, knowledge, and gendered and indigenous knowledge-systems. *Axiomathes, 31*(6), 727–741.

Goff, D. A., Kullar, R., Goldstein, E. J., Gilchrist, M., Nathwani, D., Cheng, A. C., Cairns, K. A., Escandón-Vargas, K., Villegas, M. V., Brink, A., Van den Bergh, D., & Mendelson, M. (2017). A global call from five countries to collaborate in antibiotic stewardship: United we succeed, divided we might fail. *The Lancet Infectious Diseases, 17*(2), e56-e63.

Goldberg, D. T. (1993). *Racist culture: Philosophy and the politics of meaning.* John Wiley.

Greenleaf, R. (2002). Essentials of servant-leadership. In L. Spears & M. Lawrence (Eds.), *Focus on leadership: Servant-leadership for the 21st century* (pp. 19–25). John Wiley.

Greenleaf, R. K. (1977). *Servant leadership: A journey into the nature of legitimate power and greatness.* Paulist Press.

Grint, K. (2005). Problems, problems, problems: The social construction of "leadership". *Human Relations, 58*(11), 1467–1494.

Gronn, P. (2003). Leadership: Who needs it? *School Leadership and Management, 23*(3), 267–290.

Gupta, J., Liverman, D., Prodani, K., Aldunce, P., Bai, X., Broadgate, W., Ciobanu, D., Gifford, L., Gordon, C., Hurlbert, M., Inoue, C., Jacobson, L., Kanie, N., Lade, S. J., Lenton, T. M., Obura, D., Okereke, C., Otto, I. M., Pereira, L., … Verburg, P. (2023a). Earth system justice needed to identify and live within Earth system boundaries. *Nature Sustainability, 6*, 630–638.

Gupta, J., Prodani, K., Bai, X., Gifford, L., Lenton, T. M., Otto, I., Pereira, L., Rammelt, C., Scholtens, J., & Tàbara, J. D. (2023b). Earth system boundaries and Earth system justice: Sharing the ecospace. *Environmental Politics, 1*–21. https://doi.org/10.1080/09644016.2023.2234794

Gursoy, G., Omrum, U. Z. U. N., Metan, G., Yildirim, M., Bahap, M., Demirkan, S. K., Topeli, A., Akinci, S. B., Topcuoglu, M. A., Berker, M., Hazirolan, G., Akova, M., & Unal, S. (2022). Do antimicrobial stewardship programs improve the quality of care in ICU patients diagnosed with infectious diseases following consultation? Experience in a tertiary care hospital. *International Journal of Infectious Diseases, 115*, 201–207.

Hansen, J. G., & Antsanen, R. (2018). What can traditional Indigenous knowledge teach us about changing our approach to human activity and environmental stewardship in order to reduce the severity of climate change? *International Indigenous Policy Journal, 9*(3).

Harmsworth, G. (2008). Kaitiakitanga in 2040. *New Zealand Association of Resource Management Annual Conference, Nelson, NZ, 13th–14th October.*

Hartman, E. M. (1988). *Conceptual foundations of organization theory.* Ballinger.

Havermans, L. A., Den Hartog, D. N., Keegan, A., & Uhl-Bien, M. (2015). Exploring the role of leadership in enabling contextual ambidexterity. *Human Resource Management, 54*(S1), s179–s200.

Hawken, P. (1993). *The ecology of commerce: A declaration of sustainability.* Collins Business Essentials.

Helliwell, R., & Tomei, J. (2017). Practicing stewardship: EU biofuels policy and certification in the UK and Guatemala. *Agriculture and Human Values, 34,* 473–484.

Henry, E., & Wolfgramm, R. (2018). Relational leadership: An indigenous Māori perspective. *Leadership, 14*(2), 203–219.

Hersey, P., & Blanchard, K. (1982). *Management of organizational behaviour: Utilizing human resources.* Prentice Hall.

Hibbert, P., & Wright, A. L. (2023). Challenging the hidden curriculum: Building a lived process for responsibility in responsible management education. *Management Learning, 54*(3), 418–431.

Hileman, J., Kallstenius, I., Häyhä, T., Palm, C., & Cornell, S. (2020). Keystone actors do not act alone: A business ecosystem perspective on sustainability in the global clothing industry. *PLOS One, 15*(10), e0241453.

Hitt, M. A., & Ireland, R. D. (2002). The essence of strategic leadership: Managing human and social capital. *Journal of Leadership & Organizational Studies, 9*(1), 3–14.

Hochschild, A. R. (1983). *The managed heart: Commercialization of human feeling.* University of California Press.

Hoffman, A., & Jennings, P. (2015). Institutional theory and the natural environment: Research in (and on) the Anthropocene. *Organization & Environment, 28*(1), 8–31.

Holt, R. (2020). Hannah Arendt and the raising of conscience in business schools. *Academy of Management Learning & Education, 19*(4), 584–599.

Hoon, C., & Baluch, A. M. (2020). The role of dialectical interrogation in review studies: Theorizing from what we see rather than what we have already seen. *Journal of Management Studies, 57*(6), 1246–1272.

Hoover, K. S. (2021). Children in nature: Exploring the relationship between childhood outdoor experience and environmental stewardship. *Environmental Education Research, 27*(6), 894–910.

Horikoshi, Y., Kaneko, T., Morikawa, Y., Isogai, M., Suwa, J., Higuchi, H., Yuza, Y., Shoji, T., & Ito, K. (2018). The north wind and the sun: Paediatric antimicrobial stewardship program combining restrictive and persuasive approaches in haematology-oncology ward and hematopoietic stem cell transplant unit. *The Pediatric Infectious Disease Journal, 37*(2), 164–168.

Horlick-Jones, T. (2013). Risk and time: From existential anxiety to post-enlightenment fantasy. *Health, Risk and Society, 15*(6–7), 489–493.

Hosmer, L. T. (1982). The importance of strategic leadership. *The Journal of business strategy, 3*(2), 47.

Huff, A. S. (2008). *Designing research for publication.* SAGE.

Hughes, G., O'Toole, E., Talento, A. F., O'Leary, A., & Bergin, C. (2020). Evaluating patient attitudes to increased patient engagement with antimicrobial stewardship: A quantitative survey. *JAC-Antimicrobial Resistance, 2*(3), dlaa046.

Hume, D. (1757/2007). *The natural history of religion (Critical edition by T. L. Beauchamp).* Oxford University Press.

Hunter, L., & Buchanan, S. A. (2021). Responsive stewardship and library advocacy in dystopian times: Using information from the Civil Rights Movement and *1984* to strengthen libraries. *Online Information Review, 45*(4), 853–860.

Inau, E. T., Sack, J., Waltemath, D., & Zeleke, A. A. (2021). Initiatives, concepts, and implementation practices of FAIR (findable, accessible, interoperable, and reusable) data principles in health data stewardship practice: Protocol for a scoping review. *JMIR Research Protocols, 10*(2), e22505.

Iroquois Constitution. (n.d.). http://www.indigenouspeople.net/iroqcon.htm

Iszatt-White, M., & Kempster, S. (2019). Authentic leadership: Getting back to the roots of the "root construct"? *International Journal of Management Reviews, 21*(3), 356–369.

Iszatt-White, M., Stead, V., & Elliott, C. (2021). Impossible or just irrelevant? Unravelling the 'authentic leadership' paradox through the lens of emotional labour. *Leadership, 17*(4), 464–482.

Jain, M., Bang, A., Meshram, P., Gawande, P., Kawhale, K., Kamble, P., Deotale, V., Datta, V., & Dhanireddy, R. (2021). Institution of an antibiotic stewardship programme for rationalising antibiotic usage: A quality improvement project in the NICU of a public teaching hospital in rural central India. *BMJ Open Quality, 10*(Suppl 1), e001456.

James, W. (1909/1977). *A pluralistic universe*. Harvard University Press.

Jenson, M. C., & Meckling, W. H. (1976). Theory of the firm: Managerial behaviour, agency costs and ownership structure. *Journal of Financial Economics, 3*(4), 305–360.

Johnson, J. T., Howitt, R., Cajete, G., Berkes, F., Louis, R. P., & Kilskey, A. (2016). Weaving Indigenous and sustainability sciences to diversity our methods. *Sustainability Science, 11*(1), 1–11.

Kant, I. (1784/1996). An answer to the question: what is enlightenment? In J. Schmidt (Ed.), *What is enlightenment? Eighteenth-century answers and twentieth-century questions* (pp. 58–64). University of California Press.

Kant, I. (1798). *Essays and treatises on moral, political, and various philosophical subjects*. Gale Ecco.

Kaplan, R. S., & Norton, D. P. (1996). *Using the balanced scorecard as a strategic management system*. Harvard Business School Press.

Kassinis, G., & Panayiotou, A. (2018). Visuality as greenwashing: The case of BP and Deepwater Horizon. *Organization & Environment, 31*(1), 25–47.

Katene, S. (2010). Modelling Māori leadership: What makes for good leadership? *MAI Review, 2*.

Kealiikanakaoleohaililani, K., & Giardina, C. P. (2016). Embracing the sacred: an indigenous framework for tomorrow's sustainability science. *Sustainability Science, 11*(1), 57–67.

Kelley, R. E. (2008). Rethinking followership. In R. E. Riggio, I. Chaleff, & J. Lipman-Blumen (Eds.), *The art of followership: How great followers create great leaders and organizations* (pp. 5–15). Jossey-Bass/Wiley.

Kelly, S. (2014). Towards a negative ontology of leadership. *Human Relations, 67*(8), 905–922.

Kempster, S., & Carroll, B. (Eds.). (2016). *Responsible leadership: Realism and romanticism*. Routledge.

Kempster, S., & Jackson, B. (2023). Making purpose the core work of business leadership: A guiding framework. In R. Todnem By, B. Burnes, & M. Hughes (Eds.), *Organizational change, leadership and ethics* (pp. 115–139). Routledge.

Kempster, S., Jackson, B., & Conroy, M. (2011). Leadership as purpose: Exploring the role of purpose in leadership practice. *Leadership, 7*(3), 317–334.

Kenter, J. O., & O'Connor, S. (2022). The Life Framework of Values and living as nature: Towards a full recognition of holistic and relational ontologies. *Sustainability Science, 17*(6), 2529–2542.

Kill, J. (2016). The role of voluntary certification in maintaining the ecologically unequal exchange of wood pulp: The Forest Stewardship Council's certification of industrial tree plantations in Brazil. *Journal of Political Ecology, 23*(1), 434–445.

Kirkpatrick, S. A., & Locke, E. A. (1991). Leadership: do traits matter? *Academy of Management Executive, 5*(2), 48–60.

Klettner, A. (2021). Stewardship codes and the role of institutional investors in corporate governance: An international comparison and typology. *British Journal of Management, 32*, 988–1006.

Knauß, S. (2018). Conceptualizing human stewardship in the Anthropocene: The rights of nature in Ecuador, New Zealand and India. *Journal of Agricultural & Environmental Ethics, 31*(6), 703–722.

Kopar, P. K., & Lui, F. Y. (2020). Surgeon as double agent: Perception of conflicting expectations of patient care and stewardship of resources. *Journal of the American College of Surgeons, 231*(2), 239–243.

Kotter, J. P. (1990). *A force for change: How leadership differs from management.* Free Press.

Kotter, J. P. (2001). What leaders really do. *Harvard Business Review, 79*(11), 85–96.

Kumar, S., Tadepalli, K., Joshi, R., Shrivastava, M., Malik, R., Saxena, P., Saigal, S., Jhaj, R., & Khadanga, S. (2021). Practice of antimicrobial stewardship in a government hospital of India and its impact on extended point prevalence of antibiotic usage. *Journal of Family Medicine and Primary Care, 10*(2), 991–997.

Kuttner, M., Feldbauer-Durstmüller, B., & Mitter, C. (2021). Corporate social responsibility in Austrian family firms: Socioemotional wealth and stewardship insights from a qualitative approach. *Journal of Family Business Management, 11*(2), 238–253.

Lacatus, C. (2018). Human rights networks and regulatory stewardship: An analysis of a multi-level network of human rights commissions in the United Kingdom. *British Journal of Politics & International Relations, 20*(4), 809–826.

Ladkin, D., & Taylor, S. S. (2010). Enacting the "true self": Towards a theory of embodied authentic leadership. *The Leadership Quarterly, 21*(1), 64–74.

Lane, J. E. (2002). *New public management: An introduction.* Routledge.

Landres, P., Hahn, B. A., Biber, E., & Spencer, D. T. (2020). Protected area stewardship in the Anthropocene: Integrating science, law, and ethics to evaluate proposals for ecological restoration in wilderness. *Restoration Ecology, 28*(2), 315–327.

Latour, B. (2007). *Reassembling the social: An introduction to actor-network-theory.* Oxford University Press.

Latour, B. (2017). *Facing gaia: Eight lectures on the new climatic regime.* Translated by Catherine Porter. Polity Press.

Latta, A. (2018). Indigenous rights and multilevel governance: Learning from the Northwest Territories water stewardship strategy. *International Indigenous Policy Journal, 9*(2), 1–25.

Lave, J., & Wenger, E. (1991). *Situated learning: Legitimate peripheral participation.* Cambridge University Press.

Lavine, M., Carlsen, A., Spreitzer, G., Peterson, T., & Roberts, L. M. (2022). Interweaving positive and critical perspectives in management learning and teaching. *Management Learning, 53*(1), 3–14.

Lawler, J., & Ashman, I. (2012). Theorizing leadership authenticity: A Sartrean perspective. *Leadership*, *8*(4), 327–344.

Le Grange, L. (2017). Environmental education after sustainability. In B. Jickling & S. Sterling (Eds.), *Post-sustainability and environmental education: Remaking education for the future* (pp. 93–107). Palgrave Macmillan.

Lemes, P. G., Zanuncio, J. C., Jacovine, L. A., Wilcken, C. F., & Lawson, S. A. (2021). Forest Stewardship Council and responsible wood certification in the integrated pest management in Australian forest plantations. *Forest Policy and Economics*, *131*, e102541.

Lewis, S. L., & Maslin, M. A. (2015). Defining the Anthropocene. *Nature*, *519*, 171–180.

Lliso, B., Pascual, U., Engel, S., & Mariel, P. (2020). Payments for ecosystem services or collective stewardship of Mother Earth? Applying deliberative valuation in an indigenous community in Colombia. *Ecological Economics*, *169*, e106499.

Locke, J. (1695). *Reasonableness of Christianity*. Clarendon Press.

Lovejoy, A. O. (1923/1960). The supposed primitivism of Rousseau's *Discourse on Inequality*. *Modern Philology*, *21*(2), 165–186. Reprinted in *Essays in the history of ideas* (pp. 14–37). Johns Hopkins Press.

Luthans, F., & Avolio, B. (2003). Authentic leadership: A positive development approach. In K. S. Cameron, J. E. Dutton, & R. E. Quinn (Eds.), *Positive organizational scholarship* (pp. 241–258). Berrett-Koehler.

Maak, T., & Pless, N. M. (2006). Planetary dividend: Leadership as stewardship. In S. Kempster, T. Maak, & K. Parry (Eds.), *Good dividends: Responsible leadership of business purpose* (pp. 139–153). Routledge.

MacIntyre, A. (1997). *After virtue: A study in moral theory*. Duckworth.

MacIntyre, A. (2004). Virtue ethics. In H. J. Genster, E. W. Spurgin, & J. C. Swindal (Eds.), *Ethics: Contemporary readings* (pp. 249–256). Routledge.

Mackey, J., & Sisodia, R. (2014). *Conscious capitalism, with a new preface by the authors: Liberating the heroic spirit of business*. Harvard Business Review Press.

Maeda, M., Takuma, T., Seki, H., Ugajin, K., Naito, Y., Yoshikawa, M., Yamanaka, A., Oto, Y., Minemura, A., Shoji, H., Ishino, K., & Niki , Y. (2016). Effect of interventions by an antimicrobial stewardship team on clinical course and economic outcome in patients with bloodstream infection. *Journal of Infection and Chemotherapy*, *22*(2), 90–95.

Malhi, Y. (2017). The concept of the Anthropocene. *Annual Review of Environment and Resources*, *42*(1), 77–104.

Malnight, T. W., Buche, I., & Dhanaraj, C. (2019). Put purpose at the core of your strategy. *Harvard Business Review*, *97*(5), 70–78.

Mandeville, B. (1714 – enlarged in 1723). *The fable of the bees: Or, private vices, public benefits* (Vol. 1). J. Tonson.

March-López, P., Madridejos, R., Tomas, R., Boix, L., Arcenillas, P., Gómez, L., Padilla, E., Xercavins, M., Martinez, L., Riera, M., Badia, C., Nicolás, J., & Calbo, E. (2020). Impact of a multifaceted antimicrobial stewardship intervention in a primary health care area: A quasi-experimental study. *Frontiers in Pharmacology*, *11*, 398.

Markman, G. D., Russo, M., Lumpkin, G. T., Jennings, P. D., & Mair, J. (2016). Entrepreneurship as a platform for pursuing multiple goals: A special issue on sustainability, ethics, and entrepreneurship. *Journal of Management Studies*, *53*(5), 673–694.

Martin, J. A., & Butler, F. C. (2017). Agent and stewardship behaviour: How do they differ? *Journal of Management & Organization, 23*(5), 633–646.

Mathevet, R., Bousquet, F., Larrere, C., & Larrere, R. (2018). Environmental stewardship and ecological solidarity: Rethinking social-ecological interdependency and responsibility. *Journal of Agricultural & Environmental Ethics, 31*(5), 605–623.

Mayer, C. (2019). *Prosperity: Better business makes the greater good.* Oxford University Press.

McAllister, T. (2022). 50 reasons why there are no Māori in your science department. *Journal of Global Indigeneity, 6*(2), 1–10.

McLeod, M., Ahmad, R., Shebl, N. A., Micallef, C., Sim, F., & Holmes, A. (2019). A whole-health–economy approach to antimicrobial stewardship: Analysis of current models and future direction. *PLOS Medicine, 16*(3), e1002774.

McMillen, H. L., Campbell, L. K., Svendsen, E. S., Kealiikanakaoleohaililani, K., Francisco, K. S., & Giardina, C. P. (2020). Biocultural stewardship, Indigenous and local ecological knowledge, and the urban crucible. *Ecology and Society, 25*(2), 9.

Meindl, J. R., Ehrlich, S. B., & Dukerich, J. M. (1985). The romance of leadership. *Administrative Science Quarterly, 30*, 78–102.

Merchant, C. (1980). *The death of nature: Women, ecology and the scientific revolution.* Harper & Row.

Mikhail, A. (2016). Enlightenment Anthropocene. *Eighteenth-Century Studies, 49*, 211–231.

Millennium Ecosystem Assessment. (2005). *Ecosystems and human well-being: Synthesis.* Island.

Miska, C., Hilbe, C., & Mayer, S. (2014). Reconciling different views on responsible leadership: A rationality-based approach. *Journal of Business Ethics, 125*, 349–360.

Moher, D., Liberati, A., Tetzlaff, J, Altman, D. G., & The PRISMA Group. (2009). Preferred reporting items for systematic reviews and meta-analysis: The PRISMA statement. *PLOS Medicine, 6*(7), 1–6.

Muff, K. (2013). Developing globally responsible leaders in business schools: A vision and transformational practice for the journey ahead. *Journal of Management Development, 32*(5), 487–507.

Muller, S., Hemming, S., & Rigney, D. (2019). Indigenous sovereignties: Relational ontologies and environmental management. *Geographical Research, 57*(4), 399–410.

Muzio, D. (2022). Re-conceptualizing management theory: How do we move away from Western-centred knowledge? *Journal of Management Studies, 59*(4), 1032–1035.

Nicholson, A., Spiller, C., & Pio, E. (2019). Ambicultural governance: Harmonizing Indigenous and western approaches. *Journal of Management Inquiry, 28*(1), 31–47.

Nguyen, N. H., & Shiu, C. Y. (2022). Stewardship, institutional investors monitoring, and firm value: Evidence from the United Kingdom. *Journal of Multinational Financial Management, 64*, 100732.

Nunes, C. (2017). "Connecting to the ideologies that surround us": Oral history stewardship as an entry point to critical theory in the undergraduate classroom. *Oral History Review, 44*(2), 348–362.

Nyström, M., Jouffray, J.-B., Norström, A. V., Crona, B., Søgaard Jørgensen, P., Carpenter, S. R., Bodin, Ö., Galaz, V., & Folke, C. (2019). Anatomy and resilience of the global production ecosystem. *Nature, 575*(7781), 98–108.

Obermann, J., Velte, P., Gerwanski, J., & Kordsachia, O. (2020). Mutualistic symbiosis? Combining theories of agency and stewardship through behavioural characteristics. *Management Research Review, 43*(8), 989–1011.

O'Brien, G. C., Mor, C., Buhl-Nielsen, E., Dickens, C. W., Olivier, A. L., Cullis, J., Shrestha, P., Pitts, H., Baleta, H., & Rea, D. (2021). The nature of our mistakes, from promise to practice: Water stewardship for sustainable hydropower in Sub-Saharan Africa. *River Research and Applications, 37*(10), 1538–1547.

Oldfield, F., Barnosky, A. D., Dearing, J., Fischer-Kowalski, M., McNeill, J., Steffen, W., & Zalasiewicz, J. (2014). *The Anthropocene Review*: Its significance, implications and the rationale for a new transdisciplinary journal. *The Anthropocene Review, 1*(1), 3–7.

O'Neill, J., Holland, A., & Light, A. (2008). *Environmental values*. Routledge.

Ophuls, W. (1997). *Requiem for modern politics: The tragedy of the Enlightenment and the challenge of the new millennium*. Westview.

Orlikowski, W. J. (2007). Sociomaterial practices: Exploring technology at work. *Organization Studies, 28*(9), 1435–1448.

Orwell, G. (2017). *1984*. Berkley.

O'Shannassy, T. (2021). The challenges of strategic leadership in organizations. *Journal of Management & Organization, 27*(2), 235–238.

Österblom, H. (2023). Science for a better world. In *Sounds of science: Orchestrating stewardship in the seafood industry* (pp. 197–228). Academic Press.

Österblom, H., Bebbington, J., Blasiak, R., & Folke C. (2022a). Transnational corporations, biosphere stewardship, and sustainable futures. *Annual Review of Environment and Resources, 47*(1), 609–635.

Österblom, H., Folke C., Rocha, J., Bebbington, J., Blasiak, R., Jouffray, J.-B., Selig, E. R., Wabnitz, C. C. C., Bengtsson, F., Crona, B., Gupta, R., Henriksson, P. J. G., Johansson, K. A., Merrie, A., Nakayama, S., Ortuño Crespo, G., Rockström, J., Schultz, L., Sobkowiak, M., … Lubchenco, J. (2022b). Scientific mobilization of keystone actors for biosphere stewardship. *Scientific Reports, 12*, 3802.

Österblom, H., Jouffray, J.-B., Folke, C., Crona, B., Troell, M., Merrie, A., & Rockström, J. (2015). Transnational corporations as "keystone actors" in marine ecosystems. *PLOS One, 10*(5), e0127533.

Österblom, H., Jouffray, J.-B., Folke, C., & Rockström, J. (2017). Emergence of a global science–business initiative for ocean stewardship. *Proceedings of the National Academy of Sciences, 114*(34), 9038–9043.

Outram, D. (2019). *The Enlightenment* (4th ed.). Cambridge University Press.

Pagano, F. M. (1783). *Political essays*. Verriento; Flauto.

Pagano, F. M. (1787). *Considerations on the criminal trial*. Verriento; Flauto.

Papadiamantis, A. G., Klaessig, F. C., Exner, T. E., Hofer, S., Hofstaetter, N., Himly, M., Williams, M. A., Doganis, P., Hoover, M. D., Afantitis, A., Melagraki, G., Nolan, T. S., Rumble, J., Maier, D., & Lynch, I. (2020). Metadata stewardship in nanosafety research: Community-driven organisation of metadata schemas to support FAIR nanoscience data. *Nanomaterials, 10*(10), 2033.

Partzsch, L. (2023). Introduction: The integration of development and environmental agendas. In L. Partzsch (Ed.), *The Environment in Global Sustainability Governance* (pp. 1–18). Bristol University Press.

Pascal, B. (1657). *Lettres provinciales*. Pierre de la Valleé. https:// blaisepascal .bibliotheques-clermontmetropole.eu/son-oeuvre/pascal-polemiste/les-provinciales

Patel, S. J., Wellington, M., Shah, R. M., & Ferreira, M. J. (2020). Antibiotic stewardship in food-producing animals: Challenges, progress, and opportunities. *Clinical Therapeutics, 42*(9), 1649–1658.

Patriotta, G. (2020). Writing impactful review articles. *Journal of Management Studies, 57*(6), 1272 –1276.

Pattupara, A. J., Jose, A., Panda, P. K., & Goel, V. (2019). Cocktail treatment of antibiotic, steroid, and analgesic in a tubercular case: The urgency to set up antimicrobial stewardship practices in the community. *Journal of Family Medicine and Primary Care, 8*(5), 1789.

Pearce, C., & Conger, J. (Eds.). (2003). *Shared leadership: Reframing the hows and whys of leadership.* SAGE.

Pegram, T. (2017). Regulatory stewardship and intermediation: Lessons from human rights governance. *The Annals of the American Academy of Political and Social Science, 670*(1), 225–244.

Pettit, N. N., Han, Z., Nguyen, C. T., Choksi, A., Charnot-Katsikas, A., Beavis, K. G., Tesic, V., & Pisano, J. (2019). Antimicrobial stewardship review of automated candidemia alerts using the epic stewardship module improves bundle-of-care adherence. *Open Forum Infectious Diseases, 6*(1), 412.

Pitt, A. N., Schultz, C. A., & Vaske, J. J. (2019). Engaging youth in public lands monitoring: Opportunities for enhancing ecological literacy and environmental stewardship. *Environmental Education Research, 25*(9), 386–1399.

Pless, N. M. (2007). Understanding responsible leadership: Roles identity and motivational drivers. *Journal of Business Ethics, 74*(4), 437–456.

Pless, N. M., & Maak, T. (2011). Responsible leadership: Pathways to the future. *Journal of Business Ethics, 98*, 3–13.

Porter, R. (2000). *The creation of the modern world: The untold story of the British Enlightenment.* W. W. Norton & Company.

Post, C., Sarala, R., Gatrell, C., & Prescott, J. E. (2020). Advancing theory with review articles. *Journal of Management Studies, 57*(2), 351–377.

Raisch, S., & Birkinshaw, J. (2008). Organizational ambidexterity: Antecedents, outcomes, and moderators. *Journal of Management, 34*(3), 375–409.

Rawat, Y. S. (2017). Sustainable biodiversity stewardship and inclusive development in South Africa: A novel package for a sustainable future. *Current Opinion in Environmental Sustainability, 24*, 89–95.

Reo, N. J., Whyte, K. P., McGregor, D., Smith, M. A., & Jenkins, J. F. (2017). Factors that support Indigenous involvement in multi-actor environmental stewardship. *AlterNative: An International Journal of Indigenous Peoples, 13*(2), 58–68.

Reynolds, P., & Gordon, R. (2021). *Te Āpōpōtanga: Our land, our people, our future.* Manaaki Whenau Landcare Research.

Rezel-Potts, E., L'Esperance, V., & Gulliford, M. C. (2021). Antimicrobial stewardship in the UK during the COVID-19 pandemic: A population-based cohort study and interrupted time-series analysis. *British Journal of General Practice, 71*(706), e331-e338.

Richardson, J., Steffen W., Lucht, W., Bendtsen, J., Cornell, S. E., Donges, J. F., Drüke, M., Fetzer, I., Bala, G., Bloh, W. von, Feulner, G., Fiedler, S., Gerten, D., Gleeson, T., Hofmann, M., Huiskamp, W., Kummu, M., Mohan, C., Nogués-Bravo, D., ... Rockström, J. (2023). Earth beyond six of nine planetary boundaries. *Science Advances, 9*, 37.

Riding, P. (2018). Redefining environmental stewardship to deliver governance frameworks for marine biodiversity beyond national jurisdiction. *ICES Journal of Marine Science, 75*(1), 435–443.

Rittell, H., & Webber, M. (1973). Dilemmas in a general theory of planning. *Policy Sciences, 4*, 155–169.

Robertson, J. (2015). *The Enlightenment: A very short introduction.* Oxford University Press.

Robeyns, I. (2019). What, if anything, is wrong with extreme wealth? *Journal of Human Development & Capabilities, 20*(3), 251–266.

Rockström, J., Gupta, J., Qin, D., Lade, S. J., Abrams, J. F., Andersen, L. S., Armstrong McKay, D. I., Bai, X., Bala, G., Bunn, S. E., Ciobanu, D., DeClerck, F., Ebi, K., Gifford, L., Gordon, C., Hasan, S., Kanie, N., Lenton, T. M., Loriani, S., ... Zhang, X. (2023). Safe and just earth system boundaries. *Nature, 619*, 102–111.

Rockström, J., Steffen, W., Noone, K., Persson, Å., Chapin, F. S., III, Lambin, E. F., Lenton, T. M., Scheffer, M., Folke, C., Schellnhuber, H. J., Nykvist, B., Wit, C. A. de, Hughes, T., Van der Leeuw, S., Rodhe, H., Sörlin, S., Snyder, P. K., Costanza, R., Svedin, U., ... Foley, J. A. (2009). A safe operating space for humanity. *Nature, 461*(7263), 472–475.

Rodari, S., Essilini, A., Le-Dref, G., Patoor, F., Kivits, J., Thilly, N., & Pulcini, C. (2020). Antibio'Malin: An e-health resource to raise awareness of antibiotic stewardship and resistance in France. *JAC-Antimicrobial Resistance, 2*(4), dlaa106.

Romero, C., & Putz, F. E. (2018). Analysis of corrective action requests from Forest Stewardship Council audits of natural forest management in Indonesia. *Forest Policy and Economics, 96*, 28–37.

Roth, C. G., Huang, W. Y., Caruso, A. C., Sekhon, N., Kung, D. H., Greely, J. T., Du, Y. B., Holder-Haynes, J. G., Little, J. E., Fielder, E. K., & Ismail, N. J. (2020). How to teach laboratory stewardship in the undergraduate medical curriculum? Results of a needs analysis. *American Journal of Clinical Pathology, 153*(1), 66–73.

Rousseau, J. J. (1761). *A discourse upon the origin and foundation of the inequality among mankind.* R. & J. Dodsley.

Ruddiman, W. F. (2003). The anthropogenic greenhouse era began thousands of years ago. *Climatic Change, 61*, 261–293.

Rush, L., Patterson, C., McDaid, L., & Hilton, S. (2019). Communicating antimicrobial resistance and stewardship in the national press: Lessons from sepsis awareness campaigns. *Journal of Infection, 78*(2), 88–94.

Russell, R. F., & Stone, A. G. (2002). A review of servant leadership attributes: developing a practical model. *Leadership & Organisational Development Journal, 23*(3/4), 145–157.

Ruwhiu, D., & Elkin, G. (2016). Converging pathways of contemporary leadership: In the footsteps of Māori and servant leadership. *Leadership, 12*(3), 308–323.

Salmond, A. (2014). Tears of Rangi: Water, power and people in New Zealand. *Hau: Journal of Ethnographic Theory, 4*(3), 285–309.

Sangha, K. K. (2020). Global importance of indigenous and local communities' managed lands: Building a case for stewardship schemes. *Sustainability, 12*(19), 7839.

Schaab, G. L. (2013). Relational ontology. In A. L. C. Runehov & L. Oviedo (Eds.), *Encyclopedia of sciences and religions* (pp. 1974–1975). Springer.

Scheffer, M., Carpenter, S., Lenton, T., Bascompte, J., Brock, W., Dakos, V., Van de Koppel, J., Van de Leemput, I. A., Levin, S. A., Van Nes, E. H., Pascual, M., & Vandermeer, J. (2012). Anticipating critical transitions. *Science, 338*, 344–348.

Schillemans, T., & Bjurstrøm, K. H. (2020). Trust and verification: Balancing agency and stewardship theory in the governance of agencies. *International Public Management Journal, 23*(5), 650–676.

Schwass, N. R., Potter, S. E., O'Connell, T. S., & Potter, T. G. (2021). Outdoor journeys as a catalyst for enhanced place connectedness and environmental stewardship. *Journal of Outdoor and Environmental Education, 24*, 215–231.

Seelos, C., Mair, J., & Traeger, C. (2023). The future of grand challenges research: Retiring a hopeful concept and endorsing research principles. *International Journal of Management Reviews, 25*(2), 251–269.

Serres, M. (1995). *The natural contract.* University of Michigan Press.

Serres, M. (2011). *Malfeasance: Appropriation through pollution?* Stanford University Press.

Serres, M. (2018). *The incandescent.* Bloomsbury.

Shafiq, N., Kumar, M. P., Gautam, V., Negi, H., Roat, R., Malhotra, S., Ray, P., Agarwal, R., Bhalla, A., Sharma, N., Singh, R., Sharma, G. D., Bahadur, L., Yadanapudi, N., Gupta, R., & Singh, G. (2016). Antibiotic stewardship in a tertiary care hospital of a developing country: Establishment of a system and its application in a unit-GASP Initiative. *Infection, 44*(5), 651–659.

Shevchenko, A., Lévesque, M., & Pagell, M. (2016). Why firms delay reaching true sustainability. *Journal of Management Studies, 53*(5), 911–935.

Simon, H. A. (1955). A behavioral model of rational choice. *Quarterly Journal of Economics, 69*, 99–118.

Singh, A., Lim, W. M., Jha, S., Kumar, S., & Ciasullo, M. V. (2023). The state of the art of strategic leadership. *Journal of Business Research, 158*, 113676.

Smircich, C., & Morgan, G. (1982). Leadership: "The management of meaning". *The Journal of Applied Behavioural Science, 18*(3), 257–273.

Smith, A. (1776). *The wealth of nations.* W. Strahan and T. Cadell.

Snyder, H. (2019). Literature review as a research methodology: An overview and guidelines. *Journal of Business Research, 104*, 333–339.

Sosik, J. J., Jung, D. I., Berson, Y., Dionne, S. D., & Jaussi, K. S. (2005). Making all the right connections: The strategic leadership of top executives in high-tech organizations. *Organizational Dynamics, 34*(1), 47–61.

Spiller, C. (2021). "I AM": Indigenous consciousness for authenticity and leadership. *Leadership, 17*, 491–496.

Spiller, C., Maunganui Wolfgramm, R., Henry, E., & Pouwhare, R. (2020). Paradigm warriors: Advancing a radical ecosystems view of collective leadership from an Indigenous Māori perspective. *Human Relations, 73*(4), 516–543.

Spiller, C., & Stockdale, M. (2012). Managing and leading from a Maori perspective: Bringing new life and energy to organisations. In J. Neal (Ed.), *Handbook of faith and spirituality in the workplace: Emerging research and practice* (pp. 149–173). Springer New York.

Spyropoulos, S., & Markowitz, E. M. (2021). Mechanisms of intergenerational environmental stewardship activated by Covid-19: Gratitude, fairness, and legacy motives. *Frontiers in Sustainable Cities, 3*, 105.

Steffen, W., Grinevald, J., Crutzen, P., & McNeill, J. (2011). The Anthropocene: Conceptual and historical perspectives. *Philosophical Transactions of the Royal Society A: Mathematical, Physical and Engineering Sciences, 369*(1938), 842–867.

Steffen, W., Richardson, J., Rockström, J., Cornell, S. E., Fetzer, I., Bennett, E. M., Biggs, R., Carpenter, S. R., Vries, W. de, Wit, C. A. de, Folke, C., Gerten, D., Heinke, J., Mace, G. M., Persson, L. M., Ramanathan, V., Reyers, B., & Sörlin, S. (2015). Planetary boundaries: Guiding human development on a changing planet. *Science, 347*(6223), 1259855.

Steffen, W., Richardson, K., Rockström, J., Schellnhuber, H. J., Dube, O. P., Dutreuil, S., Lenton, T. M., & Lubchenco, J. (2020). The emergence and evolution of Earth system science. *Nature Reviews Earth & Environment, 1*, 54–63.

Strauss, C. F., & Fuad-Luke, A. (2008). *The slow design principles: A new interrogative and reflexive tool for design research and practice.* [Paper presentation]. Changing the Change: Design Visions, Proposals and Tools, Torino, July. https://www.slowlab.net

Suchet-Pearson, S., Wright, S., Lloyd, K., & Burarrwanga, L. L. (2013). Caring as country: Towards an ontology of co-becoming in natural resource management. *Asia Pacific Viewpoint, 54*(2), 185–197.

Sundaram, A. K., & Inkpen, A. C. (2004). Stakeholder theory and "The corporate objective revisited": A reply. *Organization Science, 15*(3), 370–371.

Sweileh, W. M. (2021). Bibliometric analysis of peer-reviewed literature on antimicrobial stewardship from 1990 to 2019. *Globalization and Health, 17*(1), 1–14.

Tandan, M., Thapa, P., Maharjan, P., & Bhandari, B. (2022). Impact of antimicrobial stewardship program on antimicrobial resistant and prescribing in nursing home: A systematic review and meta-analysis. *Journal of Global Antimicrobial Resistance, 29*, 74–87.

Tao, Y., He, J., Wang, Y. F., & Ke, H. (2021). Strategic leadership: A bibliometric analysis on current status and emerging trends. *International Journal of Organizational Leadership, 10*(4), 439–458.

Tarim, E. (2022). Modern finance theory and practice and the Anthropocene. *New Political Economy, 27*(3), 490–503.

Taylor, A. (2017). Beyond stewardship: Common world pedagogies for the Anthropocene. *Urban Nature and Childhoods, 23*(10), 1448–1461.

Taylor, F. W. (1903). *Shop management.* Harper & Brothers.

Taylor, F. W. (1911). *The principles of scientific management.* Harper & Row.

Tey, Y. S., & Brindal, M. (2021). Sustainability stewardship: Does roundtable on sustainable palm oil certification create shareholder value? *Corporate Social Responsibility and Environmental Management, 28*(2), 786–795.

Tiri, B., Bruzzone, P., Priante, G., Sensi, E., Costantini, M., Vernelli, C., Martella, L. A., Francucci, M., Andreani, P., Mariottini, A., Capotorti, A., D'Andrea, V., Francisci, D., Cirocchi, R., & Cappanera, S. (2020). Impact of antimicrobial stewardship interventions on appropriateness of surgical antibiotic prophylaxis: How to improve. *Antibiotics, 9*(4), 168.

Tiseo, G., Arena, F., Borrè, S., Campanile, F., Falcone, M., Mussini, C., Pea, F., Sganga, G., Stefani, S., & Venditti, M. (2021). Diagnostic stewardship based on patient profiles: Differential approaches in acute versus chronic infectious syndromes. *Expert Review of Anti-infective Therapy, 19*(11), 1373–1383.

Todd, Z. (2016). An Indigenous feminist's take on the ontological turn: "Ontology" is just another word for colonialism. *Journal of Historical Sociology, 29*, 4–22.

Toole, B. (2021). Recent work in standpoint epistemology. *Analysis, 81*(2), 338–350.

Torraco, R. J. (2005). Writing integrative literature reviews: Guidelines and examples. *Human Resource Development Review, 4*, 356–367.

Torraco, R. J. (2016). Writing integrative literature reviews: Using the past and present to explore the future. *Human Resource Development Review, 15*(4), 404–428.

Tranfield, D., Denyer, D., & Smart, P. (2003). Towards a methodology from developing evidence-informed management knowledge by means of systematic review. *British Journal of Management, 14*, 207–222.

Tsing, A. (2016). Earth stalked by Man. *The Cambridge Journal of Anthropology, 34*(1), 2–16.

Tsolakis, N., Aivazidou, E., & Srai, J. S. (2019). Sensor applications in agrifood systems: Current trends and opportunities for water stewardship. *Climate, 7*(3), 44.

Tushman, M. L., & O'Reilly, C. A. (1996). Ambidextrous organizations: Managing evolutionary and revolutionary change. *California Management Review, 38*(4), 8–30.

Uhl-Bien, M. (2006). Relational leadership theory: Exploring the social processes of leadership and organizing. *The Leadership Quarterly, 17*(6), 654–676.

United Nations (2003). *Millennium ecosystem assessment: Ecosystems and human well-being – A framework for assessment.* Island Press. https://www.millennium assessment.org/documents/document.300.aspx.pdf

United Nations Environment Programme. (2021). *Making peace with nature: A scientific blueprint to tackle the climate, biodiversity and pollution emergencies.*

Van der Wees, P. J., Wammes, J. J., Jeurissen, P. P., & Westert, G. P. (2017). Stewardship of primary care physicians to contain cost in health care: An international cross-sectional survey. *Family Practice, 34*(6), 717–722.

Van Dierendonck, D. (2011). Servant leadership: A review and synthesis. *Journal of Management, 37*(4), 1228–1261.

Van Donge, W., Bharosa, N., & Janssen, M. F. W. H. A. (2022). Data-driven government: Cross-case comparison of data stewardship in data ecosystems. *Government Information Quarterly, 39*(2), 101642.

Vecsey, C., & Venables, R. W. (Eds.). (1980). *American Indian environments: Ecological issues in native American history.* Syracuse University Press.

Vera, D., Bonardi, J. P., Hitt, M. A., & Withers, M. C. (2022). Extending the boundaries of strategic leadership research. *The Leadership Quarterly, 33*(3), 101617.

Vera, D., & Crossan, M. (2004). Strategic leadership and organizational learning. *Academy of Management Review, 29*(2), 222–240.

Virdin, J., Vegh, T., Jouffray, J.-B., Blasiak, R., Mason, S., Österblom, H., Vermeer, D., Wachtmeister, H., & Werner, N. (2021). The Ocean 100: Transnational corporations in the ocean economy. *Science Advances, 7*, eabc8041.

Wæver, O. (2017). International leadership after the demise of the last superpower: System structure and stewardship. *Chinese Political Science Review, 2*(4), 452–476.

Walsh, Z., Böhme, J., & Wamsler, C. (2021). Towards a relational paradigm in sustainability research, practice, and education. *Ambio, 50*(1), 74–84.

Walumbwa, F. O., Avolio, B. J., Gardner, W. L., Wernsing, T. S., & Peterson, S. J. (2008). Authentic leadership: Development and validation of a theory-based measure. *Journal of Management, 34*(1), 89–126.

Wang, G., Devine, R. A., Molina-Sieiro, G., & Holmes, R. M., Jr. (2023). Strategic leaders and corporate social responsibility: A meta-analytic review. *Journal of Management.* Advance online publication. https://doi.org/10.1177/01492063231164991

Wang, N., Athans, V., Neuner, E., Bollinger, J., Spinner, M., & Brizendine, K. (2018). A pharmacist-driven antimicrobial stewardship intervention targeting cytomegalovirus viremia in ambulatory solid organ transplant recipients. *Transplant Infectious Disease, 20*(6), e12991.

Ward, M. K. (2011). Teaching indigenous American culture and history: Perpetuating knowledge or furthering intellectual colonization. *Journal of Social Sciences, 7*(2), 104–112.

Wei, S., Sial, M. S., Comite, U., Thu, P. A., Badulescu, D., & Popp, J. (2021). An examination to explain the mechanism of employees' environment-specific behaviour through CSR and work engagement from the perspective of stewardship theory. *International Journal of Environmental Research and Public Health, 18*(17), 9370.

West, S., Haider, L. J., Stålhammar, S., & Woroniecki, S. (2020). A relational turn for sustainability science? Relational thinking, leverage points and transformations. *Ecosystems and People*, *16*(1), 304–325.

Western, S. (2010). Eco-leadership: Towards the development of a new paradigm. In B. W. Redekop (Ed.), *Leadership for environmental sustainability* (pp. 36–54). Routledge.

Whetten, D. A. (1989). What constitutes a theoretical contribution? *Academy of Management Review*, *14*, 490–495.

White, A. C., Faulkner, J. W., Conner, D. S., Méndez, V. E., & Niles, M. T. (2022). "How can you put a price on the environment?" Farmer perspectives on stewardship and payment for ecosystem services. *Journal of Soil and Water Conservation*, *77*(3), 270–283.

Whiteman, G., Walker, B., & Perego, P. (2013). Planetary boundaries: Ecological foundations for corporate sustainability. *Journal of Management Studies*, *50*(2), 307–336.

Whyte, K. P., Brewer, J. P., & Johnson, J. T. (2016). Weaving Indigenous science, protocols and sustainability science. *Sustainability Science*, *11*(1), 25–32.

Wickert, C. (2021). Corporate social responsibility research in the *Journal of Management Studies*: A shift from a business-centric to a society-centric focus. *Journal of Management Studies*, *58*(8), E1–E17.

Wildcat, D. R. (2013). Introduction: Climate change and Indigenous peoples of the USA. *Climatic Change*, *120*(3), 509–515.

Wildman, W. J. (2006). *An introduction to relational ontology.* http://people.bu.edu/wwildman/media/docs/Wildman_2009_Relational_Ontology.pdf

Williams, A., & Whiteman, G. (2021). A call for deep engagement for impact: Addressing the planetary emergency. *Strategic Organization*, *19*(3), 526–537.

Williams, K., Lautz, T., Hendrickson, R. J., & Oyetunji, T. A. (2018). Antibiotic prophylaxis for pyloromyotomy in children: An opportunity for better stewardship. *World Journal of Surgery*, *42*, 4107–4111.

Worldwide Indigenous Science Network. (2018). *What is Indigenous science?* https://wisn.org/about/what-is-indigenous-science/

Wright, C., Nyberg, D., Rickards, L., & Freund, J. (2018). Organizing in the Anthropocene. *Organization*, *25*(4), 455–471.

Wulfson, M. (2001). The ethics of corporate social responsibility and philanthropic ventures. *Journal of Business Ethics*, *29*, 135–145.

Young, S. (2003). *Moral capitalism: Reconciling private interest with the public good.* Berrett-Koehler.

Yukl, G. (2006). *Leadership in organizations* (6th ed.). Prentice Hall.

Ziker, J. P., Rasmussen, J., & Nolin, D. A. (2016). Indigenous Siberians solve collective action problems through sharing and traditional knowledge. *Sustainability Science*, *11*(1), 45–55.

Zogning, F. (2017). Agency theory: A critical review. *European Journal of Business and Management*, *9*(2), 1–8.

Index